The Culture of Speed

Theory, Culture & Society

Theory, Culture & Society caters for the resurgence of interest in culture within contemporary social science and the humanities. Building on the heritage of classical social theory, the book series examines ways in which this tradition has been reshaped by a new generation of theorists. It also publishes theoretically informed analyses of everyday life, popular culture, and new intellectual movements.

EDITOR: Mike Featherstone, *Nottingham Trent University*

THE TCS CENTRE
The Theory, Culture & Society book series, the journals *Theory, Culture & Society* and *Body & Society*, and related conference, seminar and postgraduate programmes operate from the TCS Centre at Nottingham Trent University. For further details of the TCS Centre's activities please contact:

Centre Administrator
The TCS Centre, Room 175
Faculty of Humanities
Nottingham Trent University
Clifton Lane, Nottingham NG11 8NS, UK
email: tcs@ntu.ac.uk
web: http://tcs.ntu.ac.uk

Recent volumes include:

Informalization: Manners and Emotions Since 1890
Cas Wouters

Advertising in Modern and Postmodern Times
Pamela Odih

Phenomenological Sociology
Harvie Ferguson

The Dressed Society: Clothing, the Body and
Some Meanings of the World
Peter Corrigan

Consumer Culture and Postmodernism
Mike Featherstone

The Culture of Speed

The Coming of Immediacy

John Tomlinson

SAGE Publications
Los Angeles • London • New Delhi • Singapore

SAGE Publications Ltd
1 Oliver's Yard
55 City Road
London EC1Y 1SP

SAGE Publications Inc.
2455 Teller Road
Thousand Oaks, California 91320

SAGE Publications India Pvt Ltd
B 1/I 1 Mohan Cooperative Industrial Area
Mathura Road
New Delhi 110 044

SAGE Publications Asia-Pacific Pte Ltd
33 Pekin Street #02-01
Far East Square
Singapore 048763

Library of Congress Control Number: 2007922448

British Library Cataloguing in Publication data

A catalogue record for this book is available from the British Library

ISBN 978–1–4129–1202–0 (hbk)
ISBN 978–1–4129–1203–7 (pbk)

Typeset by Newgen Imaging Systems (P) Ltd., Chennai, India
Printed and bound in Great Britain by Athenaeum Press, Gateshead
Printed on paper from sustainable resources

For Xian Tao

. . .
Now let us sport us while we may,
And now, like amorous birds of prey,
Rather at once our time devour
Than languish in his slow-chapt power.
Let us roll all our strength and all
Our sweetness up into one ball,
And tear our pleasures with rough strife
Through the iron gates of life:
Thus, though we cannot make our sun
Stand still, yet we will make him run.

Andrew Marvell *To His Coy Mistress*

Contents

Acknowledgements viii

1 Introduction: The Cultural Significance of Speed 1

2 Machine Speed 14

3 Unruly Speed 44

4 The Condition of Immediacy 72

5 Media 94

6 Delivery 124

7 Deceleration? 146

Bibliography 160

Index 172

Acknowledgements

For a book about speed this one was slow in the making. Chris Rojek first encouraged me to address these issues in 2001 and I am deeply grateful to him for this and for all his subsequent support, first as a colleague and then, along with Mila Steele at Sage, as an editor. Thanks are also due to my colleagues in the Institute for Cultural Analysis, Nottingham. Roger Bromley in particular, for relieving me of many administrative tasks at a key point in the writing and for being a fixed point of intellectual and moral support, Dave Woods and Joost van Loon for many stimulating discussions, and everyone else for making Nottingham Trent University such a convivial place in which to work. Many other people gave me encouragement and suggestions along the way, inter alia, David Morley, Carsten Winter, Hilary Strassburger and Andreas Hepp. I am most of all indebted, for their incisive and generous comments, to Ulrich Beck and David Frisby, both of whom were kind enough to read the manuscript. Finally, of course, to Zhang Tao, who slowed me down and speeded me up in more or less equal proportions.

1

Introduction: The Cultural Significance of Speed

Sociological observations in the mouths of princes are events rare enough to attract notice. So when Charles, Prince of Wales, heir apparent to the British throne, spoke on the BBC of the need for, 'a gentler, calmer approach to life in a world which has become frenetic' he was widely reported. '[T]he aim seems to be to go ever faster, but', mused Charles, 'I often wonder, how much faster can we all go?'[1]

This is a commonplace observation of people at a certain stage in the life course and so might be passed over as simply wistful retrospection; as the tendency for people to experience the world they live in as swifter paced, more pressured, than that of their youth, or of the world described to them by their parents. '*Où sont les neiges d'antan?*' The Prince's remarks are, of course, subjective and impressionistic and, no doubt, in part nostalgic – for as Richard Sennett wisely says, 'what sensitive soul isn't?'. But there is more to it. Charles is known for statements on a range of issues, from organic farming to architecture, which express a rather complicated – and by no means platitudinous – shade of cultural conservatism. His comments on the pace of life, then, inevitably constitute an intervention in cultural politics. They give the imprimatur to a current of thought that not only regrets the demise of a world we have lost, but wants to change the one we have.

This is a current of thought that has been present in modern industrial societies since their inception, and which gained perhaps its strongest organized form, in the shape of the 'slow movement', around the turn of the present century. But in all this time it has been a minority position. Though many people routinely complain about the pace of life, and though some try to organize against it, this has never, thus far, translated into a positive social philosophy potent enough to displace speed from its central position in the cultural imagination. Acceleration rather than deceleration has been the constant leitmotiv of cultural modernity.

This book explores the different ways in which speed has preoccupied the cultural imagination of modern societies, and the way in which this imagination has shifted decisively in recent years. In doing this it takes seriously the claim implicit in Charles's intervention, that the sense of living 'a faster life' is not a sort of anthropological constant of generational succession, but a contingent state of affairs: a genuine and significant shift in temporality that occurs and accelerates specifically in modern societies.

Why should this be? Speed is not a phenomenon unnoticed in its cultural aspects before the coming of modernity, so why should modern societies be so deeply pervaded by its experience? Everywhere gestured towards, but seldom rigorously theorized, the connection between speed and cultural modernity deserves careful analysis. And we can begin with some conceptual clarification.

What is speed?

First of all, speed is fast. The English term 'speed' has a double meaning, denoting both a general calculable, *relative* rate of movement or incident – low through to high speed – and then, specifically, rapidity. This is interesting: one might even say that the concept of speed points towards its increase. From the perspective of cultural analysis, then, it is *rapid* speed, speed thought of as remarkable in its increase, that is the dominant meaning. This is not to say, of course, that things which happen slowly are devoid of interest – take for instance the concept of 'glacial time' that has been adopted to express the slow rate of change of traditional cultural attitudes and values. But it is without doubt the increase of speed that has set the cultural agenda of modernity. Indeed the recent interest in slower paced lifestyles that we are currently witnessing in the 'slow food' and 'slow cities' movements is understandable only within the broader definition of speed as fast.

The next issue to clarify is the connection of speed with physical movement. This gives us the most common, intuitive understanding of speed – swift running, fast cars – as well as the most elegant mathematical definition: SPEED = DISTANCE ÷ TIME. The relation to movement is clearly an important one, and it has its own distinct cultural implications for modernity – most notably in the application of mechanization to human mobility. However, for the purposes of cultural analysis, there is another useful definition which refers us not exclusively to movement, but to a rate of occurrence of events. When we speak of life getting faster, we are mostly thinking in terms of this broader definition. The experience of the 'speed of life' is of the rate at which things happen – or appear to happen – to us; the pace of change in our lives. 'Life getting faster' is therefore, most generally, the crowding of incident into our days and the demands this makes upon our resources of energy, time and the attribution of meaning.

Of course there are many ways in which speed as physical movement re-enters this broader definition. We may actually move our bodies faster – for example walk at a faster pace – in response to the feeling of having too much to do and not enough time in which to do it. Or the experience of the speed of mechanized transport, as it becomes integrated into our daily routines may contribute to the experience of an increasingly stressful pace of life. For example, routinely driving long distances between home and workplace generally involves the estimation of a journey time down to a precise number of minutes, typically with little margin left for error. Unforeseen traffic delays, road works, obstruction from other drivers or mechanical breakdowns may therefore produce disproportionate levels of stress for commuters as they imagine their schedules collapsing before the working day has even begun. To explain routine speeding, driving impatience and stress – or even the more extreme phenomenon of 'road rage' – we probably have to look beyond the immediate contexts of driver psychology and the human-machine interface and appreciate how these have become structurally integrated with a modern 'high speed' lifestyle.

Speed as physical movement, then, frequently interweaves with speed as rate of incident. However the latter has some analytic precedence. We can, of course, experience time pressure, haste, hurry and rush – all of these essentially cultural-phenomenological rather than physical descriptions – without ever stirring from our office desk. And what we might call 'sedentary speed' becomes increasingly significant when we try to account for the integration of media technologies into our everyday lives. So to understand the culture of modern speed in its broadest terms we need to approach it as a context in which, in various modes, events crowd into our daily lives. Some of these modes involve increasing physical mobility, but others might be better understood as an increase in the rate of 'delivery' of experience.

A third fundamental set of issues has to do with how cultural speed is *regarded*. An increasing pace of life has both its critics and its enthusiasts, but it is rarely regarded neutrally. Speed is always a matter of cultural value. But, like much else in modern societies, the attribution of value here is not a straightforward issue. Speed exhibits different aspects, it offers both pleasures and pains, exhilarations and stresses, emancipation and domination. And frequently these aspects appear to us so intertwined that it seems impossible, as individuals, to say whether an increasing pace of life is, in essence, a good or a bad thing. It is rather something to be shrugged at as, 'just the way life is today', or to be addressed in the market-derived social calculus of upsides and downsides.

This ambiguity over the value of speed is felt in the language we use to describe it. In English at least, there is a rich array of meanings, nuances, connotations and derived expressions attaching to the terminology of speed which seems to reflect our mixed feelings towards it.

On the one hand, there is a good deal of terminological evidence of cultural disapproval, or at least suspicion, of the life lived at too rapid a pace. A fast talker may be quick witted, but is suspected of deceitful intent – probably trying to pull a fast one; almost certainly out to make a fast buck. Similarly, work done at speed – a quick fix – is suspected of shoddiness and marked down compared to a methodical 'slow but sure' approach. To indulge in a 'quickie' – whether in terms of alcohol or sex – speaks of yielding to desires and temptations which one might feel shifty about admitting to publicly.

However this disapproval doesn't always amount to a direct rejection of the value of speed. If Aesop's tortoise enjoys moral approval it is, ultimately, because he won the race: it is the hare's overconfidence and subsequent indolence, rather than its innate dynamism that is disapproved of. 'More haste less speed', in a similar way, warns against a certain type of ill-considered and counterproductive disposal of energy and effort rather than attacking the goal of speed itself.

Indeed, on the other hand, there is a wealth of positive associations which reach back to the archaic meaning of speed as success or prosperity – as in 'God send you good speed' – and of 'quick' as meaning 'alive' – as in 'the quick and the dead'. This association with vitality and life energy is the one that has survived most into contemporary language. To be quick – quick witted, quick on the uptake – is to be lively, alert, intelligent. Such a person is liable to succeed in life – to have their career 'fast-tracked' and, perhaps, to end up living life in the fast lane. If we aspire to this sort of career success and prosperity we need to get up to speed with the latest developments in our field. Clearly the underlying cultural metaphor here is of life as a competition, as a race to achievement. We may, of course, disapprove of this sort of attitude to life, regarding it as part of the insidious ideology of western capitalist-consumerism, or more simply as a rather unreflective 'heads down' conformity to the modern rat-race. And, indeed, if this were all that was implied, a life lived at speed could scarcely be deemed a particularly rich or virtuous one. However, this would be to neglect the deeper existential associations – though frequently cashed, it has to be said, in the vulgar currency of material accumulation – of speed.

For example, to 'quicken' is also 'to give life or vigour, to rouse, to animate, to stimulate' (OED). In an archaic usage it is to kindle a flame, to make a fire burn brighter – in a sense, to bring light into the world. When the Virgin Mary 'quickened in her womb' she reached the stage in her mysterious pregnancy at which the first movements of the foetus – of a biological life which was to become a principle of spiritual life – could be felt. These associations are, to be sure, slightly remote from the contemporary discourse of speed, but they nonetheless point us towards a significant evaluative connection between speed, energy, dynamism, vitality and (pro)creativity.

There may be something rather particular to the Judeo-Christian tradition here. It is notable that sloth – 'laziness, reluctance to make an effort' – makes it into St Thomas Aquinas's list of the seven deadly sins, while there is no specific censure of impatience or impetuosity. (Although to be *quick tempered* gets dangerously close to the sin of anger and certainly does not imitate the forbearance of God who, viewing things *sub specie aeternitatis* is, of course, 'slow to anger'.)

Beyond these particularities, however, the association of speed with vigour and vitality seems to be quite general. Speed as a measure of physical prowess and sporting achievement has been common in most cultures. Running was originally the single event of the ancient Olympics.

But more significantly, to maintain a certain brisk pace to life itself, in the sense of making the most of the enigmatic finite gift of existence, or of actualizing our human potential – at least of not squandering it in brutish indolence – has been widely considered a virtue.

Whilst it may be unwise – hasty, even – to draw any strong lessons from these commonly expressed cultural values, they do point us towards two other important questions. One of these is the question of how values and attitudes towards speed may be changing, of how older implicit senses of the appropriate pace of life may be losing ground to new sensibilities and even associated senses of social virtue. This is something we shall consider later in the book. But, more immediately, there is the question of how these diverse, ambivalent and frequently contradictory common attitudes and values have been shaped into more or less coherent, if generally implicit, narratives in the complex cultural discourse of modernity.

Speed in the record of modernity

It has to be said here that these narratives have not been significantly shaped as the result of direct social or cultural-theoretical analysis. One of the most curious facts about speed is that, despite its being central to the cultural experience of modern societies, it is hardly ever directly and independently addressed in the major social scientific accounts of modernity. In the writings of the classical sociologists – witnesses to the most profound historical step change in both physical and social velocity that occurred during the nineteenth century – the phenomenon of speed crops up, at best, as an adjunct to other debates and issues.

In Durkheim, unless vaguely inferred as a constituent part of the division of labour characteristic of advanced societies, speed is entirely invisible. In Marx, there is a good deal more attention, most notably in the various discussions throughout *Capital* and in the *Grundrisse* of the importance of the speed of 'turnover time' for the realization of profit in the overall theory of the circulation of capital. Thus, for example, Marx writes in the *Grundrisse*:

> In as much as the circuits which capital travels in order to go from one of [its] forms into the other constitute sections of circulation, and these sections are travelled in specific *amounts of time* (even spatial distance reduces itself to time; the important thing e.g. is not the market's distance in space but the speed – the amount of time – by which it can be reached), by that much the velocity of circulation, the time in which it is accomplished, is a determinant of...how often capital can be realized in a given time. (1973: 538)

Marx develops these ideas on the next page in a famous passage which has come to represent more generally the inherently accelerating and globalizing tendencies of capitalism:

> Thus whilst capital must on the one side strive to tear down every spatial barrier to intercourse, i.e. to exchange, and to conquer the whole earth for its

market, it strives on the other side to annihilate this space with time, i.e. to reduce to a minimum the time spent in motion from one place to another. (1973: 539)

Clearly speed is important to Marx not only in terms of its place in theoretical political economy, but also in understanding developments in the order of modern spatiality (Harvey, 1999) and in the interpretation of the rise of new technologies – particularly communications and transportation systems. And, in a famous passage from *The Communist Manifesto*, Marx and Engels *imply* a context of *cultural* acceleration in their discussion of the turbulence and dynamism of the bourgeois era:

> Constant revolutionising of production, uninterrupted disturbance of all social conditions, everlasting uncertainty and agitation distinguish the bourgeois epoch from all earlier ones. All fixed, fast-frozen relations . . . are swept away, all new-formed ones become antiquated before they can ossify. All that is solid melts into air. (1969: 52)

But in all of these cases the references are oblique and the experience of speed is noticed primarily as the backdrop to other dramas: the dynamic but contradictory nature of capitalist economic development and the class antagonisms that are inherent in this.

Of the classical sociologists it is Max Weber who gives us perhaps the most explicit reference to speed as a dimension of modern life in his discussion of the nature of bureaucratic organizations. In *Economy and Society* he compares the social relations of this 'ideal-type' organizational form with the characteristics of machinery:

> The fully developed bureaucratic apparatus compares with other organizations exactly as does the machine with the non-mechanical modes of production. Precision, speed, unambiguity, knowledge of files, continuity, discretion, unity, strict subordination, reduction of friction and of material and personal costs – these are raised to the optimum point in the strictly bureaucratic administration. (Weber, 1978: 973)

Weber goes on to observe that in modern bureaucracies which have eliminated the particularism and the interpersonal conflict and compromise inherent in traditional organizations like collegiate bodies, 'official business is discharged precisely and with as much speed as possible' (1978: 974). And it scarcely matters that this was not in fact empirically correct: that, as Frank Parkin points out, 'Real bureaucracies, far from living up to Weber's model of "precision, speed and unambiguity" are likely to be cumbersome, slow and full of muddle' (Parkin, 1982: 36). For whatever the epistemological status of the construct of the 'ideal type' (Parkin, 1982: 30f.; Morrison, 1995: 270f.), Weber's discussion of bureaucracies has a quite separate status as a reflexive constituent of the broad cultural imagination of modernity, in which, as we shall see, speed becomes deeply linked to ideas of reason, progress, order and regulation. Yet, just as in the case of Marx, Weber's reference to speed, though deeply significant in its associations, is merely incidental to his other concerns.

We might fairly say, then, that the great systematic social theorists took the increasing speed of their societies, if not quite for granted, at least as analytically inseparable from the social dynamics – industrial production, capitalism, individualism – and the social contexts – mass society, urbanism, rationalism, secularization – which they saw as constitutive of modernity. For interest in the actual social *experience* of speed in this stage of modernity we have to turn from systematic theorists to the 'sociological impressionism' (Frisby, 1991) of a theorist like Georg Simmel.

For example, the final chapter of Simmel's monumental *Philosophy of Money*, published in 1900, contains a number of significant references to the idea of a shift in the tempo and rhythm of modern societies and specifically a section on, 'The pace of life, its alterations and those of the money supply' (Simmel, 1978: 498–512 ff.). Here Simmel analyses various aspects of, 'the significance of money in determining the pace of life in a given period' arguing, overall, that an increase in the supply, rate of circulation and geographical concentration of money has not only economic but psycho-logical consequences. A dynamic money economy adds to the 'restless flux' of modern existence, at the same time, 'enhancing the variety and richness of life' and producing, 'a constant sense of disorder and psychic shock' which can result in 'break downs, irritations and the compression of mental processes'. In one of his most vivid examples, of the life of the stock exchange, he writes:

> Its sanguine-choleric oscillations between optimism and pessimism, its nervous reaction to ponderable and imponderable matters, the swiftness with which every factor affecting the situation is grasped and forgotten again – all this represents an extreme acceleration in the pace of life, a feverish commotion and compression of its fluctuations, in which the specific influence of money on the course of psychological life becomes most clearly discernible. (Simmel, 1978: 506)

However even in Simmel's rich and penetrating essays on culture, speed appears only as an ancillary aspect of other phenomena which he treats in elaborate and dazzling detail. As with the analysis of money, so with the reference to speed in his analysis of modern fashion. Though the phenomenon of fashion involves, as a necessary aspect, 'its rapid and complete transitori-ness', for Simmel its essence lies in the contradiction between this, and the fact that, 'each individual fashion . . . makes its appearance as though it wished to live forever' (Simmel, 1997a: 203). In a similar way, speed, as the increasing pace of modern life, appears in one of Simmel's most famous essays, not as the direct focus of analysis, but as the implied context for the intensity of mental stimulation involved in the shift from rural to urban existence: 'the rapid crowding up of changing images . . . . The unexpectedness of onrushing impressions' of metropolitan existence (Simmel, 1997b: 175).

With one or two notable exceptions, social and cultural theory throughout the twentieth century has not been significantly more interested in directly broaching the issue of acceleration. Alvin Toffler, whose popular text

Future Shock contains one of the rare explicit discussions of an increasing 'pace of life' could more or less accurately claim that, 'it has received no attention from either psychologists or sociologists' (Toffler, 1971: 42). Speed is scarcely mentioned in the Frankfurt School's critique of the legacy of the Enlightenment; it is virtually ignored by functionalists, structuralists and post-structuralists alike. Even in the existential-phenomenological tradition of Heidegger, Sartre or Merleau-Ponty, in which the crux of analysis of the human condition is its situation in relation to the ontological dimensions of time and space, the experience of speed, arguably the most dramatic nexus of these dimensions, is passed over. Perhaps even more strikingly, the vast corpus of representations of speed in the texts of popular culture has hardly any specific critical recognition in the broad discourse of cultural studies in either its Marxist or its post-modern inflexions. Finally, the analysis of globalization, that great preoccupation of the close of the twentieth century, though it dwells at the core of its theorization on the complex connectedness that issues from the social compression of time and space (Giddens, 1990; Robertson, 1992; Castells, 1996; Held et al., 1999; Tomlinson, 1999) nonetheless takes the speed of globalizing dynamics pretty much for granted.

There are, of course, some exceptions.[2] But, and this is my point, these do not, on any estimate, amount to a concerted confrontation by the main tendencies in twentieth-century social and cultural analysis with the issue of speed. The century, indeed, stands curiously framed, at its beginning and its end, by the two most significant critical encounters with speed, entirely contrasted in their response but twinned in their marginality from the mainstream. The Italian Futurists, and in particular, Marinetti, as we shall see in Chapter 3, establish a reckless, hyperbolic celebratory discourse of machine speed which, though it has its own legacy in the ensuing cultural imagination, deliberately sets itself at odds, both politically and intellectually, with the serious analytical trends of modernity. And at the century's close, Paul Virilio's coruscating critical essays on speed, power and violence, almost mirror images in their contrast with the braggadocio of Marinetti, are characterized by their idiosyncrasy. Though Virilio's name is, perhaps, the one most commonly invoked in relation to the culture of speed today, his work has, as he admits, developed in relative isolation. In an interview with Neils Brugger in 1991, Virilio said:

> I stand rather alone in insisting that speed is clearly the determining factor. In my capacity as a social analyst, I do not wish to deliver monologues, but to partake in a dialogue. For the past twenty-five years, my work has nevertheless been solitary. To say that speed is a determining factor in society requires proof, an effort that is starting to exhaust me. (Virilio, 2001b: 83)

However, the fact that the academic recording of cultural modernity has for the most part subsumed speed to other concerns, does not mean that there has been no serious encounter in the wider body of cultural texts which make up the record of modernity. On the contrary, speed is powerfully inscribed, not just in the creative imagination of writers and artists of the modern period, but more significantly in the written and unwritten 'institutional narratives' that have given form, meaning and value to the modern experience. It is these broad cultural narratives that this book will explore.

The shape of the discussion

The book has a simple structure. Essentially I will try to tell three stories. Or, to be more precise, I will try to trace two established narratives of modern speed and to suggest the elements of a third, only recently emergent.

In the first story, (Chapter 2) speed is made to appear against the background of the most dominant institutionalized understanding of the meaning of modernity: as the conquest of nature by mechanism, the unproblematized belief in open-ended progress, the unstoppable advance and spread of the capitalist market economy and the fundamental shift in culture from an agrarian-rural to an industrial-urban context of experience. What is essential to this story is the way it seeks to *discipline* the inherently violent and unstable impulses of social and economic modernity – of which speed is the prime emblem – in a culture of rational regulation. This story, I will argue, has been the most successful one in shaping the cultural meaning of speed; and it is one that, despite a recent loss of confidence amongst intellectuals, continues to have considerable influence both in the public discourse of our political leaders, and in the commonsense understandings of many ordinary people.

But then in the second story (Chapter 3) speed is encountered as it escapes discipline and regulation. Here the focus is on the complicated and frequently dark association between the risks, dangers and implicit violence of speed and the – quintessentially modern – sensual-aesthetic experiences and pleasures it can afford. This is a discourse which embraces a range of transgressive and rebellious impulses chafing the smooth surface order of institutional modernity. And out of this is formed a narrative of speed which is 'unruly' both in its orientation and in its expression. Subversive and impetuous, conjoining hedonism with a peculiar sort of existential heroism, this discourse constantly teeters on the brink of collapse into violence and chaos.

Because of this constitutional instability, this second narrative has never displaced the first from its position of discursive dominance. However, though constantly threatened by absorption and incorporation, 'unruly speed' has for most of the twentieth century maintained a strong grip on the cultural imagination. And so the two stories have co-existed not exactly in symbiotic relationship, but on account of the complex appeal of speed across other fault lines in cultural modernity, for example those of the political left/right divide. Gramsci was an early admirer of the Futurists, despite their Fascist tendencies and Lenin enthusiastically embraced the 'scientific' speed-regulation of Taylorism.

In fact neither narrative finally triumphed, for both became overtaken by events, by the coming of a new condition which I go on to argue is re-configuring the modern culture of speed. The premise here – and indeed the central claim of this book – is that we can identify an emergent cultural principle of contemporary globalized and telemediated societies: what I shall call, exploiting all the ambiguity of the term, the principle of 'immediacy'.

The condition of immediacy is not smoothly continuous with the earlier modern culture of speed. In certain ways it grows out of the general acceleration of practices, processes and experience associated with the institutional and technological bases of modernity and interpreted, until around the last couple of decades, by the discourses of regulated and unruly speed. But there is a shift occurring. In significant ways, and particularly as a consequence of the ubiquitous influence of telemediation, immediacy alters the cultural terms of speed's impact, undermining some earlier presumptions and installing new commonplace realities. In the process, the emerging condition of immediacy produces new possibilities and problems which eclipse those of an earlier era of the culture of speed. The attempt to grasp the coming of immediacy and its implications for broader cultural sensibilities and values occupies most of the rest of the book. In Chapter 4 I sketch some indications of the condition of immediacy along with some contextual frameworks for understanding its emergence. And in Chapters 5 and 6 I explore the implication of immediacy in the contexts, respectively, of the increasing telemediation of everyday experience, and the changing forms of the commodification of culture.

In the final chapter, I return, briefly, to the issue with which this chapter began: the possibility of social and cultural deceleration. Here we will explore a little of the impulses and arguments of the contemporary 'slow movement', but we will be more concerned with broader questions of cultural value. Beside the obvious question of the practicality of slowing the pace of modernity, we will examine the more complicated one of whether general deceleration would be, overall, a good thing.

The small print

Qualifications and provisos tend to detract from the clarity of purpose that is aimed for in an Introduction. But the scope of the discussion and the generalizations involved in a book like this are so broad that I can't avoid issuing some brief circumscriptions at the outset. Although the discussion is most at home in the sociology of culture, the particular style of cultural analysis I favour is fairly interdisciplinary in its approach and eclectic as to both sources and examples. This always risks trespassing, in a way that may be annoying, on the territory of specialists with deeper understandings and knowledge of particular cases or of the intricacies of different theoretical approaches. But this is a risk which has to be taken in this mode of analysis and nothing much is to be gained by trying anxiously to hedge one's bets.

On the other hand, there are a few points which would probably benefit from a disclaimer at the outset, just so as to avoid misunderstanding.

The first is the question of the cultural-geographical scope of the discussion, which really maps on to the range of relevance of the idea of 'global modernity'. The cultural patterns, forces and experiences that I focus on, and take my examples from, are predominantly those of western 'developed' industrial economies. To the extent that these cultural trajectories have become, for good or ill, globalized ones, the discussion has relevance for the experiences of increasingly extensive urbanized, industrialized sectors of non-western societies. But what the discussion does not broach – simply because it is beyond our practical bounds – are the differences in the experience of speed and immediacy that may attach either to the inherent economic unevenness and inequality of capitalist globalization, or to the distinctive cultural contexts which may inflect modernity in ways not imagined in the western experience.

Secondly, the issue of technology. In several places the discussion of speed becomes involved in questions of the cultural reception of technologies, particularly, in Chapters 5 and 6, of new media technologies. These issues bring the discussion into contact with debates within the sociology of science and technology about the intrinsic nature of technological processes and artefacts and, particularly, about the interface between the social and the technological. These are debates which have been fiercely fought over in the last couple of decades (see, inter alia, Bijker and Law, 1992; Grint and Woolgar, 1997) and which are challenging for our understanding not only of the ontological status of technologies, but of wider issues of social causality and, in the case of the influential 'Actor Network Theory' (Callon, 1987; Latour, 1992), of the attribution of agency beyond the human world.

In the interests of clarity I have generally avoided becoming caught up in these, often abstruse, debates. And I have felt justified in doing so. This is because the focus of my discussion is not on the precise ways in which technologies impact on the social world, but upon the ways in which tech-nologies, as the perceived 'vehicles' of an increasing cultural acceleration, have been received and interpreted within the broad narratives I describe: quite a different issue. However my discussion does not remain agnostic on all these points, particularly on the key one of 'technological determinism'. Where this issue presses hardest on the discussion – notably in Chapter 6 – I try to clarify my position in reference to some of these debates.

However, it is worthwhile saying here that overall I adopt a fairly conventional sociological attitude which can be summarized as follows. Technological determinism as the view that technologies have an independent causal (not to say, monocausal) role in the production of social forms, practices and relations seems obviously false. This is because technologies never appear other than as embedded within other contexts: chiefly the political-cultural and economic ones which surround their research and development and their conversion into technological 'products' (see Williams, 1983: 128ff.). However, neither does it seem plausible to think, as those of a resolutely social-constructivist persuasion apparently do, that the novel *material* qualities possessed by new technologies – which are, after all, the key to their attraction – should be understood as *entirely* a function of social interpretation or as 'textually' constructed. This seems to me not only to push the general position of social constructivism to implausible lengths, it also engages extremely poorly with the lived experiences of ordinary people in their everyday interactions with technologies. It seems to me, on the contrary, that it is necessary, in order to avoid an equal and opposite mystification to that involved in technological determinism, to recognize that technologies as they appear as objects within the flow of cultural experience, possess independent inherent properties which define, to some extent, the possibilities and meanings of their use. Without such a recognition, it seems difficult to imagine either how cultural interpretations of technologies ever get off the ground, or – perhaps more important – how moral agency can ever be exercised in relation to their appropriate use.

Thirdly, a matter that can be dealt with more briefly, historical periodization. In understanding speed as a modern phenomenon I focus on the period of industrial modernity beginning around the turn of the nineteenth century and continuing, in certain aspects, into the world of today. Within this period I move pretty freely back and forth in my deployment of examples to trace the different cultural narratives of speed. I also suggest that our current condition of 'immediacy' in certain crucial ways marks a departure from an earlier era of 'mechanical speed'. Apart from obvious scruples as to the dating of examples, none of this is, nor is intended to be, historically rigorous, at least in respect of periodization. I do not, for example, engage with arguments about the precise periodization of modernity on different criteria, nor with the status of broad and loose temporal categories such as the 'epoch' or the 'era' (for a discussion, see Tomlinson, 1999: 33f.). I take refuge here in the general position that cultural change is never particularly susceptible to neat periodization anyway, since it always involves rather complicated shading and overlapping. More generally, although it employs historical perspective in interpreting culture, this is decidedly not a history of modern speed, but an attempt to understand, in perspective, its contemporary cultural significance.

Lastly, the use of examples from imaginative texts. In a few places, notably in Chapters 2 and 5, I make use of examples from novels, short stories, poems, films and, in one case, an opera. There are two reasons to do this: first, because non-factual texts are clearly significant parts of the cultural narratives of speed that I shall explore; and secondly, because imaginative writings and productions seem to me to be, amongst other things, often wonderfully refined historical stories of human experience. The novelist, poet, librettist or film director can often grasp the phenomenology of an event with a sharpness, clarity and resonance which makes the efforts of social and cultural analysts appear (as they indeed often are) clodhopping. And so I don't feel the need to justify the inclusion of such examples in a broadly sociological account, nor to dwell on their epistemological status. But I do want to register the inadequacy of the way in which I, of necessity, employ these examples, 'turning them to account' in the service of the more prosaic discourse of academic argument. All that can be said in mitigation is that cultural analysts, however leaden their appropriations may be, clearly cannot afford to assume the 'data' of imaginative texts to be off limits – either as the specialist domain of textual criticism (which anyway is quite different in its aims and practices), or on account of scruples over compromising their integrity as works of art. The pragmatic answer to this may be just to accept the instrumental handling of these examples as cultural data, as something done in good faith, and then to read the novel or watch the movie.

There are no doubt other vulnerabilities in the analysis, and the keen-eyed reader will need, and get, no more prompting from me in identifying them. So now let's gather pace.

Notes

1 The context of the remark, made in a *Songs of Praise* religious broadcast on 11 September 2005, was a comparison of the relatively slower pace of life in the north as compared to the south of Britain. Stephen Bates: 'Charles tells high-speed Britain to learn from the north' *The Guardian* 12 Sept. 2005, p. 4.

2 The issue of speed is of course *implicit* in the social-theoretical treatment of time (Adam, 1990, 1998; Hassard, 1990) but it largely remains so, as it does in social-theoretical analysis of time–space compression (Giddens, 1984, 1990; Harvey, 1989). There are more explicit treatments in the critical literature on modern time organization, for example Rifkin (1987) and Eriksen (2001) and in cultural history, for example the seminal work of Kern (2003) (originally 1983) on the period spanning the end of the nineteenth century. And there is also an interesting genre of journalistic treatments, for example, Gleick (1999) and Kreitzman (1999). With such a wide potential interdisciplinary field, there are no doubt many others which I have failed to notice. But I don't aim at the encyclopaedic here. The point is to notice how overall, and in comparison with other pre-occupations in the condition of modernity, the social-scientific interest in speed has been remarkably sparse.

2

Machine Speed

> Away, with a roar and a shriek and a rattle, from the town, burrowing among the dwellings of men and making the streets hum, flashing out into the meadows for a moment, mining in through the damp earth, booming on in darkness and heavy air, bursting out again into the sunny day so bright and wide; away, with a shriek and a roar, and a rattle, through the fields, through the corn, through the hay...through the hollow, on the height, by the heath, by the orchard, by the park, by the garden, over the canal, across the river, where the sheep are feeding, where the mill is going, where the barge is floating, where the dead are lying, where the factory is smoking.... Away with a shriek and a roar and a rattle, plunging down into the earth again, and working on in such a storm of energy and perseverance...until a ray of light upon the wet wall shows its surface flying past like a fierce stream. Away once more into the day, and through the day, with a shrill yell of exultation, roaring, rattling, tearing on, spurning everything with its dark breath. (Charles Dickens: *Dombey and Son*, 2002: 309–310)

Dickens's evocation of speed in Paul Dombey's railway journey between London and Birmingham is remarkable for the way in which it grasps the ambiguous nature of modern machine velocity. The onward rush of the locomotive also stands for the implacable impetus of mechanization in general: tearing up the social as well as the physical landscape. But more than this, its roaring progress between light and darkness captures the mixture of promised enlightenment and emancipation on the one hand and rapaciousness and violent confusion on the other.

Dombey and Son was conceived in 1844 and written and published in 19 parts, beginning in the year 1846 and concluding in 1848, the year of revolutions in Europe and of Marx and Engels's *Communist Manifesto*. Its creation spanned that period of extraordinary unregulated financial speculation in Britain known as the second railway boom or, more popularly, 'Railroad Mania'[1] and Dickens took some of his inspiration from these events. There is an inherent ambiguity in Dickens's attitudes which mirrors the ambiguous depiction of the speed of the locomotive. *Dombey and Son*, though in essence a domestic novel, contains some of Dickens's sharpest invective against the cold, calculative attitudes representative of the new capitalist institutions of his time; yet he is perhaps even more withering in his satire on the entrenched backward-looking conservative values which these were displacing. Although he despises personal avariciousness and the excesses of speculation, he admires the self-made entrepreneurs and engineers of his age – such men as the architect and railway promoter (and designer of the Crystal Palace), Joseph Paxton, with whom he collaborates on the planning of a new radical newspaper to challenge *The Times*, and to represent the liberal-progressive vision of the new industrial class. *The Daily News*, which Dickens edits for its first 17 issues in 1846 is directly supported by capital generated out of the railway boom. Though it is advertised as representing, 'Liberal politics and thorough independence', it is notable that it will, in particular, carry, 'Scientific and Business Information on every topic connected with Railways, whether in actual operation, in progress, or projected' (Ackroyd, 1990: 485). In December of 1847 Dickens shares, to huge acclaim, a platform at the Leeds Mechanics' Institute with the great locomotive engineer and 'father of the railways' George Stephenson (Ackroyd, 1990: 539).

Speed thus enters Dickens's literary world, as it does the modern cultural imagination, via a set of quintessentially modern impulses which, despite their internal tensions and incoherencies, become yoked together to form a powerful cultural narrative that has held sway from the mid-nineteenth until at least the mid-twentieth century: machines, money, progress. The elaboration of this narrative, and the way that it becomes woven into the interpretation of modern metropolitan life, is the theme of this chapter.

Machines

The ebullient, almost frantic, insistent rhythms of Dickens's prose absolutely match his subject. There is no danger of over-estimating the significance of mechanization in the modern experience of speed, and the railways were by far the most culturally significant form in which mechanization was initially experienced. As Eric Hobsbawm put it, '"railway" became a sort of synonym for ultra modernity in the 1840s' (Hobsbawm, 1999: 111). The railways mark a watershed in the human experience of speed. As is often observed, until the application of steam locomotion to railway transport beginning in the 1820s,[2] no one had ever experienced a speed faster than that of a galloping horse. By the 1840s, the time of Paul Dombey's journey, trains in England were reaching top speeds of between 60 and 70 miles per hour and averaging between 20 and 30 miles per hour over all journeys (Schivelbusch, 1980: 193). Although the sheer dramatic increase in achievable velocity was remarkable, and was experienced as little short of a marvel,[3] this alone was not the main issue. Of greater significance was undoubtedly the shift in the *type* of speed: from a velocity of 'nature' to one of machinery. Ian Carter summarizes a widely held view that, 'Victorian railways drove to the heart of the modern impulse as they demonstrated humankind's increased control over nature' (Carter, 2001: 15).[4]

Perhaps the most direct way in which control over nature was felt was in the potential to *sustain* motive power over distance – a key advantage of mechanical speed over natural speed. A fast horse could outpace the early locomotives over short distances, but the fact that horses tired and required long periods of rest was the single most important limitation on the further development of literal 'horsepower'. And this was consequently the prime reason for the rapid decline of the stage-coach system in England, once the railways became established. Schivelbusch quotes a contemporary authority on the new railway transport, Nicholas Wood, writing in 1832:

> The greatest exertions have been used to accelerate the speed of the mails (which have hitherto been the quickest species of conveyance), without being able to exceed ten miles per hour; and that only with the exercise of such destruction of animal power, as no one can contemplate without feelings of the most painful nature; while upon the Liverpool Rail-way, an average rate of fifteen miles is kept up with the greatest ease. (Schivelbusch, 1980: 11)

It was the natural limitation of animal power which had made single figure miles-per-hour speeds over any reasonable distance seem 'immutable' in the early nineteenth century – even given the super-efficiency of the staging posts' ostler teams, 'as professionally adept as the best modern motor-racing pit crews' (Setright, 2002: 8) in changing horses.

The displacement of the stage-coach by the steam train is thus emblematic of a shift from 'natural' speed to machine speed felt in qualitative as well as quantitative terms. Schivelbusch argues that, before the coming of industrial modernity, transportation had a 'mimetic' relationship with natural forces, 'Ships drift with water and wind currents, overland motion follows the natural irregularities of the landscape and is determined by the physical powers of the draft animals'. He goes on to quote Charles Babbage,[5] writing in the 1830s on the 'eotechnology' of wind and water power: 'We merely make use of bodies in a state of motion; we change the directions of their movement, in order to make them subservient to our purposes, but we neither add to nor diminish the quantity of motion in existence' (Schivelbusch, 1980: 12). In contrast with this mimesis of nature, machine motive energy is an artifice which actually *exerts* itself upon the natural world. Steamships no longer have to wear and tack, but cleave through the oceans in straight lines; the cuttings, tunnels and embankments of railway construction force new flat and level paths through landscapes that had seemed permanent and God-given in their natural features.

In this sense machine power as it is embodied in the railways actually alters the way in which people regard nature (Macnaughton and Urry, 1998: 207f.). Nature is no longer seen as an order which possesses decisive limiting power over human ambition, an order that may be harnessed, but which ultimately has to be deferred to. Suddenly human ingenuity deploying mechanical power appears to overcome the natural order. Early-nineteenth-century writing abounds with observations of this. 'The Railway Companion' of 1833 describes a 'new era ... ushered to the wondering world':

> It was the birth struggle of a giant power, destined ere long to bear down, like the rushing of a mighty torrent, all existing barriers, and *give a direction hitherto*

unknown to the leading features of our social institutions; to annihilate – or at least immediately extend – the bounds of time and space; to convert our hills and valleys into level planes. (quoted in Freeman, 1999: 44, emphasis added)

This is an interesting passage, and not only because it is one of the earliest instances of the deployment of the idea of 'annihilation' in relation to time and space – an idea made famous in Marx's phrase 'the annihilation of space by time' in the *Grundrisse* (Marx, 1973: 524, 539).[6] Although continuing to use the imagery of nature to describe the awesome mechanical power of the railway – for what other metaphors were available? – the passage extends the observation of the physical/spatial transformations brought about by the railways into the realm of social institutions. The barriers it refers to are thus not only those of land formations, but more general resistances to the achievements of human will and desire.

Mechanical speed is thus unprecedented in its sheer physical power, but it is other features distinguishing it from the speed simply appropriated from natural forces that open up its wider implications. Chief amongst these are the core engineering notions of control and regulation.

The initial experience of machine power was by no means one of consummate rational order and control. In what Lewis Mumford (1946) characterized as the 'Paleotechnic Age' of the early industrial revolution, the predominant experience of the smoke, fire, grime and toil of the iron foundry, the mill and the factory was probably one of barely controlled uproar and confusion. This is captured in the term Humphrey Jennings (1995) appropriated from John Milton as the title of his 'imaginative history of the industrial revolution': *Pandaemonium*. One of the contemporary accounts which Jennings presents vividly depicts this in a description of the Black Country of the West Midlands in 1830:

The earth seems to have been turned inside out. Its entrails are strewn about.... The coal which has been drawn from below ground is blazing on the surface. By day and by night the country is glowing with fire, and the smoke of the ironworks hovers over it. There is rumbling and clanking of iron forges and rolling mills. Workmen covered in smut, and with fierce white eyes, are seen moving amongst the glowing iron and dull thud of forge hammers...the grass had been parched and killed by the vapours of sulphureous acid thrown out by the chimneys; and every herbaceous object was of a ghastly grey. (James Naysmith quoted in Jennings, 1995: 172)[7]

Although one might equally apply this sort of description to areas of industrial blight in the twenty-first-century world – to some cities in China for example – the imagination gets its force from its dramatic contrast with the bucolic landscape within which it is initially haphazardly set. What redeems this infernal vision is the promise that these forces can be tamed and contained in a rational-progressive – and moreover, wonderful – industrial order.

And in some ways this promise becomes fulfilled with extreme rapidity. In particular the development of machine toolmaking by people like Naysmith during the 1830s and 1840s dramatically accelerated the pace of industrial production and the scope for realizing invention.[8] The Great Exhibition of 1851 – just over 20 years after Naysmith's description of the elemental chaos of the iron foundry – is an extraordinarily confident and (literally) spectacular demonstration of the triumph of mechanical modernity (as well as, like all subsequent international exhibitions and fairs, the unabashed promotion of free-trade capitalism). As Andrew Wilson says, it is difficult to describe the sheer scale of the event without producing a 'catalogue of hyperboles'. Over 100,000 exhibits fill the area of Hyde Park enclosed – along with its very trees – by Joseph Paxton's Crystal Palace, the revolutionary glass-house construction which itself seemed to have turned earth-bound cast-iron into light. Twenty thousand advance season tickets are sold, a balloon ascent organized to coincide with the opening ceremony (which was controversially closed to the public) attracts a crowd of half a million, and daily attendances of over 100,000 are common. Between 1 May and the end of the exhibition on 11 October, over six million visitors are officially recorded (Wilson, 2002: 137f.).

What is most striking is that, in contemporary accounts, it is the exhibits of locomotives and manufacturing machinery that are the most popular. Thus, for example, Henry Mayhew writes:

> The machinery...has been from the first the grand focus of attention.... Round the electro-plating [and at] the steam brewery, crowds of men and women are continually ascending and descending the stairs; youths are watching the model carriages moving along the new pneumatic railways...indeed, whether it be the noisy flax-crushing machine, or the splashing centrifugal pump, or the clatter of the Jacquard lace machine, or the bewildering whirling of the cylindrical steampress, – round each and all are anxious, intelligent and simple minded artisans, and farmers, and servants and youths and children clustered, endeavouring to solve the mystery of its complex operations. (Mayhew and Cruikshank, '1851 or the Adventures of Mr and Mrs Sandboys', quoted in Jennings, 1995: 258–9)

Mayhew's liberal account introduces an element of class critique, insisting that the working class visitors – the 'shilling people' – have a keener interest in, and grasp of the significance of, the mechanical exhibits than the 'lounging gentlefolk' since they possess, by dint of their occupations, more direct experience of, 'the acquisition of power over natural forces so as to render them subservient to human happiness'. And there is a clue here to the enduring power of the cultural imagination of mechanical processes and their related speed.

The working class is of course – and knows itself to be – at the sharp and dangerous end of machine production and on the bad side of the economic deal that accompanies it. And so, as Wilson observes, there is a paradox in the way working people crowd to see the cotton spinning machines, 'demonstrated in anodyne, clean conditions in a southern exhibition chamber' (Wilson, 2002: 138).[9] The answer may be that they are even more keenly aware of the emancipations that machinery – 'gleaming incarnations of progress and progressivism' – offers from a greater drudgery on the land

and in hand production (Wilson, 2002: 138).[10] Despite the often appalling conditions of industrial labour, as the nineteenth century progresses the prevailing popular sentiment is anything but Luddite.

Indeed a new popular hero – the mechanical engineer – emerges. Figures like Brunel, Boulton, Watt, Naysmith and Stephenson – though exaggeratedly eulogized in Samuel Smiles's *Lives of the Engineers* of 1861, are none the less genuinely popular figures. For, quite apart from their accomplishments, their biographies represent the possibility of a more general escape from the old orders and fixed destinies of class and nature through sheer merit: personal ingenuity and industry. Dickens, despite his ambivalence towards the Great Exhibition, and his withering satire of Utilitarianism in the figure of Gradgrind in *Hard Times*, none the less promotes individual engineering heroes – the ironmaster Mr Rouncewell in *Bleak House* and the engineer Daniel Doyce in *Little Dorrit* – as the modest, clever, hardworking meritocracy to whom the future belongs.

It is this powerful mixture of demonstrable material progress through machine industry and a cluster of new (potentially) emancipatory and quasi-democratic ideas and values – the modern principles of control, planning, organization and regulation – that comes to form the central motif and the legitimating ideology of maturing industrial modernity as it moves into the twentieth century. And this is an ideology which co-exists with, but is never eclipsed by, a developing and organizing class consciousness.

To illustrate the development of this constellation of ideas, and its significance for the cultural imagination associated with mechanical speed, we can stay on the railways and consider an iconic cultural product of the first part of the twentieth century.

Night Mail, a documentary film made in 1936 for the British GPO Film Unit[11] is arguably one of the definitive cultural texts of early-twentieth-century industrial modernity. Produced by John Grierson, directed by Basil Wright and Harry Watt and featuring verse by W.H. Auden and a score by Benjamin Britten, this short film has become a classic of the British documentary movement.

The film is a celebration of mechanical velocity in the delivery of modern communication and also in the territorial 'binding' of the nation into one modern culture by the transport and communications technologies of the time. What it shows is the journey of the overnight mail express – the 'T.P.O. Down Special'[12] – from London Euston to Glasgow, on which mail from intervening stations and locations is collected and sorted as the train speeds northwards.

As the mail express's journey proceeds, so the film unfolds many of the main characteristics of the cultural imaginary of mechanical velocity. First, there is an obvious focus on the exercise of mechanical power overcoming – 'eating up' – distance, with the locomotive, in the words of Auden's verse, 'shovelling white steam over its shoulder'. This is emphasized in recurrent shots of the actions of pistons, wheels and connecting rods, the rush of wind and the pulsating, accelerating rhythm of Britten's score.

This is a speed tied to concerted effort and, particularly, to the overcoming of obstacles – for example the steep gradients of the Pennines on the later part of the journey. It is a pretty basic image of work in Bertrand Russell's famous definition but, contrary to Russell's slightly cynical view of the virtues of labour,[13] it is one glossed here as a co-operative social enterprise which is at the same time both mundane and in a certain sense, *noble*. The clue to this signification is that the exercise of mechanical power is shown within the context of other quintessentially early-modern themes. Goal orientation, organization, planning and time–space regulation are continually stressed in the sequences showing the precise timetabling of the Night Mail and its co-ordination with connecting trains, or in the routines of sorting the letters or the famous sequence showing the high-speed mechanical collection and delivery of mail bags from the trackside. These sequences also display an ideology of teamworking and of the disciplined co-ordination of mechanical and labour power in the achievement of a common goal.[14] And related to this is a modern heroic image of labour in the human-machine ensemble and a sense of the exhilaration of velocity. Though it appears here in very muted tones, there are also at least distant echoes of the Futurists' obsession with the heroics of machine speed – a theme we shall come to in the following chapter.

But if we were pushed to identify the central theme of *Night Mail*, we might say it is, above all, a film about the *closing of the gap* between a point of departure and a point of arrival. The goal, the effort, the technology, the exhilaration of mechanical velocity that is celebrated here all constellate around this key theme in the modern imagination: demolishing distance, establishing communication, connecting localities. For the Night Mail's journey crucially documents and affirms, in its dependable, precisely organized regularity, both the technologically achieved connectedness and the cultural unity of the nation-state: not merely across distance, but across rural and urban, class, regional and even 'national' divides.

A cultural text such as *Night Mail*, then, offers an interpretation of the specific social value of rational mechanical speed: its promise to overcome the material realities of space, distance and separation – contexts which are defined in this discourse as *obstacles* to the fulfilment of human needs and desires. Speed is therefore a good, not merely in and of itself, but as a prime mark of social *progress*.

Progress

The association of mechanical speed with progress is deep-seated but it requires some teasing out. Although, as Robert Nisbet (1980) shows, the idea of progress has a long and complex history reaching back to the classical world, it undoubtedly takes off as a social ideology with the era of industrial modernity.[15] And its significance here is perhaps not so much in the specific formulations of social scientists like Comte or Herbert Spencer,[16] so much as in its popular appeal as a powerful story that can be read easily in the direct comparison of the empirical conditions of life. This comparison is set out with great clarity, curiously by a thinker more often associated with barbed criticism of, rather than enthusiasm for, commercial and industrial modernity, Ralph Waldo Emerson: 'Who would live in the stone age or the bronze or the iron or the lacustrine? Who does not prefer the age of steel, of gold, of coal, petroleum, cotton, steam, electricity and the spectroscope?' (Emerson, 'The Progress of Culture', quoted in Nisbet, 1980: 203). It is the way in which this forces a choice for the modern upon us – a choice that cannot be refused without seeming irrational or deliberately obtuse – that is the key to the power of the ideology of progress.

Of course this forced choice obscures all manner of more subtle discriminations of value, leaves out of account all questions of the social and cultural costs of industrialization; ignores entirely the political-economic *context* of technological change. But despite all this, it contains a clear proposition about the *general* historical relationship of technology to the improvement of human material well-being that is difficult to deny – and which has only relatively recently been at all widely doubted.[17] Well into the twentieth century, as Nisbet shows, what now appear as incredibly Panglossian ideas of progress were more or less commonly accepted. He cites, for example, one Professor Alexander Mackendrick writing in the *Hibbert Journal* in 1927:

> The remarkable increase in the efficiency of industry through the achievements of science and the multiplication of tools and machinery seems to justify the belief that the age of plenty has dawned.... It is now fairly certain that the power of production and the means of transport are such that the entire human race might be comfortably housed, clothed and nurtured. (Nisbet, 1980: 298)

This was by no means an uncommon view in the first part of the twentieth century and, though such simple confidence in progress – particularly amongst intellectuals – has since steadily declined,[18] it would be quite incorrect to dismiss the ideological power of the idea even in the more ironic and sceptical climate of the twenty-first century.

Mechanization has had a well-documented affinity with the idea of social progress, but the question remains of how speed itself becomes so closely identified with improvement in the social order and the quality of life. It is not self-evident: a faster pace of life is not *by definition* a benefit of, or contributor to, progress.

One answer to this is in the simple association of the speed of mechanical processes, compared to hand and animal power, with delivering improvements. The speed of mechanical manufacturing, transportation and domestic technologies is obviously – in principle – liberating not just of effort, but of *time*. Both in the workplace and in the home, 'labour-saving' mechanisms have the potential to liberate human lives from both drudgery and tedium. Of course the context of capitalist production has meant that this potential has by no means been properly or equally realized. But despite all that we can say about the enforced time-discipline of the industrial labour contract, or about the issue of time poverty in developed economies, we cannot pass lightly over the emancipatory impact of machines. Anyone doubting this needs only to consider the steady movement of labour across all societies from agricultural to industrial-commercial employment. Just as in Europe in the nineteenth century, in a country like China today internal labour migration demonstrates unequivocally that, despite all the exploitation, hardships, health risks and so forth of industrial employment, aspirations for a better life track the path from the land to the factory. The speed of mechanical processing is intrinsic to this aspiration, a speed which represents self-betterment in urban industrial employment compared with the slow, unchanging, laborious and impoverished life of the peasant. And it is the speed of mechanical production which also promises the delivery and affordability of the material goods – the refrigerators, washing machines, televisions, cars and mobile phones – which are not just the tokens, but the actual material benefits of 'progress'.

The intrinsic benefits of mechanical production in delivering the fruits of material modernity, then, tends to bind speed in with progress. To this extent, an increase in the pace of life, though it may not be particularly attractive in itself, may appear as a matter for pragmatic acceptance as part of the cultural 'bargain' with modernity. This is not, however, a seamless identification and, under scrutiny, the ideological slippage between the notions of 'labour saving' and 'time saving' becomes, as we shall later see, both apparent and significant.[19]

However we can add a second layer of association which bolsters the ideological linkage between speed and progress. This is the quasi-moral connection that I referred to in Chapter 1 between dynamism – as opposed to stasis – and visions of the human good. The ideological nub of progress, which appeals equally to social reformers – 'progressives' by definition – as to capitalist entrepreneurs is its *impatience* with the way things are, and the intuition that the human good lies in a struggle for improvement. Change thus comes to be valorized over continuity – one of the other defining characteristic shifts of modernity – and once this is accepted, then the speed of change becomes pretty much a self-evident good. Of course this cultural drive towards change is often tempered and controlled by other modern social discourses: planning, scheduling, bureaucratic management and so on. Equally, modern political institutions by and large come to favour reform over sudden – or worse, permanent – revolution. But underlying all this, there is a fundamental tacit consensus in modern societies that progress should be as swift as possible. If progress is defined as change for the better, then delay is always a matter for either apology or rationalization. Modern political conservatives might advocate the preservation of 'traditional values', but they realize that it would be suicidal to campaign on a ticket promising a slower rate of progress. Similarly, the celebration of the virtues of a less 'driven' social existence in various contemporary 'slow movements' is always implicitly a celebration of such virtues as 'progressive' ones.

The rhetorical force of the association of speed with progress – its appeal to a general human aspiration for betterment and an impatience with circumstances that are 'holding us back' – is pervasive of modern political discourse. Tony Blair launched the British General Election campaign of 2005 with a speech promising, as the core of his political programme for the next five years, the 'acceleration of progress'. This is political rhetoric of course – appropriate to a party that has held power for two terms and intends to offer more or less more of the same. But the point to note is that the rhetoric works upon a *moral* ground that connotes speed with dynamism as a social virtue. This is rather clear in Blair's authoritarian Christian-inflected 'New Labour' version of social democracy which blesses rapid technological advance, energetic entrepreneurialism and a high-paced consumerist lifestyle as features not just of material, but of (albeit in an ill-defined sense) *moral* betterment.

This moral underpinning of mechanical speed combines with the material benefits it offers and its sheer excitement, to construct a hugely powerful cultural narrative of social acceleration. We can understand this better if we consider the difficulties facing cultural critics of mechanization. The problem for opponents of industrial modernity in the nineteenth century is that, measured against the exuberance of the culture of machine velocity, their critique so often appears carping and regressive. Consider John Ruskin's invective against the railway entrepreneurs responsible for the construction of the Matlock and Buxton railway line in Derbyshire in the 1860s:

> There was a rocky valley between Buxton and Bakewell, once upon a time, divine as the vale of Tempe; you might have seen . . . Apollo and all the sweet Muses of the light walking in fair procession on the lawns of it. You cared neither for Gods nor grass, but for cash . . . . You Enterprised a Railroad through the valley – you blasted away its rocks, heaped thousands of tons of shale into its lovely stream. The valley is gone, and the Gods with it; and now every fool in Buxton can be at Bakewell in half-an-hour, and every fool in Bakewell at Buxton; which you think a lucrative process of exchange – you Fools Everywhere.
> (Ruskin, from *Fors Clavigera*, 1871, quoted in Jennings, 1995: 325)

Ruskin's main target – pretty much like that of present day environmentalists opposing the construction of a new motorway – is the commercial interests involved.[20] But he compromises this in his high-handed distain for the benefits of better and speedier communication. Compared with the prevailing popular discourse of mechanical progress, then, his appeal to classical antiquity in the description of the aesthetic-environmental loss sustained appears vapid and out of touch with the times.

Even less convincing is the campaign by William Wordsworth – another early conservationist (Bate, 1991) – against the Kendal and Windermere Railway which would penetrate into the heart of his adopted Lake District. Wordsworth was Poet Laureate at the time of this proposal in 1844 and, hoping to use the influence of his position, he wrote a letter of protest to the Prime Minister, William Gladstone, enclosing a short poem which was published, along with a letter, in the *Morning Post* the following day. The poem begins:

> And is no nook of English ground secure
> From rash assault? Schemes of retirement sown
> In youth, and 'mid the busy world kept pure
> As when their earliest flowers of hope were blown,
> Must perish; – how can they this blight endure?[21]

These lines get straight to the heart of Wordsworth's key objection, which is that the opening up of the Lake District to mass tourism – to 'swarms of pleasure hunters, most of them thinking that they do not fly fast enough through the country which they have come to see' – will damage it not just as an environment but as a place of 'retirement' – a retreat from the busy world which depends on its seclusion (quoted in Bicknell, 1984: 196). Like Ruskin, Wordsworth's enemies were the railway speculators and the 'Thirst of Gold that rull[ed] o'er Britain like a baneful star' (Freeman, 1999: 98). But he rather disastrously focused his argument against them on their claim to be providing easy and cheap access for the common people to share the beauties of the Lakes: 'the molestation of cheap trains pouring out their hundreds at a time along the margins of Windermere' (Wordsworth quoted in Bicknell, 1984: 192). This objection involved him in arguing that the 'humbler classes' would not be able to appreciate these beauties properly since they did not possess the requisite refinement of sensibility: 'a vivid perception of romantic scenery is neither inherent in mankind, nor a necessary consequence of even a comprehensive education'. Such a sensibility, 'is not to be implanted at once...it must be gradually developed' (1984: 188–9). Admitting the rights of the 'uneducated classes' to recreation and improvement, but discounting the possibility that this gradual process of cultural refinement could develop through day excursions to the Lakes from the neighbouring manufacturing towns, Wordsworth proposed that the workers, 'make little excursions with their wives and children amongst [their] neighbouring fields...where they can be trained to a profitable intercourse with nature' (1984: 191). As it were, on the nursery slopes of aesthetic appreciation and well clear of Ullswater or Windermere.[22]

As may be imagined, the argument did not go down well. Wordsworth, though past his radical prime, still saw himself as somehow aligned with the common people against the avaricious entrepreneurs and was genuinely hurt by the suggestion that he argued out of self-interest: that having found his idyll, he just wanted to keep the noisy masses out. But it was impossible to make the case for conservation in these aesthetic terms without coming hard up against a popular democratic impulse which the railway entrepreneurs had firmly on their side.

However, despite their failure to come to terms with the emerging popular democracy of the time, and the politics of social amenity, Ruskin and Wordsworth nevertheless raise, in their politically inept interventions, an important question of the *value* of speed in relation to other social goods: a question that remains as unanswered in the cultural discourse of the New Labour enterprise economy as in the heat of nineteenth-century industrial capitalist expansion, and which is only now gaining recognition in the environmental and 'slow' movements. The problem is that this issue of value struggles to emerge clearly given the overwhelming popular power of the discourse of progress which has dominated the culture of mechanical modernity. Where the issue of the social value of increased speed *does* emerge more sharply, however, is where it is posed at the productive heart of industrial capitalism: in the key nexus of time and profit, and in the workplace culture which this engenders.

Money

The impact of technologies is always conditioned by the socio-economic context of their application, and there can be little doubt of the significance of the context of capitalism to an understanding of mechanical speed. For its many critics, and indeed equally for its admirers, capitalism is *the* determining context, so much so that to advance explanations of social and cultural change that don't proceed directly from a perspective of political economy is often judged to fall into profound error, if not ideological mystification. Part of the challenge of a broader cultural assessment of the influence of capitalism is, indeed, to resist the pull towards a facile economic determinism, whilst recognising that capitalism is deeply implicated in the general acceleration of modern cultures. The problem facing cultural analysis is to distinguish and clarify the precise nature of this implication, particularly as capitalism is complexly interwoven with other aspects of modernity. In what ways, then, can capitalism be connected with increasing speed? The question can be approached in several ways.

At the most general level, capitalism is often seen as the *primum mobile* driving the development and application of machinery in the areas of industrial production and transportation and, as a result, producing the increase in the pace of life that mechanization brings. The case of the development of the railways in nineteenth-century Britain that we have been considering is an obvious example, and one to which Marx devotes considerable attention in *Capital* (Marx, 1976, 1978). According to this argument, though the railways appear as the fruits of human ingenuity and as part of the general emancipation of humanity from the constraints of nature – and though they *genuinely do* have this aspect – their underlying economic function is in the speeding up of the time taken for the transit of goods: thus the acceleration – optimally to the speed of 'the twinkling of an eye' – of the circulation time of capital (Freeman, 1999: 92f.).

A closely related line of argument concerns the influence of particular capitalist interests in the promotion of mechanized transportation. Schivelbusch, for instance, draws attention to the influence of the 1815 Corn Laws in Britain on the development of coal-powered locomotive transport.

The Corn Laws were intended to protect the interests of British agriculture by restricting imports of foreign corn. These laws – passed by a parliament dominated by the interests of agricultural capital – proved hugely unpopular in their unintended consequence of forcing the price of bread to levels damaging to both consumer and producer. But, according to Schivelbusch, they had the additional unforeseen consequence of driving on the development of mechanical power as a replacement for horsepower. As the price of grain for animal feed rose, so the early industrial capitalists turned their attention and resources increasingly to developing steam-powered locomotion. Schivelbusch maintains that the high cost of grain was, 'a recurrent and standard argument' in the promotion of the 'Railway Movement' in Britain from the 1820s, quoting from Thomas Graham's *A Treatise on Internal Intercourse and Communication in Civilised States* (1834):

> The landed capitalists of Britain...have by the taxes on corn and provisions more than doubled the price of animal labour...to avoid the effects of these taxes the monied capitalists of Britain have been for years devoting their capital to the promotion of those inventions by which taxed animal power may be dispensed with. (Graham quoted in Schivelbusch, 1980: 9)

Where opinion polarizes, this vigorous, dynamic, catalysing character of the capitalist system – its power to drive changes in technology and in cultural practices – is either seen as its prime and vindicating virtue, as the guarantor of social progress and prosperity, or contrarily, as the mark of its rapacity and its indifference to human or environmental well-being in the blind pursuit of profit. The central puzzle of capitalist culture however is that it combines, in varying proportions and dependent on the complexion of its political regulation, *both* of these elements. But, in whatever way they are governed, there is, undoubtedly, an inherent tendency for capitalist societies to produce an increase in social speed and the pace of life.

The simple, overall, explanation of this is, of course, that speed is the outcome of the pursuit of the maximization of profit. But this can be understood in relation to three different aspects of capitalism: in the character of the relations of production and work practices it promotes; in the acceleration of the market process (particularly in respect of finance capitalism); and in the sphere of consumption. Here I shall focus on the first of these, leaving most of the discussion of the other two until Chapters 4 and 6 respectively, and the contemporary period of capitalist modernity, where their implications are most sharply evident.

'Time is money' is surely one of the most succinct encapsulations of the spirit of capitalism.[23] The elegant reductionism of the phrase sets the parameters of debate about how one's time should (quite literally) be 'spent' in the hardnosed terms of profit margins and wages, and brooks no airy-fairy utopian argument. If it tends to conjure the image of a nineteenth-century cotton master, thumbs in broadcloth waistcoat pockets, driving his mill-hands, we should not be mistaken. This equation is not just the particular sentiment of a bygone unrestrained free-market entrepreneurialism, but a deeply structured operative principle of capitalist culture. It is inescapably present in twenty-first-century globalized capitalism in the long hours and forced pace of working in the 'lightly' regulated labour markets – the sweatshops – of South and East Asia and Latin America to which so many manufacturing and assembly operations have migrated. But it is equally with us in the West, in the culture of ostentatious work performance – breakfast meetings, 'last to leave the office syndrome' – that developed within corporate culture towards the end of the twentieth century. And more generally it exists as one of the core 'economic realities' that are so often invoked in policy debates.

A prime example of the latter is the debate within the European Union over working hours, that was marked in May 2005 by the vote of Members of the European Parliament to end the 'opt-out' available to member states of a measure restricting the maximum working week to 48 hours. The issue has most relevance to the United Kingdom, which originally negotiated the opt-out and which currently has the longest working hours in Europe. Here the debate falls between left-wing Labour and Green MEPs, union leaders, and the liberal press on the one hand – who argue for the need to restrict the growing culture of long working hours both on grounds of health and safety and to maintain the 'work–life balance' – and the representatives of business, robustly supported by the New Labour government on the other – who vigorously resist restrictions in the name of 'flexible labour markets' and the need to compete in a globalized capitalist market. What is interesting about this debate (apart from the fact that it displays so starkly the disengagement of the UK from the social democratic welfare consensus of most of the rest of western Europe) is the way in which it demonstrates the dominance of capitalist culture in defining the value of human time. The case for deregulation and 'flexibility' is sold to workers *purely* in economic terms. For example, the defence of the 'opt out' offered by the then chairman of the Confederation of British Industry, Sir Digby Jones was:

> It gives employees choice in the hours they work, allowing them to generate wealth for their families and companies to generate wealth for the nation. People need the opportunity to aspire and earn extra money if they want to. (quoted in *The Guardian*, 12 May 2005)

Leaving aside the familiar rhetorical elision of the interests of capital and labour and the emphasis on 'choice' (presumably excluding the choice to work fewer hours for similar wage rates), what is evident is that nowhere does this discourse recognize that time – that is to say the temporal *existence* of human beings – can be valued in anything other than financial terms. And what is more striking is that the response of organized labour, in the shape of the British Trades Union Congress, seems bound by the same terms of debate. The main argument put forward by the TUC in launching a campaign to end the 'opt-out' is that long working hours are, 'damaging to productivity'. Time is money.

Working long hours in itself does not, of course, necessarily entail working faster, but it seems very likely to contribute to an increased pace of life, particularly as it leaves less time in the day or week to negotiate all the other demands of a modern life – from the 'pledged time' of family commitments, travel, maintaining one's property, paying bills and so on, to the more subtle cultural 'duties' of routine communication, interaction with media technologies, self-presentation and consumption. We will come back to these increasingly significant time demands in Chapter 6.

But, for the present, staying with the experience of working life, it is clear that capitalism entails a perpetual struggle over the resource of time in which the interests of capital as buyer, and labour as seller, are in a structured opposition. This struggle historically has been – as it continues to be – variable in its tactics and emphasis: fought over the length of the working day, over the demands for security of employment as against the flexibility to hire and to lay-off at will (the optimal conditions for the capitalist), over payment for sick leave or holidays and so on. And amongst these the issue of speed emerges in the particular struggle over the *pace of work*, that is to say the drive to extract as much productive value from the worker's time as possible.

Nowhere is this struggle more directly focused than in the ideas of 'Scientific Management' propounded in the early years of the twentieth century by American engineer Frederick Winslow Taylor, particularly in his book, *The Principles of Scientific Management* (1911). Lampooned by Charlie Chaplin in the film *Modern Times*,[24] 'Taylorism' has become synonymous with the use of the time-and-motion study, intense worker scrutiny and the rigid differentiation of tasks to eliminate all 'wasted' actions from work processes and to maximize task efficiency. Although most generally thought of as a rather crude precursor to modern management and organizations theory – and one that has, it is often argued, now been superseded – Taylorism is more properly understood as one of the formative, and indeed enduring, strategies in the disciplining of the workforce within modern capitalism (Braverman, 1974; Hardt and Negri, 2000).

Harry Braverman, in what is perhaps the *locus classicus* of the critique of work relations in twentieth-century capitalism, points out that Taylorism, for all its 'scientific' pretensions proceeds, 'not from the human point of view but from the capitalist point of view, from the point of view of the management of a refractory workforce in a setting of antagonistic social relations' (Braverman, 1974: 86). The significance of Taylorism, then, lies not in its relationship to technological progress – indeed Taylor's most well-known example is of the most basic sort of manual labouring task, loading pig-iron. Its significance is more deep-seated: 'a theory which is nothing less than the explicit verbalization of the capitalist mode of production' (Braverman, 1974: 86).

This verbalization can be read through Taylor's blunt, no-nonsense engineer's style in which he expresses with almost disarming candour the standpoint of the capitalist interest. His starting point is that, 'the greatest prosperity can exist only as the result of the greatest possible productivity of the men and machines of the establishment' (Taylor, 1967: 12). And, 'the greatest obstacle to the attainment of this standard is the slow pace which [the workers] adopt, or the loafing or "soldiering", marking time as it is called' (Taylor, 'Shop Management', quoted in Braverman, 1974: 97). Deliberate slow working, indeed, constitutes, 'the greatest evil with which the working people of both England and America are now afflicted' (Taylor, 1967: 14) and the whole thrust of *The Principles of Scientific Management* is aimed at its elimination.

Taylor distinguished between two types of deliberate slow working. The first, which he calls, 'natural soldiering' is, 'the tendency of the average man (in all walks of life)...toward working at a slow easy gait'. The second – 'systematic soldiering' – 'is done by the men with the deliberate object of keeping their employers ignorant of how fast work can be done' (Taylor, 1967: 21). Taylor's discussion of 'soldiering' is an odd mixture of candid recognition that the workers are pursuing their rational interests on the one hand – for example in resisting the inevitable drop in rate for piecework measured at a fast pace – and a moral appeal to the (undefined) principle of 'a fair day's work' (Braverman, 1974: 97) and to the supposed (but fallacious) mutuality of purpose of the worker and employer on the other. There is neither moral nor psychological complexity here. What there is, however, is one of the clearest statements that management within capitalism is a matter of the control of the speed of the worker. The critique of Taylorism has generally focused on the deskilling of labour and the loss of control of the worker over his or her activity. But it is clear that these effects are all in the cause of increasing the pace of work. Thus Taylorism might reasonably be characterized as a set of techniques concerned with the shift in the locus of control of *working tempo* from the craftsman or labourer to the manager.

It is this core concern that has endured in the legacy of Taylorism to contemporary management theory and practice, particularly in low-pay/ low-skill employment such as that of the food service industry. For example, Royle's study of labour relations in McDonald's restaurants in Europe describes the character of 'McWork' as follows:

> [S]tandardisation and higher productivity are ensured through new technology and the systematic planning of each job, broken down into the smallest of steps. The corporation's industrial engineers measure and plan the equipment layout and scheduling in terms of seconds of working time using computerised time study methods. The worker's skills are eliminated and the work is labour intensive with the machinery making the cooking decisions. Lights and buzzers tell workers when to turn burgers or take fries out of the fat. Computerised cash registers do most of the thinking for till and window workers, separating hand and brain in classic scientific management style.... One German floor manager stated, 'Anyone can learn this job. There's no challenge for workers, only speed and exactitude'. (Royle, 2000: 58–9)

Working practices in fast food restaurants like McDonald's (see also, Ritzer, 2000; Schlosser, 2002) involve forms of worker control which recall in a rather striking manner some of the core aspects of Taylorism. Even the stress on leadership and teamwork – keeping up with the collective pace of the 'crew' – and the quasi-moral coercion which this represents – recalls Taylor's appeal to the team spirit of the sports field (Taylor, 1967: 13).

Whilst there can be no doubt, then, that there is inherent pressure to increase the pace of workplace life in capitalism, there are, however, a number of factors that prevent the realization of a completely Taylorized work regimen across the board. In the first place, by no means all industries lend themselves to the sort of banally routinized division of labour, surveillance and team-work pressure as McDonald's. In the second place, capitalist enterprises and their management systems come in all shapes and sizes and with great variety both in their zeal and their competence to extract the maximum productivity from their workforce. And, perhaps most significantly, employees, in all but the most extreme of coercive situations,[25] become skilled in 'playing the system' so as to maintain control over their working tempo: 'In imposing time discipline, capitalists unintentionally stimulated new forms of time-resistance such as goldbricking, working by rule, signalling the approach of supervisors...and stretching authorised breaks' (Tilly, 2002: 182).

A classic depiction of this is found in Alan Sillitoe's novel of British working-class life in the 1950s, *Saturday Night and Sunday Morning*. The hero, Arthur Seaton, an independently minded worker in a time of growing affluence and full employment, is a lathe operator in a bicycle factory. Though capable of a very high pace of work, he is equally skilled in maintaining his optimum piecework rate:

> At a piecework rate of four-and-six a hundred you could make your money if you knocked-up fourteen hundred a day – possible without grabbing too much – and if you went all out for a thousand in the morning you could dawdle through the afternoon and lark about with the women and talk to your mates now and again.... Though you couldn't grumble at four-and-six a hundred, the rate-checker sometimes came and watched you work, so that if he saw you knock up a hundred in less than an hour [the foreman] would come and tell you one fine morning that you had been dropped by sixpence or a bob. So when you felt the shadow of the rate checker breathing down your neck you knew what to do if you had any brains at all: make every move more complicated, though not slow because that was cutting your own throat, and do everything with a deliberate show of speed. (Sillitoe, 1973: 29–30)

Working the system in this way is of course an obvious, widely practiced and entirely rational response. But what is most significant is Arthur's attitude to the system itself. He has no developed political views – certainly he is no socialist – and in fact he has no stance of principle towards capitalism overall. Rather he responds entirely pragmatically, with an intuitive, rather aloof sense of what Braverman calls the 'antagonistic social relations' that characterize his working life: 'you earned your living in spite of the firm, the rate checker, the foreman and the tool-setters...most of the time you didn't give a sod about them but worked quite happily for a cool fourteen nicker' (1973: 31).

What most allows him this luxury of indifference is the clear-cut and *limited* nature of his 'contract' with the capitalist system. He looks for no preferment or promotion and, as a skilled and productive worker in a time of high labour demand, has no fear of redundancy. And he certainly has no expectation of a 'career' or of 'job satisfaction'. Shorn of these anxieties and constraints, employment becomes a simple exchange of time, skill and physical effort for wages. Most importantly, his employment has a quite limited reach into the rest of his life, allowing him to compartmentalize his existence in a reasonably agreeable way: forty-two hours a week in the factory, and cash-in-hand wages at the end of the week, buying Friday and Saturday night's enjoyment in the pub and Sunday afternoons, 'fishing...in the cool shade of the willow-sleeved canal'.

Time – time spent at work – is certainly money for Arthur Seaton, but in a clearly delimited sense. He makes the best bargain available with the alienation of his labour and retains a cynically detached sort of autonomy. The example is instructive if we compare the increasing reach of capitalism and its associated technologies into the rest of everyday life that has occurred in the period between the mid-1950s of the novel's setting and today. Arthur's world[26] was one in which there were no computers, no email, no internet, no call centres, no mobile phones, no supermarkets, shopping centres or Sunday trading; a world in which only one of the two British television stations carried advertising, a world before the invention of cash machines or credit or debit cards – and, for the working class at least, a world in which the personal ownership of cars, telephones, mortgages or even bank current accounts was rare enough to be the cause of comment. All these commonplaces of everyday life in present day industrial societies are, undeniably, the fruits of vigorous capitalist growth and the markers of a broad rising affluence. And yet all these advances in one way or another also extend the reach of economic imperatives into other spheres of life, and as a result, attenuate temporal autonomy, so increasing the experienced speed of everyday life. Just *how* they do this – either in terms of the time consumed in the 'servicing' of a high level of consumerism, the increasing integration of employment performance with personal identity and self-esteem, or the sheer time-demands of interfacing with communications technologies – is something we shall have to leave – time being short – until later in the book.

So, to summarize, it seems undeniable that capitalism, considered as a pure system of production and exchange, will, if left unconstrained, tend to drive the speed of workplace life according to a brutal competitive logic. This is a crucial consideration in assessing the sources of modern social speed, for employment within the capitalist order is the key social dynamic, *the* defining context, of most of our lives.[27] But, of course, constraints on capitalism – at least in the industrial democracies of the West – there clearly are. Whether in the form of state regulation, the resistance of workers (either in the organized form of unions or simply in the ingenuity or recalcitrance of individuals) or – never to be overlooked – in the simple incompetence of management, the impetus of capitalism meets daily obstacles. In order to understand the full impact of capitalism on the modern experience of speed, then, we need to look beyond the sphere of production to the practices of exchange and consumption that we will explore in later chapters.

The metropolis

A city made for speed is made for success. (Le Corbusier, 1971)

If the antithesis between a fast and a slow pace of life maps broadly on to the urban–rural divide, this, of course, is because city life is quintessentially *modern* life. The city is the place where the forces and fruits of modernity – capitalist enterprise, machine industrialism, the concentration of populations and the energy of their everyday activities, the traffic of crowds and vehicles, the constant encounter with strangers and with cultural difference, and the kaleidoscopic display of commodities and experiences for purchase – all come together. It is in the modern city that the acceleration of cultural pace has its 'natural' setting, and the experience of urban life typically displays the classic ambiguities of modernity – simultaneous vivacity and stress – in tempo as in so much else. Who could imagine modern speed as a general condition without also imagining the backdrop of the cityscape?

There is, however, a practical problem in coming to terms with the data of urban modernity and this is that it contains an *embarras de richesse*. Too many significant forces intersect here, there is too much evidential detail, too dense a pattern presents itself in the weave of metropolitan life. So as not to be daunted by this complexity we can focus on Le Corbusier's big, bold and confident – in fact rather simple – argument about the relationship of speed to urban life and let that pose some questions for us.

Le Corbusier's great modernist polemic on urban planning, *l'Urbanisme* (a title not entirely happily translated as *The City of Tomorrow*)[28] is a tour de force of single-mindedness. Writing in 1924, Le Corbusier (Charles-Edouard Jeanneret) is utterly convinced of the need radically and dramatically to re-construct the great cities – 'the spiritual workshops in which the work of the world is done' – to meet the challenge of 'the machine age'. The crux of this challenge is speed.

Le Corbusier's (apparent) attitude to speed is recorded in a well-known passage from the book's Foreword, describing the experience of the traffic on the Champs Elysées in the autumn of 1924:

> Motors in all directions, going at all speeds. I was overwhelmed, an enthusiastic rapture filled me. . . . The simple and ingenuous pleasure of being in the centre of so much power, so much speed. We are part of it. We are part of that race whose dawn is just awakening. We have confidence in this new society. . . . We believe in it. (Le Corbusier, 1971: 5)

Marshall Berman (1983), in an interesting and influential reading, stresses this moment of epiphany. At one point Le Corbusier has the sensibility of 'the familiar Baudelairean man in the street, dodging and fighting the traffic' and at the next moment he 'speaks from *inside* the traffic.... Now instead of being menaced by it, he can be a believer in it, a part of it' (1983: 167). In Berman's reading, Le Corbusier, with all the zeal of the convert to modernity, emerges as a slightly mad lyric visionary. This vision is to solve all the political and psychic contradictions of modern urban life at a stroke by the destruction of the old chaotic unplanned city where people and machines randomly and perplexingly mingle: 'We must kill the streets!'

Le Corbusier's writing is full of this sort of gesture, and it doesn't do to take him too seriously. *L'Urbanisme*, like the earlier *Towards a New Architecture* of 1923, is hugely polemical, and frequently both hyperbolic and ironical in style (Donald, 1997; Gold, 1997). The problem with focusing on the polemical high spots is that Le Corbusier's project gets confused with other rather different currents in the modernity of the time; with the Italian Futurists for instance – a very different kettle of fish as we shall see. Berman aligns Le Corbusier with Marinetti as a 'modernolator', and David Inglis (2004: 215), in an otherwise fascinating exploration of the automobile in French intellectual thought, makes the same mistake of suggesting his affinities with the Futurists. Describing his project for a 'contemporary city of three million inhabitants', however, Le Corbusier explicitly disavows this comparison: 'This is no dangerous futurism, a sort of literary dynamite flung violently at the spectator' (Le Corbusier, 1971: 178).

In point of fact Le Corbusier employs so many different rhetorical 'voices' in his writing that it's not surprising that such confusions arise. I am rather labouring these points of interpretation because it seems to me that there is an underlying dominant voice – let's call it the voice of the practical, rational architect – of the *planner* – that is the key both to Le Corbusier's wider architectural influence and to his contribution to the twentieth-century cultural discourse of machine speed.

Time after time, Le Corbusier expresses the issue of speed in the old unplanned city as a *problem* requiring an architectural and a planning solution. He discusses the problems of traffic congestion, traffic accidents, fatigue and 'nervous sickness', and he dwells quite alarmingly on the issue of atmospheric pollution from exhaust gases: 'Already in the month of May in the Champs Elysées half the chestnuts lining the avenue have their leaves withered... Only May!...Year in, year out, and unperceived by us, our lungs absorb these dangerous gases. But the martyred trees cry out, "Beware!"' (1971: 199).

But the core problem, the one from which all these others derive, is the inadequacy to the demands of modern machine speed of cities which have grown organically from medieval origins. The first chapter lays out the problem in formal terms as a choice between the curve and the straight line: 'The Pack Donkey's Way and Man's Way':

> [A] modern city lives by the straight line, inevitably; for the construction of buildings, sewers and tunnels, highways, pavements. The circulation of traffic demands the straight line; it is the proper thing for the heart of a city. The curve is ruinous, difficult and dangerous; it is a paralysing thing. (1971: 18)

Actually Le Corbusier is intervening here in a rather older aesthetic debate about the virtues of straight or crooked streets initiated by a book – 'a most wilful piece of work' – by the Viennese architect Camillo Sitte in 1889.[29] Le Corbusier's bile against Sitte's rather nostalgic celebration of the charms of the irregular is consistent with his polemical style – as is the high moral tone adopted. But his obsession with geometry, with the straight line and the right angle – which was eventually to pass[30] – are less important than his conflation of rationality and order with *functionality*. Le Corbusier is famous for his uncompromising stress on the relation of form to function, encapsulated in dictums like, 'The house is a machine for living in', 'A town is a tool' and 'The street is a traffic machine'. It is this functionalism – one might even say instrumental rationality – that is most significant in forming his discourse in relation to speed.

For when it comes to his practical proposals, Le Corbusier provides the classic example of rational deduction – 'a continuous train of thought taken to its logical conclusion' (1971: 181) – but one based on an unexamined premise: 'One can only come to this conclusion; that the city which can achieve speed will achieve success – and this is an obvious truth' (1971: 190–1). What does success mean? Compared to Camillo Sitte's Aristotelian principle of city planning, 'to facilitate happiness' (Frisby, 2001: 194), Le Corbusier is both pragmatic and prosaic. Success is clearing away the clutter of the old *Cité* to allow room for the serious work of the *hommes des affairs*: 'Men of *business* have now definitely concentrated in the centres of towns. The rhythm which actuates business is obvious; it is speed and the struggle for speed' (1971: 96, emphasis in original). Success lies in providing the conditions for this pulse of business: 'This is the ideal city. A model city for commerce!' (1971: 190).

But Le Corbusier is by no means a self-conscious apologist for capitalism. He ends his book by declaring his independence of political-economic alignment: 'I am an architect; [and this work] is not dedicated to our existing Bourgeois-Capitalist Society nor to the Third International. It is a technical work' (1971: 301). This is surely a sincere and, in a sense, an entirely accurate self-assessment. His attitude to capitalism is naïve: 'business' is a sort of 'given' of everyday life that naturally has to be prioritized since it produces wealth and gives employment. On this basis it is justified – rational – to raze 600 acres of the historic centre of Paris, from Montmartre to the Seine, to provide space for a high-density 'gridiron' business development of skyscrapers – a 'vertical city' serviced by a 'speedway' which will be the 'GHQ of Business'. The 'Voisin Plan'[31] envisages this high-rise business hub as a French rationalized version of New York or Chicago. And the rationalization is one aimed at facilitating rapid communications:

> Work begins, and speeded up by efficient organization, goes on busily in luminous and even radiant offices...Everything is concentrated in them: apparatus for abolishing time and space, telephones, cable and wireless; the banks, business affairs and the control of industry; finance, commerce, specialization. (Le Corbusier, 1971: 184–7)

In part this is a reasonably accurate prediction of the modern downtown business hub. But where Le Corbusier's vision is wildly over-optimistic is in his supposition that the combination of speed and planning will deliver quality of life. He predicts that the super-efficiency of the new city will mean a shorter working day, finishing 'perhaps...soon after midday. After which, the city will empty as though by a deep breath' (1971: 191).

Although Le Corbusier has been characterized as applying Taylorism to architecture (Mcleod, 1983), in a curious way his attitude to capitalist labour-time is not unlike Arthur Seaton's. The necessity of work is something simply, ineluctably, inertly *there* at the core of our social existence: an activity to be expedited quickly and efficiently, rather than criticized, after which we can go quickly home to enjoy 'the hours of repose'. Unlike Arthur, however, he thinks of leisure as another activity to be planned and organized. And so the successful city is one in which social amenity – in the garden suburbs of mass cellular-system housing set amongst sporting and exercise facilities and communal allotments – is integrated with working life to provide a healthy rational, ordered modern lifestyle.

Had it not been for the largely disastrous experience of the modernist planned housing schemes of the 1960s and 1970s[32] which it inspired, it is not at all unlikely that we may have looked back on Le Corbusier's vision of an urban pastoral with more warmth. Despite its – in retrospect – obvious flaws, there is something both initially plausible and attractive in the central idea that speed, the energy of capitalist industry and new technologies can – with the application of reason and planning – deliver a better quality of life. And, indeed, this is what is most instructive in the example of Le Corbusier's work. Despite all the scorn heaped upon the modernist vision by later urban planners, the deep grammar of modernism – faith in reason, order and progress, optimism, energy and the engineer's enthusiasm to *intervene* – have continued as key aspects of our political institutional culture. And this is not simply the triumph of hope over experience. Engineering and planning 'solutions' have definitively shaped – and continue to shape – both the urban environment and the urban cultural imagination.

But what is also instructive – because it also represents a more general aspect of early modern regulatory discourse – are those elements of modern urban culture which the problem-solving stance either passes lightly over, or deliberately turns its face away from: ungovernable desire, desultoriness and danger. Le Corbusier's ideal metropolis is populated by rational, orderly and law-abiding beings who stick to their allotted places and paths both in the social and the spatial orders:

> Great men and our leaders install themselves in the city's centre. There too we find their subordinates of every grade, whose presence there at certain hours is essential, though their destinies are circumscribed within the narrower bounds of family life.... Finally there is industry with its factories thickly grouped... about the great centres: and working in these factories are multitudes of workers...who spend their lives between suburban factories and garden cities. (Le Corbusier, 1971: 102)

No one trespasses in this city. The constant accidental social mixing which Le Corbusier sees as so wicked and chaotic in the old Paris – 'the dangerous magma of human beings gathered from every quarter by conquest, growth and immigration' – is planned away, and with it the dangerous aspects of speed – dangers of social and cultural collision. We get little sense that Paris was either a class-antagonistic or a culturally or ethnically vibrant city in the 1920s. Similarly, there is no space for the 'fast living' in which the wealthy mingle with the *demi-monde*. Indeed there are few temptations: shops and cafés are occasionally mentioned, but their cultural significance is barely recognized. It is as though Walter Benjamin's arcades, the 'primordial landscape of consumption' (Gilloch, 1996: 123) – and perhaps even the *Bon Marché* – were, like Baudelaire's *souterrains*, imagined as simply part of a general dysfunctional clutter that could be cleared away to reveal the true spirit of Paris, which, for Le Corbusier, 'is fundamentally limpid and beautiful' (1971: 31).

Probing Le Corbusier's rhetoric discloses perhaps less of an ominous obsession with social hygiene, than a simple indifference and insensitivity to the social anthropology of street life; and it is because of this that his vision of urban speed is at once powerful and banal. There is not a glimmer of recognition of the fundamental ambiguities of modern existence: the simultaneous horrors and attractions, the mix of stress and excitement, of urgent opportunity and casual insouciance that is the quick of urban life.

It is not that he does not recognize *problems* that attend a modern lifestyle: he comments, for instance on the nervous energy used up in the office routine of a shorthand typist, by which, 'she slowly wears herself out'. His perspective on this is, predictably, therapeutic: he prescribes healthy outdoor exercise and gentle work in the communal gardens (Le Corbusier, 1971: 206). Considered both in context and in retrospect, this is not quite so simple-minded as it appears. As Stephen Kern (2003) documents, there was, from at least the 1880s, a string of extravagantly alarmist prognoses of the effects of the pace of modern life on the human nervous system. In one of the earliest and most influential, *American Nervousness: Its Causes and Consequences* (1881), George M. Beard introduced the concept of 'neurasthenia' into psychotherapeutic discourse:

> Beard argued that the telegraph, railroads, and steam power have enabled businessmen to make 'a hundred times' more transactions in a given period than had been possible in the eighteenth century; they intensified competition and tempo, causing an increase in the incidence of a host of problems including neurasthenia, neuralgia, nervous dyspepsia, early tooth decay and even premature baldness. (Kern, 2003: 125)

Compared with this, and even wilder pathological speculations that continued into the twentieth century, Le Corbusier's implicit faith in the resilience of the human constitution – given an orderly, planned restorative regimen – seems reasonably vindicated. But what he entirely missed – as indeed did the prophets of neurotic disaster – was the way in which 'nervous excitement' can be understood as a complex *cultural* response to urban modernity – as, indeed, a way of life.

The theorist most frequently credited with a nuanced appreciation of the culture of early urban modernity, its relation to the money economy and, in particular, the response to the nervous stimulation provided by metropolitan life is Georg Simmel. In his well-known essay 'The Metropolis and Mental Life' (1903), Simmel offers a penetrating analysis of the influence of the urban environment on the formation of a specifically 'metropolitan type of individuality'. Key to this is what he famously describes as the 'blasé attitude' – an 'incapacity to react to new sensations with the appropriate energy.... the blunting of discrimination' in which 'no object deserves preference over any other' (Simmel, 1997b: 178). The blasé attitude is a direct response to the increased pace of life in cities – 'the intensification of nervous stimulation which results from the swift and uninterrupted change in...stimuli' (Simmel, 1997b: 175). This tempo is contrasted by Simmel with the slow, habitual and even rhythm of rural life:

> the rapid crowding of changing images, the sharp discontinuity in the grasp of a single glance, and the unexpectedness of onrushing impressions. These are the psychological conditions which the metropolis creates. With each crossing of the street, with the tempo and multiplicity of economic, occupational and social life, the city sets up a deep contrast with small town and rural life. (1997b: 175)

The blasé attitude is associated with other features of the emergent social psychology of urban interaction – the 'calculating attitude' arising from relations dominated by the money economy and the phenomenon of interpersonal 'reserve' as a way of dealing with the anonymity of everyday encounters and the 'touch and go elements of metropolitan life' (1997b: 179). All these can be seen as subtle insights into social-psychological *pathologies* of high-tempo urban existence, but as David Frisby (2001: 151) acutely observes, 'we are observing pathologies of metropolitan existence as increasingly *normal* features of urban interaction'. Simmel offers us not so much a clinical diagnosis or a moral-political indictment of the pathologies of urban life (and to this extent he cannot be considered a direct antagonist of the modernism exemplified by Le Corbusier) as a *cultural analysis* of, 'the inner meaning of specifically modern life and its products, [of] the soul of the cultural body' (Simmel, 1997b: 175).[33]

In this his sociology leans more towards the phenomenological sensibilities of the novelist than of the scientist. And, in fact, we can turn to a novelist of the modern condition, Robert Musil, for a more distilled impression of the experience of metropolitan speed.

The opening chapters of Musil's epic novel *The Man Without Qualities* paint a vivid picture of the rush of life in Vienna in 1913. On the first page

Musil sets the scene in impressionistic terms of the intersecting rhythms and speeds of traffic and pedestrians:

> Automobiles shot out of deep, narrow streets into the shallows of bright squares. Dark clusters of pedestrians formed cloudlike strings. Where more powerful lines of speed cut across their casual haste they clotted up, then trickled on faster and, after a few oscillations, resumed their steady rhythm. (Musil, 1995: 1)

Later, in a striking passage, he goes on to describe the popular 'daydream' of an even more accelerated high-tech metropolis:

> – a kind of super-American city where everyone rushes about , or stands still, with a stopwatch in hand. Air trains, ground trains, underground trains, people mailed through tubes special delivery, and chains of cars race along horizontally, while express elevators pump masses of people vertically from one traffic level to another; at the junctions people leap from one vehicle to the next, instantly sucked in and snatched away by the rhythm of it, which makes a syncope, a pause, a little gap of twenty seconds during which a word might be hastily exchanged with someone else. Questions and answers synchronise like meshing gears; everyone has only certain fixed tasks to do; professions are located in special areas.... Other parts of the city are centres of entertainment, while still others contain the towers where one finds wife, family, phonograph and soul. (Musil, 1995: 27)

Stephen Kern interprets this as, 'a caricature of Europe speeding out of control, heading towards war' (Kern, 2003: 127) but it could equally be read as a lampoon of the sort of high-speed heroic functionalism – an odd blend of the Nietzschian ideal of the *Übermensch*[34] with Taylorism – which lay in the hinterland of Le Corbusier's pristine planning vision. What is more striking about Musil's imagination, though, is the way it grasps precisely the *resistance* of the dynamism of modern life to planning. Dismissing these daydreams as superficial fantasies, he goes on:

> Presumably it is up to us to...come up with a plan for us all. If all that high-speed business doesn't suit us, let's try something else! For instance, something quite slow-moving, with a veiled billowing, sea-slug-like, mysterious happiness and the deep cow-eyed gaze the ancient Greeks admired. But that is not how it really is; we are at the mercy of our condition. We travel in it day and night, doing whatever else we do, shaving, eating, making love, reading books, working at our jobs as though those four walls were standing still: but the uncanny thing is that those walls are moving along without our noticing it, casting their rails ahead like long, groping, twisted antennae, going we don't know where. (Musil, 1995: 28)

This sense of the ungovernable impetus of modern-urban speed – of being carried along by the 'Juggernaut of modernity' (Giddens, 1990) at precisely the same time that we live out the repeating, familiar routines of our quotidian lives, could hardly be a greater contrast to Le Corbusier's faith in order, planning and foresight, in 'a society that goes to work in a positive way and *controls itself*' (Le Corbusier, 1971: 18). And yet *both* perspectives are important for understanding the constitution and experience of metropolitan social speed.

Conclusion

What the social phenomenology of Musil or Simmel reveals is that speed is much, much more than the simple application of machine technology to social or economic practices and processes – and more even than the generalized cultural attitude that underpins this application. Metropolitan speed is no less than the experienced interface between a human lifeworld governed by the biological constitution and temporal frame of our existence, and the complex, ungovernable dynamics of the modern institutions into which we are inserted and which sweep us along even as we struggle to construct and enact our life projects.

Le Corbusier clearly had no such grasp of the nature of the social forces which were shaping his world and which ultimately must frustrate his plans for a patterned, regulated, speed-efficient metropolis. None the less, his project remains exemplary in that it demonstrates how powerful the informing narrative of order, control and regulation are in the very consti-tution of the institutional modernity in which we have – at least until comparatively recently – been immersed. As Stephen Kern (2003: 129) nicely puts it, all the sophisticated cultural critique, the intellectual dissent and the anxiety over the accelerating pace of life, 'cannot negate the fact that the world opted for speed time and again'. And a major part of the reason for this is that speed presents itself in its functional, developmental aspect – as the prime condition for economic growth and for the delivery of material improvement in everyday life – in the most impeccably rational, progressive terms. This sort of speed is the energetic, dutiful offspring of a good marriage between liberal capitalism and progressive engineering.

However this is not the only progeny of mechanical modernity. Machine speed has a rival sibling, whose wilful fancy turns, as we shall now see, towards other far less improving, instrumental or prudential pursuits.

Notes

1 To give just some sense of this level of wild speculative investment and construction, by 1848 no less than five railway companies had built lines to Brighton (Wilson, 2002: 72).

2 Although Richard Trevethick's first steam railway locomotive ran as early as 1804, the first scheduled passenger service, covering the 25 miles between Stockton and Darlington, began in 1825. Probably of most significance in establishing the viability of the railways was the Liverpool and Manchester Railway, opened in 1830. This line, on which George Stephenson's famous 'Rocket' ran, was the first to use exclusively mechanical power and to utilize a proper railway station.

3 As Freeman (1999: 38f.) notes, the most frequent metaphor used to grasp the entirely novel experience of movement at such speeds was that of 'flight'. For example, he cites Fanny Kemble's reaction to her journey with George Stephenson in 1830 on the Liverpool and Manchester Railway at a speed of 35 miles per hour: 'It was impossible to conceive, she went

on to say , what "the sensation of cutting the air was": when the eyes were closed it was exactly as if in flight' (Freeman, 1999: 40). As Freeman goes on to say, the metaphor of flight often took on, 'a less comfortable dimension in the depiction of the railroad train as a projectile' – a cannon ball, a bullet, or, of course, a rocket.

4 For reasons of scope, I have had to restrict the discussion to the case of railways in Britain, the place of their birth. There is an extensive literature on the history of British railways (see, inter alia, Clapham, 1950; Robbins, 1962; Simmons, 1968; Perkin, 1970; Simmons and Biddle, 1997), but a rather smaller one on their cultural history. Of these the ones I draw most on are: Ian Carter's excellent *Railways and Culture in Britain* (2001) which, as its sub-title suggests, sees them as epitomizing the general advance of modernity; Michael Freeman's comprehensive and erudite *Railways and the Victorian Imagination* (1999) and Wolfgang Schivelbusch's indispensable classic study, *The Railway Journey* (1980) which extends beyond the British experience. Simon Garfield's very readable *The Last Journey of William Huskisson* (2002) gives a nice snapshot of railway enterprise in the 1820s and Bryan Morgan's *The Railway-Lover's Companion* (1963) is a rich anthology of literary sources and contemporary cultural observation.

5 Babbage is famous for his attempts to design a mechanical 'difference engine'. Beginning in the 1820s, so coinciding with the birth of the railways, these attempts anticipated the modern computer, the emblematic speed technology of our age, by over a century. For a fascinating assessment of Babbage's significance, see Spufford and Uglow (1996).

6 And, more recently, as an encapsulation of the dynamics of the globalization process, Freeman (1999: 247) traces the earliest use of the phrase to the *Liverpool Railway Companion* of 1833.

7 As Raymond Williams points out, this is an account written 'not just by rural or literary people at some distance from it'. James Naysmith was an industrialist and the inventor of the steam hammer. See the essay 'Socialism and Ecology' in Williams (1989: 211).

8 See Marx's discussion of the key mid-century technological development of, 'the production of machines by machines' by which he says modern industry, 'stood on its own feet'. Marx uses the example of Naysmith's steam hammer (Marx,1976: 384f.). See also the more detailed discussion of Knowles (1921: 74f.).

9 The whole issue of the relationship of the British working class to the Great Exhibition is a complicated and fascinating one (see, inter alia, Davis, 1999; Gurney, 2001). Clearly they are not in any meaningful sense properly included or represented, either in the organization and planning of the event, nor, even allowing the concessionary 'shilling days', as paying spectators. But though the Exhibition clearly belongs to the modernizing industrial capitalist interest, the event can also in part be read as an attempt by the liberal and moderately reformist elements of the upper-classes to engage with the working class, via education – if only to avert the threats of social revolution seen across Europe in 1848. This is seen, for example, in the abortive attempt by the Bishop of Oxford's 'Central Working Classes Committee' (supported by Prince Albert) to exercise influence on the Royal Commission's planning. And, the key point for the argument here, despite sceptical radical opinion on both the left and the right – both Marx and Carlyle condemned it – Mayhew's assessment of the sober enthusiasm for the exhibition of ordinary people motivated by the rational desire for self-improvement is almost certainly correct.

10 Walter Benjamin took a much more jaundiced view of the working classes' attendance at world exhibitions (like that of the Paris 1855 exhibition), seeing them as, 'the high school in which the masses, dragged away from consumption, learned to empathize with exchange value: "look at everything, touch nothing"' Benjamin, 'Das Passagen-Werk' quoted in Frisby, 1985: 254. But I think this, quite apart from the way it can be read as exaggerating the susceptibility of 'the masses' to ideological manipulation, simply misses something rather obvious about the practical and aesthetic attractions of invention and machinery.

11 During the 1930s the General Post Office (GPO) Film Unit, under the directorship of John Grierson, became a focus for leftist artists and intellectuals, employing, amongst others, W.H. Auden, Benjamin Britten, the painter William Coldstream and the directors Basil Wright,

Alberto Cavalcanti and also Humphrey Jennings – the compiler of *Pandaemonium* and one of the co-founders of the 'Mass Observation' movement.

12 'TPO' for 'Travelling Post Office'. The first travelling post office – a converted horsebox utilized to enable the sorting of mail whilst the train was on the move – ran on the Grand Junction Railway in 1838. By 1852 the mechanical bag exchange system was introduced which remained in use on the British railway system, little modified, until its eventual withdrawal in 1971. Although improved acceleration and braking capabilities of modern locomotives, along with other developments in postal delivery practices made the mechanical exchange apparatus obsolete, the TPO continued to run into the 1990s as a mobile sorting office, see Blakemore (1990). The 'Up-Special TPO' – running in the opposite direction to the Night Mail – achieved fame in 1963 when it became the victim of the 'Great Train Robbery', an event chiefly remembered today for the colourful fugitive criminal Ronald Biggs.

13 In his essay 'In Praise of Idleness' written around the same time as the making of *Night Mail*, Russell says,

> Work is of two kinds: first, altering the position of matter at or near the earth's surface relatively to other such matter; second, telling other people to do so. The first kind is unpleasant and ill paid; the second is pleasant and highly paid. (Russell, 1967: 11)

It's a nice point, and Russell's main statement of the socialist case for the reduction of the working day to no more than four hours retains a good deal of force. However he not only offers too simplistic a view of the nature of what we might call 'managerial labour' – certainly not so pleasant as he assumes – he also overlooks the element of genuine 'dignity in labour' – for example in the satisfactions of precise human-machine co-ordination and in team working – that the film, despite some over-romanticizing, captures.

14 Although these themes now seem so distant from the representation of working life, they in fact continued to occupy a central place in the British Documentary movement right up into the 1970s. An important example is the work of the British Transport Commission's Film Unit, set up in 1949 following the nationalization of transport by the post-war Labour government. Under the direction of Edgar Anstey, this group produced an extraordinary range of informational, promotional and training films. Films like *Snowdrift at Bleath Gill* (1955), *Train Time* (1952) and *Work in Progress* (1951) typify the celebration of energetic progressive industry of this generally left-leaning group. For examples of this corpus, now held in the National Film and Television Archive, see the BFI's 'British Transport Films Collection'.

15 On the connection between the idea of progress and the general 'time consciousness' of modernity see, for example, Delanty, 1999: 38f.

16 In particular, the association of the idea of progress with the social-evolutionary thinking which Spencer represents. Although it may be worth noting, if only as a sidelight, that Spencer began his career as an engineer on the London and Birmingham Railway.

17 Thus, for example, Jacques Ellul's relentless critique of the delusions of technological advances none the less recognizes that there is an undeniable 'material basis' to progress: 'For modern man with his peculiar orientation – which has material possessions and "stomach" as the central values – the period of great hopes indeed arrived' (Ellul, 1964: 193). Ellul correctly says that comparisons of quality of life are difficult because of inherent problems of incommensurability across historical epochs. However it is ultimately his Catholicism – 'the primacy of the spiritual' – that prevents him from fully conceding the deep material attractions of industrial progress.

18 For discussions see, inter alia, Alexander, 1990; Lasch, 1991; Sztompka, 1993; McQuire, 1998.

19 See the discussion of convenience goods in Chapter 6.

20 On the issue of the expropriation of land for railway construction during the Railroad Mania in the mid-nineteenth century see Freeman, 1999: 31f.

21 'Sonnet on the Projected Kendal and Windermere Railway', Wordsworth (Bicknell, 1984: 185).

22 The letters can be found in an Appendix to Wordsworth's *Guide to the Lakes* (Bicknell (ed.), 1984). For a useful summary of the issue see, 'Wordsworth's Arguments against the Kendal and Windermere Railway' (www.mthyoke.edu/course/rschwart).

23 As is often the case with famous sayings, the origins of 'Time is Money' are obscure. Though the phrase is often attributed to Benjamin Franklin, it was almost certainly used before his time. Teresa Brennan (2003) gives it to the fifteenth-century thinker, Alberti. There are several variations extant: Edward Thompson (1991: 352), for instance quotes Henry Fielding in 1751: 'To the upper Part of Mankind Time is an Enemy, and... their chief Labour is to kill it; whereas for the others, Time and Money are almost synonymous'. In one of the most interesting uses, George Gissing exploits the reversibility of the term: 'Time is money – says the vulgarest saw known to any age or people. Turn it round about and you get a precious truth – money is time.... With money I buy for cheerful use [in writing] the hours which would not in any sense be mine; nay, which would make me their miserable bondsman' (Gissing, 1953: 216).

24 Chaplin's 1936 film depicts in comic form the alienation of the factory worker under constant surveillance and time pressure, particularly in a famous sequence depicting the abortive use of an automatic mechanical 'feeding machine' to increase workers' production line efficiency.

25 As, for example, in the extreme competition for employment in sweatshop labour in high population, developing counties. In this regard it should be noted, however, in Taylor's defence, that he was opposed to sweatshop labour and saw his scientific principles as a way of ameliorating this sort of crude physical exploitation. This may have been one of the reasons why figures like Lenin became attracted by Taylorism.

26 And the world of my childhood. I grew up in the same street in which Alan Sillitoe lived and in which he set the novel, and my father and mother both worked in the Raleigh bicycle factory during the 1950s.

27 And this is a context that reaches beyond the workplace. Consider Tilly's observation that capitalist time-discipline created the phenomenon of the 'rush hour' 'when many people were travelling between home and workplace because multiple firms summoned and dismissed their workers simultaneously' (2002: 181).

28 Besides being a hostage to fortune which has not dealt kindly with it, the translation does not grasp the point, made in the 1945 Preface, that *l'Urbanism* was primarily intended as a critique of contemporary architectural practice. Le Corbusier in point of fact eventually changed his mind about quite a number of his individual recommendations – for instance the controversial proposals for class-divided housing – but he is remarkably consistent in his central convictions about order, balance and rational planning: 'Principles... which have never been departed from' (1971: xi).

29 See David Frisby's (2001: 195) discussion of Sitte's position in relation to the 'shallow modernity' involved in the plans for the re-development of Vienna by Otto Wagner.

30 Le Corbusier's only church, The Chapel of Notre Dame du Haut, Ronchamp, built in 1957, is marked by its entirely curvilinear design, with sloping and curving ceilings and floors, and, in fact, containing no parallel planes whatsoever. Ironically it was the use of reinforced concrete – the 'brutal' material with which his style of modernism is so inextricably linked today – that allowed him to produce such flowing structures.

31 Emphasizing the link between urban planning and the automobile, the *Plan Voisin* is named after its sponsor, the now forgotten Voisin motor-car company. Both Peugeot and Citroën had turned Le Corbusier down.

32 For critiques of Le Corbusier's legacy and of its inappropriate application in urban planning see Jacobs (1961), Holston (1989), Hall (1996) and Gold (1997). Lodder (2006) gives an interesting account of Le Corbusier's place within the various strands of utopian thinking in the modernist movement. See also Kristin Ross's comments (1995: 53–4) on the enduring dominance of the demands of automobile circulation in Parisian urban planning during the 1960s – see for example, George Pompidou's statement that, 'Paris must adapt itself to the automobile. We must renounce an outmoded aesthetic' (Ross, 1995: 54).

33 A comparable analysis of the experience of metropolitan life can be found in Walter Benjamin's famous encapsulation – in his discussion of Baudelaire – of the modern urban experience as one of 'shock':

> Fear, revulsion, and horror were the emotions which the big-city crowd aroused in those who first observed it.... Moving through this traffic involves the individual in a series of shocks and collisions. At dangerous intersections, nervous impulses flow through him in rapid succession like the energy from a battery. (Benjamin, 1979a: 176–7, see also, Wolin, 1982: 226ff.)

Benjamin's analysis of modernity has a much more directly critical-comparative edge – for instance in the way in which he speaks of the development of a defence in consciousness against shocks as, a 'disintegration' and as being, 'at the cost of the integrity of [experience's] contents', or explicitly of, 'the deterioration of experience'. Or, again, in his explicit connection of the shock experience with Marx's comments on the worker's experience of machine production (Benjamin, 1979a: 177). Despite this – and the fact that Benjamin extends his analysis to the media technologies of his time – photography, film – it seems to me that Simmel's more dispassionate phenomenology in an odd way retains rather more resonance today.

34 See, for instance, John Gold's discussion of the influence of the architect and Nietzsche enthusiast Henry van de Velde in the formation of the modernist notion of the 'New Man': 'a product of the era of machine invention. He eats, sleeps, works and amuses himself efficiently, sweeping aside irrelevant objects despite their apparent glamour' (quoted in Gold, 1997: 35).

3

Unruly Speed

In the aspects of the culture of machine speed we have explored so far, the dominance of the great modern cultural values of reason, order and progress has been inescapable. Even where the core social impetus has been capitalist development, the haste and rapaciousness implicit in the profit motive has been contained within, and to some degree constrained by, a social ideology stressing order, control, management, planning and coordination. Speed as an increase in the pace of life has therefore most generally been represented, justified and experienced as a necessary aspect of the bending of nature (including human nature) to human design in the cause of progress.

Rationality is not, however, the be-all-and-end-all of modernity. Alongside the reasoned course of velocity-as-progress, there has developed quite a different imagination of machine speed, associating it with the far less indisputably rational elements of excitement, thrill, danger, risk and violence. Before we can generalize about the cultural significance of speed we surely have to pay attention to this other unruly child of mechanical modernity. And then – crucially – we need to ask how these two discourses relate to each other.

'Time and space died yesterday'

If we were to choose an event emblematic of the emergence of this more sensational discourse of machine speed, it might be the publication in *Le Figaro* of Filippo Tommaso Marinetti's 'Futurist Manifesto' in 1909. The date has some significance. The beginning of the Futurist movement a few years before the outbreak of the First World War allowed it a peculiarly pure enthusiasm for the mixture of excitement and violence of machine-speed, unchastened by the horrors of twentieth-century mechanical warfare that were swiftly to follow. And, equally important, 1909 stands within a particularly compressed moment in the technological development of modernity. This is two years before Frederick Taylor published his *Scientific Management* but already new, far less earth-bound senses of the human relationship with machine technology are emerging – senses corresponding to the shift, in Lewis Mumford's analysis, from the 'paleotechnic' to the 'neotechnic' age. It is a new type and experience of machinery and energy – of objects and vehicles sleek, clean, powerful, beautiful and desirable – that inspire the Futurist moment. So in the same year that Bleriot flew across the English channel, the Model 'T' Ford started in production, the first Pathé Newsreel appeared, and the Indianapolis racetrack opened, Marinetti's florid, 'incendiary' polemic pronounced that:

> the world's magnificence has been enriched by a new beauty; the beauty of speed. A racing car whose hood is adorned with great pipes, like serpents of explosive breath – a roaring car that seems to ride on shrapnel is more beautiful than the *Victory of Samothrace*.... Time and Space died yesterday. We already live in the absolute, because we have created eternal omnipresent speed.... We will sing the vibrant nightly fervour of arsenals and shipyards blazing with violent electric moons;... adventurous steamers that sniff the horizon; deep-chested locomotives whose wheels paw the tracks like the hooves of enormous steel horses bridled by tubing; and the sleek flight of planes whose propellers chatter in the wind like banners and seem to cheer like an enthusiastic crowd. (Marinetti, 1973a: 22)

Italian Futurism was a complex, composite and frequently internally incoherent body of artistic, cultural and political ideas (Apollonio, 1973; Perloff, 2003) but there is no disputing its obsession with speed. Some of the artists associated with the movement – notably the painter Giacomo Balla, the musician and painter Luigi Russolo and painter and sculptor Umberto Boccioni – made serious and interesting technical attempts to capture the dynamism of this new speed. Despite this, the wider significance of Futurism judged purely as a corpus of artistic work contributing to modernism remains a matter of dispute.[1] But it is Marinetti himself who epitomizes the cultural spirit of Futurism, which was, after all, his own coining. Robert Hughes (1991: 40) nicely sums Marinetti up as, 'a singular creature, sired as it were, by Gabriele d'Annunzio out of a turbine, inheriting the tireless and repetitive energy of the latter and the opportunistic dandyism of the former ... the first *agent provocateur* of modern art'.

There can be no doubt that it is Marinetti's inflammatory, proto-Fascist prose that is most remembered today, if only for its sheer excess: 'We will glorify war – the world's only hygiene – militarism, patriotism ... and scorn for women. We will destroy the museums, libraries ... we will fight moralism, feminism, every opportunistic or utilitarian cowardice' (Marinetti, 1973a: 22). As is well known, Marinetti developed a complicated political, artistic and personal relationship with Mussolini's Fascism (Tisdall and Bozzolla, 1977: 200ff.) and the Fascist inclinations of the Manifesto are evident enough. Despite this, it obviously cannot be taken literally as a political programme that any voter might seriously be expected to subscribe to: 'Come on! set fire to the library shelves! Turn aside the canals to flood the museums! ... Take up your pickaxes, your axes and hammers and wreck, wreck the venerable cities pitilessly.'[2] And, indeed, actual Italian Fascism ultimately turned its aesthetic face away from Futurist iconoclasm, towards a more hackneyed, populist, Roman-imperial grandiosity. Rather, the *form* of a manifesto – what might be seen as the archetypal genre of Futurism[3] – was an attempt, skilfully exploiting the mass media of the time, to present a body of artistic and cultural ideas, 'as if it were a political campaign' (Tisdall and Bozzolla, 1977: 9).

One way of understanding Marinetti's significance, then (without it being entirely coloured by his Fascist leanings), is to see him as mixture of performance artist and cultural entrepreneur: simultaneously a publicist for genuine new cultural ideas and a self-publicist. Both in his personality – he famously described himself as *'la caffeina dell'Europa'* (the caffeine of Europe) – and in his untiring cultural-political agitation, his theatrical stunts and his hyperbolic, gestural prose, he epitomized his own vision of a 'new man' with all the energy and 'heroic' sensibility of the machine age. This vision was undoubtedly narrow and partial in the sense that it represented the perspective of a sector of society able romantically to enjoy the fruits of the new technology without coming into much contact with the harsh realities of its production.[4] And this position of privilege no doubt had some bearing on the rather gross cultural-political values which he espoused.

However, for all his privilege, excess, egocentricity and bombast, it would be wrong to see Marinetti as either self-absorbed or monstrously idiosyncratic. He was a sharp cultural observer and he clearly had his finger on an important pulse in modern society. Furthermore he expresses this perception vividly in a later manifesto, 'Destruction of Syntax – Imagination without Strings – Words-in-Freedom' (1913):

> Those people who today make use of the telegraph, the telephone, the phonograph, the train, the bicycle, the motorcycle, the automobile, the ocean liner, the dirigible, the aeroplane, the cinema, the great newspaper (synthesis of a day in the world's life), do not yet realize that these various means of communication, transportation and information have a decisive influence on their psyches. (quoted in Tisdall and Bozzolla, 1977: 8)

Whatever his faults in cultural-political judgement, Marinetti was prescient in his grasp that these new technologies of mobility were to have deep consequences for human self-understanding. He even goes on to anticipate one of the core themes of cultural globalization: the simultaneously liberating and perplexing 'opening up' of local life to wider horizons of experience:

> An ordinary man can in a day's time travel by train from a dead little town of empty squares, where the sun, the dust and the wind amuse themselves in silence, to a great city bristling with lights, gestures and street cries. By reading a newspaper the inhabitant of a mountain village can tremble each day with anxiety, following insurrection in China, the London and New York suffragettes... and the heroic dog sleds of the polar explorers. The timid, sedentary inhabitant of a provincial town can indulge in the intoxication of danger by going to the movies and watching a great hunt in the Congo. (quoted in Tisdall and Bozzolla, 1977: 8)

The key contribution of Futurism for understanding the culture of machine speed then, is that it absorbed, expressed and gave artistic focus to the cluster of new experiences and impressions which, very early in the twentieth century, were emerging in relation to new technologies.

To this extent, the particular judgements and pronouncements it made – and it can probably be counted as the most opinionated movement in modern art – are of less interest than its success in grasping and *thematizing* the new celebratory culture of machine speed. We can identify three such themes which have been particularly important formative elements of the modern – twentieth century – cultural imagination. For convenience of discussion, and recognizing that this loses something of the rhetorical *brio* of the Futurist style, we can express these as three general propositions:

1. That the sensual-aesthetic experience to be derived from fast machines is valuable and desirable in itself and that the risk and danger associated with speed offers satisfactions beyond those generally sanctioned within mainstream society.
2. That courting this risk and danger has an 'existential' / heroic / transgressive dimension.
3. That speed and violence are inextricably intertwined.

Now it is very tempting to bundle these themes together to constitute what might be thought of as a sort of counter-narrative of modern machine speed: in various degrees, impetuous, improvident, anti-rational, amoral and subversive. This is tempting, not only because they seem, at least intuitively, to be interrelated, but also because the contrast between each of them and the dominant institutional, rational-progressive discourse of machine speed seems to lend them a certain coherence. However, it is wise to resist this temptation. Partly because the coherence of entities twinned in adversity so often proves spurious. Partly because there is so much potential for over-statement and conceptual slippage here – particularly when it comes to the connection between ideas like danger and violence. And mostly because totalizing does not promise to be the best way of approaching the complex integration of each of these themes into the everyday experience of speed as an increasing pace of life. So, in a deliberately un-Futurist spirit, let us take things coolly, and one at a time.

'Adrenalin rush': the sensuality of machine speed

The Futurist celebration of machine speed poses for us the tricky question of accounting for its sensual attractions and satisfactions. The question is a tricky one for two reasons. First, because the attempt to answer it faces us with a whole range of difficult theoretical issues linking the body, the psyche, non-human entities and the understanding of cultural experience, which we can't realistically hope to address thoroughly here. And secondly because pursuing these intriguing issues can easily make us lose focus on our main project of accounting for the place of 'unruly speed' within the overall cultural imagination of modernity. And yet it's difficult to avoid the rather assertive – and genuinely puzzling – issue of why modern people find machine speed pleasurable in itself, not simply as a means to an end. So, rather than taking the issue head on as a problem to be definitively resolved, my strategy will be to sketch three ways in which the question *might* be answered, and to see what implications these have for a broader cultural account.

Let's begin with what we might call the brain chemistry answer. My own knowledge of brain chemistry is, to say the least, rudimentary; and I will assume, as a condition of the tacit reader – writer compact, that yours is not significantly better. If I were to suddenly launch into a technical description, using terms like 'adrenocorticotrophin' or 'neurotransmitter' you would be right to think that this was an inappropriate shift in discourse. But, like me, you will have no difficulty in grasping the register of Jeremy Clarkson's deployment of similar technicalities:

> We .... crave the rush of adrenaline, the endorphin highs and the buzz of a dopamine hit. And the only way we can unlock this medicine chest is by taking a risk .... We don't drive fast because we're in a hurry; we drive fast because it pushes the arousal buttons, makes us feel alive, makes us feel human. (Clarkson, 2004: 30)[5]

Leaving aside, for the moment, the actual claim involved here, we can concentrate on the particular mixture of technical and existential ('alive'; 'human') vocabulary. One reason why this does not jar is that brain chemistry terms have acquired a non-technical acceptation. They only, as it were, *gesture* towards a physiological explanation; to all intents and purposes these are ways of describing new forms of experience. 'Adrenaline' here refers not to the hormone secreted by the adrenal glands but to a modern-human mode of being. This everyday deployment of quasi-technical language is an interesting example of the reflexivity of modernity,[6] and it adds to the semantic range of modern culture, but it doesn't in itself take us that much further in understanding the sensual attractions of speed.

One view, of course – and this is partly implicit in Clarkson's claim – is that there is not much more to understand. The 'buzz' of speed is just a fact of sensory experience, like the pleasure of the warmth of the sun on your face or the wind in your hair. Dogs after all – some dogs – seem to find pleasure in hanging their heads out of car windows and experiencing the sense of rapid movement and we don't feel the need to invoke cultural mediation in understanding this.

Well, this really is a question of level of analysis. The simple fact of sensory experience is of course an answer, and one that may be perfectly satisfying when it comes to the behaviour of dogs. But what makes it less satisfying in the case of human beings – what pushes us to look for higher level accounts – is not so much a hierarchical distinction between human and non-human experience, as the inescapability, in the human case, of a cultural context, of a context of meaning. To say, as Jeremy Clarkson does, that speed makes us 'feel alive', to associate it with the ideas of risk and thrills, is already to enter a cultural discourse. And this is to demand interpretation beyond the level of the senses.

The language of psychoanalysis – itself a peculiarly modern way of linking physiology with cultural interpretation – offers a second type of answer, and takes us somewhat further in understanding the pleasure of machine speed. Although Freud himself offers little directly of relevance, the film scholar Peter Wollen (1998, 2002) points us towards the work of the object-relations theorist Michael Balint whose book *Thrills and Regression* (1959) contains an analysis of the thrills, 'connected with high speed'. Balint was a pioneer in theorizing a psychology of motility, drawing on Freudian ideas of infantile sexuality relating to, for example, 'being rocked and swinging on the one hand, romping, wrestling, getting wild on the other' (Wollen, 2002: 114). As Wollen observes, these categories of regressive sexuality[7] are suggestive for understanding the pleasurable aspects of driving more generally. But it is Balint's approach to the thrills associated with speed that is most interesting. According to Balint, such thrills involve the following experiential structure:

> (a) some amount of conscious fear, or at least an awareness of real external danger; (b) a voluntary and intentional exposing of oneself to this external danger and to fear aroused by it; (c) while having the more or less confident hope that the fear can be tolerated and mastered, the danger will pass, and that one will be able to return unharmed to safety. This mixture of fear, pleasure and confident hope in the face of an external danger is what constitutes the fundamental element of all thrills. (Balint, quoted in Wollen, 2002: 77)

What this adds to the plain sensory explanation is not simply the element of an edge of danger. Rather, we are invited to think of thrills as complex emotional states in which the danger is at once recognized, balanced and (at least partly) discounted; in which fear is called up yet mastered, and so made enjoyable. This delicate, deliberate balancing is the difference, as it were, between thrills and terrors. This is well observed, and Balint offers the further insight that the pleasure involved is not related to any extrinsic goal – such as winning a race – but is an end in itself. In Balint's psychoanalytic terms, thrills are thus auto-erotic; in less Freudian-indebted vocabulary they are, as Peter Wollen nicely puts it, 'intransitive'.

Balint made the distinction between those people who actively seek out and enjoy thrills, whom he called 'philobats'; and those who avoid the trauma and risk attendant upon them: 'ocnophiles'. Such a categorical distinction may be intuitively appealing – in the same way that the terms 'extrovert' and 'introvert' help us sum up clusters of personality traits – and this way of thinking makes some degree of sense when referred to different patterns of infantile regression. However, outside of this psychoanalytic framework it suffers from all the problems of dualistic thinking, not least that it is too broad a generalization to cope with either the range and complexity of both direct and vicarious thrill phenomena, or the much broader integration of a symbolic discourse of machine excitement into modern culture. However, none of this detracts from the main virtue of Balint's approach: that it makes intelligible one of the most intriguing elements of the attractions of machine speed – its frequent courting of danger – without disposing this either to some curious design fault in the hard-wiring of human consciousness, to a psychology of dark (self) destructive impulses or even to the disciplinary regimes of industrial capitalism.[8] This is an important point if we are to understand the wide appeal of apparently risky speed, particularly within automobile culture.

The third type of explanation of the attractions of machine speed can be thought of – admittedly taking the term rather broadly – as 'ergonomic' pleasure. This refers to the satisfactions – partly sensual, partly aesthetic – gained from fluent, skilled and even elegant control and mastery of the machine. As with all these explanations, it is car driving which is the prime example, and here we can think of such actions as the slick gear shift, the precision of braking and finding the best line into a fast corner, the feeling of response from the engine as you change down in a well-judged overtaking manoeuvre and so on. What seems to unite these sorts of satisfaction is a feeling of deft action on the part of the driver which elicits immediate perceptible responses from the machine. The important thing to grasp about this is the qualitative difference from the experience of thrilling speed. Although this sort of ergonomic pleasure is generally dependent on its taking place at speed,[9] this is not necessarily the sort of on-the-edge speed that produces the emotional balancing act of thrills. It's an altogether cooler process. Ergonomic satisfaction is based in the coordination – the fit – between the human body and the fast machine.

One source of interest in this line of thinking is that it touches on a much bigger question about the way we should best conceptualize human–machine interaction. So far we have implicitly conceptualized it as a fairly simple process involving two entirely discrete entities, the embodied human and the machine. In this – the commonsense understanding – the human being, the driver, is the operator and the car merely the tool. What pleasure there is to be derived from this process lies simply in the satisfaction of a skilled operation.

However it's not entirely clear that this is the best way of thinking about it, particularly of grasping the phenomenology of driving. That legendary figure of automobile culture Enzo Ferrari once described the ideal constitution of the racing driver in terms which seem to anticipate the ideas of 'cyborg culture': 'Between man and machine there exists a perfect equation: fifty per cent machine and fifty per cent man' (quoted in Bayley, 1986: 34). Some accounts of everyday driving also quite explicitly suggest an experience of the dissolution of the perceived boundaries between body and machine: 'It was as though I became the car, or the car became me, and which was which didn't matter any more' (quoted in Sheller, 2004: 226).[10] And even where the experience is not so vividly expressed, grasping the ergonomic pleasure of this very particular multilevel engagement between body and machine suggests that some degree of shading between the embodied human and the machine may be called for. The question is, how far can we plausibly go with this intuition?

It is perhaps not surprising that Marinetti's febrile embrace of 'Mechanical Splendour' extended as far as to imagine merging with it in, 'the enthusiastic imitation of electricity and the machine; essential concision and synthesis; the happy precision of well-oiled thoughts' (Marinetti, 1973b: 154) or in what he elsewhere called, 'the dreamt-of metalization of the human body'. And indeed this was not an uncommon artistic conceit of its time. For example, the German artist Willi Baumeister, a friend of Le Corbusier, developed, between 1924 and 1931, a series of *Maschinenbilder* in which the machine serves as a metaphor for the 'New Man' (Chapter 2, p. 38). Baumeister believed in the unity of human beings and machines: 'Our existence has a new foundation, the machine' (quoted in Green, 2006: 104). Proto-cyborg fantasies – including those exploiting the erotic connotations of the internal combustion engine – also provided inspiration for some of the major artists of the early-twentieth-century avant-garde, such as Francis Picabia and Marcel Duchamp (Hughes, 1991: 48f.). Perhaps the most useful way of understanding such ideas, apart from seeing them as the artistic reflection of the technological forces of their time, is as, in the most positive sense, imaginatively provocative. Fantasies of human-machine hybrids rather outrageously oblige us to reconsider our ideas of what are the actual boundaries between people and their environment. And I think this is also the appropriate way to understand the more recent interest in cyborg culture (Haraway, 1991; Featherstone and Burrows, 1995; Lupton, 1999; Urry, 2000: 70f.).

But for our present purposes what is at stake is the less dramatic and far-reaching proposition that the experience – and perhaps the practice – of driving would benefit from conceptualization in a more integrated fashion. A particularly clear-sighted argument to this effect is provided by Tim Dant in developing his concept of the 'driver-car'. The 'driver-car' is a concept intended to grasp a particular form of social being, a symbiotic relationship that is constituted in actions connected with automobile culture. Dant contends that thinking in terms of this 'assemblage' is the best way of understanding the new patterns and forms of social action that the car has introduced into everyday modern life. The driver-car 'is neither a thing nor a person; it is an assembled social being that takes on the properties of both and cannot exist without both' (Dant, 2004: 74). Conceptually combining human and non-human entities in the form of assemblages has some distinct advantages for understanding how each of these entities contributes its own properties to a social situation: most importantly, it directs more attention than has traditionally been the case to the properties of technologies 'acting' as parts of complex technical-social-economic systems. As Dant is aware, this approach, if exaggerated, can lead to rather implausible attributions of equivalence between the categories of humans and things.[11] However, for the purpose of capturing the phenomenology of machine speed it is a useful way of thinking.

For not only does it help us to grasp the pleasurable sensation of being 'at one' with the machine as a single entity-in-motion, it also casts some light on the surprising lack of inhibitions – once one comes to think about it – involved in routine driving. The feeling of being integrated with the machine helps to establish the tacit trust relations (Giddens, 1990) necessary to maintain the act of driving – involving what Dant describes as, 'the embodied orientation to a world of rapidly moving objects from a sitting but rapidly moving position' – as a normal part of everyday life. For example, the blurring of a sharp distinction between body and machine helps us to effectively bracket out the potentially fatal risks of collisions even at relatively low speeds. And it is only in the limit condition of a crash that the (literally) sharp boundary between flesh and metal asserts itself. Thus as elements of 'driver-cars' we are enabled both to enjoy machine speed without necessarily thrill-seeking, and, more importantly, to cope with the demands of a modern, automobile-dependent social existence. This is a significant consideration. The pleasures available from driving are for most people inextricably intertwined with its routine necessity and the many frustrations associated with this. This integration, moreover, may prove to be a more general feature of the relationship between 'unruly speed' and 'rational-progressive speed'.

Let us now draw the threads of this discussion together. The sensual attractions of machine speed, I have argued, need to be taken seriously. But purely physiological explanations – the appeal to 'adrenalin' – though apparently tough-minded, none the less invariably demand cultural contextualization. One such context is that of the psychology of thrill-seeking and another the 'ergonomic' pleasures to be derived from the experience of merging body and machine functions. Each of these contexts combine bodily experience with culturally embedded meanings. But we can add a third context which in the long run may prove to be decisive for understanding the culture of speed. This is the integration of a system of pleasure into a system of necessity. Machine-speed competence is a virtually indispensable modern accomplishment which provides the overarching context within which we must understand the seemingly wayward – even transgressive – pleasures of speed. This is an argument I will return to towards the end of this chapter. But now we need to explore the transgressive aspects of speed culture along a different line.

Speed-heroism

> The oldest of us is thirty . . . when we are forty, other younger and stronger men will probably throw us in the wastebasket like useless manuscripts – we want it to happen! . . . .The oldest of us is thirty: even so we have already scattered a thousand treasures . . . thrown them impatiently away, with fury, carelessly, unhesitatingly, breathless, and unresting . . . .Look at us! We are still untired! Our hearts know no weariness because they are fed with fire, hatred and speed! (Marinetti, 1973a: 23–4)

Marinetti's celebration of youth has generally been understood in the context of its Fascistic colouring, but in fact it can be seen both to grow out of earlier artistic attempts to *épate le bourgeois*[12] and to prefigure a much broader theme in twentieth-century modernity: the association of the category of 'youth' with rebellion, impetuosity and transgression. The involvement of speed in this is complex in that it combines what we can call speed-inflected dispositions – impatience, daring, restlessness, defiance of authority – with thrill-seeking interaction with speed-machines, and the forming out of this of a counter-cultural narrative of existential heroism.

This is famously captured in the expression, 'Live fast, die young', popularly associated with the iconic figure of James Dean (Gilmore, 1997). Dean's career – particularly his role in the film *Rebel without a Cause* – and early death (aged 24) in 1955 at the wheel of his Porsche Typ 550 Spyder seemed perfectly to illustrate the maxim.[13] The phrase which Dean admired and ultimately enacted was actually coined in Nicholas Ray's 1949 film, *Knock on any Door*, starring Humphrey Bogart. The complete line spoken by the actor John Derek – 'Live fast, die young and leave a good-looking corpse' – adds a wisecracking aesthetic dimension, but it is the more succinct formulation that has passed – along with the figure of Dean – into cultural history.[14]

A curious popular mythology has grown up around celebrity auto-fatalities like those of Dean, Jackson Pollock, Jayne Mansfield, Grace Kelly, Albert Camus, Marc Bolan, François Sagan and Princess Diana. This tends to mix a simple curiosity about the details of glamorous or transgressive lifestyles with often wild speculation and rumour about the circumstances of the death, extending to even more dubious morbid-erotic fascinations (Brottman, 2001).[15] But leaving these dark-romantic connotations aside, we can see that 'live fast, die young' is among the great epitomes of recent times. The phrase seems so elegantly to summarize the reckless, intuitive insouciance of modern youth culture, that analysing it risks pedantry.

But let's risk it anyway. What does 'fast' imply here? Well certainly a commitment to pleasure-seeking and being careless of conventional law and morality (as in the now rather quaint 'racy'), but also perhaps deliberately exposing oneself to risk and, more generally, being intent on packing into life as much experience as possible. An early death is perhaps what is risked in this life-strategy, but if that were all there was to it, there is little that is particularly heroic here, or indeed threatening to dominant social mores. What, after all, separates the hell-raising exploits of a film star from those of any other young person self-centredly out for a good time, other than superior financial resources and the suspicion of a talent squandered?

The heroic element arises where to 'die young' signals not self-indulgence, nor merely self-negligence, but a more deliberate, principled contempt for the bottom line of the social contract, self-preservation itself. The crux of the value orientation contained in the phrase is thus a peculiarly modern version of carpe diem. Living for the moment is heroic in an existential sense because it insists – admittedly frequently in a less than fully baked form – on the value of exposing oneself to all that life can offer, as opposed to settling for the comfortable anaesthesia of the typical bourgeois life course.

The transgressive challenge of a fast-short life is the implicit refusal of a slow-extended life of plodding, cautious, mortgaged, humdrum material acquisition. This is dangerous *not* because it is scornful of the bargain of labour time for material reward upon which capitalist-modernity is established, for this is easily countered with the rather compelling rebuke that the world owes no one a living. It is dangerous because it calls into question the fundamental assumption on which this bargain is struck: the privileging of the extension rather than the intensity of existence. In modern secular cultures in particular, where no paradise beckons, length of days is the bedrock of social value – as is witnessed in the uncomprehending outrage, indeed the sense of an unforgivable existential betrayal of trust, towards the actions of suicide bombers.

Intensity of experience, then, is the crux of a fast life – existentially heroic since, unlike the case of the aspirant religious martyr, it looks for no heavenly reception, no reward beyond the act itself.

The connection between speed-heroism and youth is thus definitional, but many questions remain as to its actual cultural force. The cynical-cyclical view that this amounts to no more than the theatrical gestures of hormonally charged juvenility can, of course, point to all those ageing rock stars whose ravaged longevity is an embarrassment to the memory of lyrics in which they, 'hoped they'd die before they got old'. But this somehow misses the point. Much more significant is the susceptibility of speed-heroism to incorporation by the dominant cultural ideology.

This is a familiar theme of cultural critique but none the less an important one. The history of the cultural industries in the twentieth century is in large part a history of the attempt to translate the transgressive energy of youth into a customer base. Young people's cultural preoccupations and their associated heroes – in music, cinema, sport – have generally been easily incorporated into consumption practices, and marketeers have found no problems in handling rebellion and waywardness. Indeed, as Chris Rojek (2001) has argued, the notion of 'celebrity' itself, in dividing heroes off from ordinary social life, is inherently bound up with transgression. So the incorporation of the 'live fast, die young' ethic into superficial consumer imagery presents no great difficulties. Whether one sees the value-added component in this sort of incorporation – the effective cooling out of genuine dissent – as deliberate, or merely as a happy accident for the culture of capitalism, the result has been much the same.

However we shouldn't be content with a cynical view of the incorporative power of the market. The more subtle question concerns the compatibility of the transgressive values of unruly speed with the much broader social ideology of velocity-as-progress. This is a more complex issue than the simple commodification of heroism – or indeed anti-heroism. We can see what is at stake if we briefly consider a different type of speed-heroism, that associated with sporting prowess, particularly with the pursuit of speed records. Two of the most notable twentieth-century figures here were the father and son Malcolm and Donald Campbell. Both established speed records on both land and water, Malcolm Campbell during the 1930s and Donald during the 1960s. But, as in the case of James Dean, death in the pursuit of speed is the ultimate guarantor of celebrity here. And so it was his death in an attempt on a new water speed record of 300 mph on Coniston Water in the Lake District on 4 January 1967 that fixed Donald Campbell's place in popular memory.

There is plenty of heroic-myth potential in Campbell's story. His own hero worship of his father Malcolm – an archetypal figure of British late-imperial endeavour, known as the 'Speed King' in the 1930s – coupled with a sense of duty to continue the dynastic line in the face of competition from America were responsible for his embarking on speed records after his father's death. Campbell displayed all his father's characteristic 'stiff upper lip' courage (at a time when such attitudes were beginning to appear anachronistic); but this was combined with a deeply superstitious attitude which has led to speculation that he had a premonition of his death.[16] The drama of Campbell's death is further enhanced by the controversy that has always surrounded the causes of the crash, and that though items of his clothing and his lucky mascot rose to the surface, his body was not recovered from the depths of Coniston Water until 2001. And above all, by the fact that the spectacular instant of destruction of his speedboat – 'Bluebird' – is recorded on film along with his haunting final words: 'The hull is up. I'm going. I've gone . . . .' But despite these prime constituents of cult status, Donald Campbell's death is entirely different to that of James Dean.

The difference is that Campbell died, as it were, as martyr to the cause of speed-as-progress. The whole culture of speed record attempts is, indeed, intelligible only against the background of that cluster of social values – technological progress, order, control, planning, co-ordination and the overcoming of obstacles – which characterize the dominant narrative of modern speed which we discussed in Chapter 2. The speed-heroism of Campbell displays a certain 'nobility' which is entirely different from the transgressive charisma of Dean. In interviews before the attempt, Campbell described breaking the speed record as, 'a job to be done, a man-sized job' and said that it would, 'prove British leadership in engineering terms' and that 'the British when they make their minds up can jolly well overcome all obstacles and achieve anything'. His death may have signalled a disregard for personal survival but, unlike Dean's, this was entirely goal-oriented and, in a sense, rational-instrumental: a calculated risk. Questioned on this, Campbell replied that, 'You do it with your eyes open, you take the risks'. Speed-heroism of this kind, then, presents no threat to mainstream cultural values; rather the reverse, it serves to sanctify them.

In contrast with this, the ethic of 'live fast, die young' – where it amounts to more than a stylistic gesture – seems inherently resistant to incorporation into the cultural mainstream, for the key reason, discussed above, that it so profoundly opposes the values of progress, particularly as translated into a life project of slow, prudential, measured, accumulation, but also because it stands opposed to the conventional model of heroism that had served as its underlying moral fable. The puzzle remains then of why this potentially radical counter cultural impulse has been so effectively *contained* within modernity, even at the point at which an earlier sacrificial-heroic morality has so clearly eroded. One simple answer, of course, may be that it is an impulse which is inherently transient, something which people grow out of. But there may be a more interesting answer: that the energy and impatience that characterizes the 'fast short life' has mutated into behaviour patterns that are at once more banal and more consistent with contemporary economic demands for an accelerated pace of production. This possibility, which raises some of the inherent contradictions of modern-speed culture, is something we will return to at the end of the chapter. But before this I want to broach the darkest aspect of unruly speed: its association with violence, aggression and, specifically, war.

Violence and war

This connection is of course something we can trace back, at least, to the Futurists. Marinetti's *Manifesto* had claimed that, 'Art . . . can be nothing but violence, cruelty and injustice' and advocated 'violent spasms of action and creation' (1973a: 23). These statements can no doubt be interpreted as stylistic metaphors or as the deliberately excessive language of the artist bent on outraging the cultural establishment. But he had also explicitly set out the movement's intention to, 'glorify war – the world's only hygiene' (1973a: 22). In a much later manifesto, on the Italian invasion of Ethiopia in 1935, he elaborates on this:

> War is beautiful because it establishes man's dominion over the subjugated machinery by means of gas masks, terrifying megaphones, flame throwers and small tanks. War is beautiful because it initiates the dreamt-of metalization of the human body. War is beautiful because it enriches a flowering meadow with the fiery orchids of machine guns. War is beautiful because it combines the gunfire, the cannonades, the cease-fire, the scents, and the stench of putrefaction into a symphony. War is beautiful because it creates new architecture, like that of the big tanks, the geometrical formation flights, the smoke spirals from burning villages, and many others. (Marinetti quoted in Benjamin, 1979b: 243–4)

This is a specious argument for the aesthetics of warfare, more or less on a level with Lieutenant-Colonel Kilgore's well-remembered words in *Apocalypse Now*: 'I love the smell of napalm in the morning.' But there is also a connection here between machine speed and violence that goes beyond dubious artistic metaphor. Certainly in the case of Marinetti, and probably for others, the new mechanized warfare of the twentieth century exercised a *personal* attraction which was intrinsically linked to the intoxications of speed. Marinetti wrote to Gino Severini in 1914 of the need for, 'direct collaboration in the splendour of this conflagration'. It was as much, then, for the accelerated thrills of actual combat, as to represent the processes of war, that in July 1915, Marinetti along with other prominent members of the Milan group of Futurists – Boccioni, Russolo, Sant'Elia and others – enlisted in the Italian army. Appropriately, they joined the Lombard Volunteer Cyclist Battalion, 'the speediest division' (Tisdall and Bozzolla, 1977: 178).

The experience and indeed the consequences of actual warfare – Boccioni, Sant'Elia and several other Futurist artists were killed; Marinetti, Russolo and many others injured – were of course quite different from the aesthetic imaginings of pure, splendid creative destruction. Moreover, the motivation of the artist-volunteers can't be solely attributed to an aesthetic creed, but surely comprised an admixture of other commonplace feelings – the patriotism and naïve youthful heroics,[17] the simple sense of obligation and peer-pressure – which sent millions of other young European men to their deaths in the trenches. None the less, it is the Futurists once more, for all their hyperbolic rhetoric and posturing, who force us to confront the perplexing connection between speed and violence that has characterized twentieth-century modernity. And the issue here is not the aesthetisization of war, but the question of what sort of elective affinity may exist between machine speed and the real violence of modern warfare.

War is, of course, a special category of organized violence and as such straddles to some extent the divide between the ruly and the unruly aspects of machine-speed culture. In one sense the deployment of war machines from the tank to the laser-guided missile and Global Positioning Satellite controlled weaponry during the twentieth century simply exemplifies a certain 'rational' progression in technique. This is intelligible in terms of Sun Tzu's famous dictum that, 'speed is the essence of war'. Sun Tzu's *The Art of War*, written during the 'Warring States' period of Chinese history (403–221 BC) has retained its readership amongst military (and indeed, business) strategists in the modern era not on account of its Taoist precepts, but because it offers clear practical advice on how to win wars without bank-rupting the state. 'A speedy victory is the main object in war' writes Sun:

> When the army engages in protracted campaigns, the resources of the state will fall short . . . your weapons are dulled and ardour dampened, your strength exhausted and treasure spent . . . . There has never been a protracted war which benefited a country. (Sun, 1998: 23)

Speed is the essence of war, then, in both economic terms and in the crucial strategic aspect of gaining the initiative. The deployment of fast machines is obviously rational in so far as they enable the rapid, efficient and cost-effective prosecution of war. And this stress on speed has been a defining feature of wars fought by the most technologically advanced states in the twentieth century – from Hitler's Blitzkrieg ('lightning war') to the 'shock and awe' tactics of the Iraq war of 2003.

But, on the other hand, modern wars can clearly be seen as the most dramatic examples of the *failure* of institutional rationality. On no realistically broad system of accounting can the military and political gains accruing to victory be reconciled with the 'butcher's bill' of twentieth-century wars,[18] to say nothing of their huge economic and environmental costs. And the phenomenon of what Anthony Giddens calls the 'industrialisation of war' (Giddens, 1990) in the twentieth century can of course be seen as contrary to rationality in several other senses. Not only does it destroy the faith – founded on Enlightenment reason – in the progressive potential for modern societies to move beyond age-old war fighting into a new pacified age; it actually transforms the nature of war into a practice demonstrably *less rational* than the wars fought at a lower level of technology in pre-modern societies. As Giddens and others have pointed out, the apotheosis of this is the development of weapons of mass destruction ('WMDs') – in particular, nuclear weapons – so awesome in their power that the strategic benefits of their actual deployment becomes negated, indeed unthinkable. The famous acronym for the strategy of nuclear deterrence through 'balance of terror' during the superpower Cold War, 'MAD' ('Mutually Assured Destruction') expresses this irrationality. As Mary Kaldor succinctly puts it:

> A nuclear war would be one in which force is applied in the extreme in a matter of minutes. But what rational purpose could ever justify their use?...Do not nuclear weapons nullify the premise of modern warfare – state interest? (Kaldor, 1999: 28)

But whilst (thus far) shrinking from this ultimate apocalyptic threshold, modern states have, of course, continued to wage technically advanced wars[19] in which speed has continued to grow in significance. The theorist who has most provocatively tracked this trajectory is Paul Virilio. Since the mid-1970s, in a series of books, articles and journalistic interventions on the interpretation of actual conflicts, Virilio has developed a complex and wide-ranging analysis of the relationship between speed, technology, cultural representation (particularly cinema) and what he calls the 'pure war' of twentieth-century modernity.

It is impossible to encapsulate Virilio's work briefly and I shall not try.[20] But simply to pick out one dominant, recurrent theme, Virilio argues in *Speed and Politics* that the increasing speed of modern weapons delivery systems, linked to high-speed communications technologies is producing a shift in the very ontology of warfare. Wars are now not so much about gaining, holding and pressing the initiative in terms of *territory*, as in terms of *temporality*. Because of the speed and accuracy of modern weapons – approaching 'the speed of light with laser weapons' – there are now, according to Virilio, 'no longer *geostrategic strongpoints*, since from any given spot we can now reach any other, no matter where it may be, in record time and within several metres' (1986: 134). This means that strategic advantage now belongs not to occupied points of territory, but to what he calls the 'vector in permanent movement', to a 'delocalized' force – for example a missile – combining magnitude and direction capable of striking anywhere. 'All that counts is the speed of the moving body and the undetectability of its path' (Virilio, 1986: 135). Hence what is now strategically crucial is superiority in the control of the combined speed and precision of delivery of weapons. Indeed it is the *threat* of such superiority, particularly having the perceived edge in terms of the vital minutes of a preemptive attack, that counts. Thus, 'The invasion of the instant succeeds the invasion of territory. The countdown becomes the scene of battle' (1986: 138).

Virilio draws not only strategic but also political inferences from this shift in the terrain of war from space to time. For instance, he points out that the time for political reflection and deliberation shrinks along with the shrinking in reaction time available, potentially to a point at which automatic computer protocols will, of necessity, supplant human decision making. In typical style, this analysis of the undermining of politics forced by a technological *fait accompli* is elaborated beyond actual warfare scenarios to more general speculations about a diminishing political sphere:

> The loss of material space leads to the government of nothing but time. The whole geographic history of the distribution of land and countries would stop in favour of a single regrouping of time, power no longer being comparable to anything but a 'meteorology'. In this precarious fiction, speed would suddenly become a destiny, a form of progress. (Virilio, 1986: 141)

Anyone who has read Virilio will recognize in this passage his tantalizing way of combining dramatic overstatement and deliberate ambiguity over the status of his claims (a few pages later he writes that, 'the violence of speed *has become* the world's destiny') with a subtle insight. If we can live with the stylistic exuberance and the ellipsis,[21] there is a truth to be grasped here: that government is indeed in many ways becoming preoccupied with dealing with, and anticipating, the speed of events rather than, as it were, with simply patrolling the bounds of territory.

Virilio wrote *Speed and Politics* in 1977 within the context of the Cold War, the Strategic Arms Limitation Talks (SALT) and the White House-Kremlin telephone hotline – a context dominated by the threat of escalation in superpower tensions or perhaps even of the accidental precipitation of a nuclear Armageddon. But, though both the geopolitical situation and the weapons and communications technologies have changed dramatically since, much of what he has to say remains relevant, and has been elaborated upon, rather than revised, in his discussions of more recent conflicts, particularly the 1991 Gulf War (*Desert Screen: War at the Speed of Light*, 2001a), and the 1999 Kosovo conflict (*Strategy of Deception*, 2000a). In much of this more recent work Virilio charts the increasing military significance of the 'absolute velocity' or the 'speed of light' of electronic communications. Here he argues, for example, that we are witnessing, 'the supremacy of weapons of communication above the supremacy of weapons of destruction' (2001b: 86) and that, 'the locale of war is no longer the geosphere, military geography, the realm of geostrategy, but the "infosphere" cyberspace' (2000b: 47). These arguments in fact take the relevance of Virilio's work quite beyond the epoch of machine speed and into what I will discuss as the emergent realm of immediacy and fluidity. And in this connection we shall revisit Virilio in a later chapter.

But for now perhaps what is most strikingly percipient about Virilio's writings on speed and war is the way in which the preoccupation with preparedness, rapid response and *preemption* have not only increased in the post-Cold-War period, but have spilled over from war fighting strategy into the realm of everyday life. In 1977 he wrote:

> The blindness of the speed of means of communicating destruction is not a liberation from geographical servitude, but the extermination of space as the field of freedom of political action. We only need refer to the necessary controls and constraints on the railway, airway or highway infrastructures to see the fatal impulse: the more speed increases, the faster freedom decreases. (Virilio, 1986: 142)

The immediate context of these remarks is what Virilio calls, with a dual meaning, the 'State of Emergency' that prevailed during the superpower tensions of the 1960s and 1970s. But his claim that freedom decreases in proportion with increase in speed has striking resonance for the current, post-9/11, open-ended 'state of emergency' declared by President Bush as the 'War on Terror'. Developing his point about the 'miniaturization of space as a field of action', Virilio goes on to say, 'An imperceptible movement...made by a "skyjacker" brandishing a cookie box covered with masking tape, can lead to a catastrophic chain of events that until recently was inconceivable' (1986: 143). Substitute a box cutter as the weapon and the chain of events can be read as linking the catastrophe of the World Trade Center attack with the US invasion of Afghanistan, the Iraq war, the Madrid train bombings, the 2005 London tube bombings....

But it is vital to be clear what is being claimed here. It is not that speed itself is the *primum mobile*. For clearly there are quite different issues, combining mutual cultural-religious hostility, fanaticism, social injustice, superpower hegemony and old-fashioned political-economic interests, which provide compelling enough explanations. But the point is that the speed at which politically inflected violent events can occur – or, more accurately, the state's perception of the threat of such speed – has produced an increasingly common civil culture of fear and insecurity which allows the constraints on civil liberties which Virilio points to.

Some of these are relatively minor incursions – the increase in security screenings in airports, restrictions on carrying everyday objects like scissors or nail files or hand cream in carry-on luggage, having to eat airline meals with plastic knives and forks, or the rather ludicrous indignity – once an emblematic speciality of the United States, but now likely to become the global norm – of being required to remove one's belt and shoes at the barrier.[22] But these trivialities are given a deeper cultural significance when seen against the background of the increasingly routine institutionalized suspicion of everyone (everyone being in theory a potential terrorist).[23] This suspicion is articulated technologically in the ubiquity of surveillance cameras in public places and the emerging deployment of bio-metrics (iris recognition, finger prints, genetic profiling) in the confirmation of identity, and personally, in the expansion in the numbers and powers of security personnel to be found in all public spaces.

There are, of course, much broader questions of surveillance and control by the modern state to be considered here, but an important factor in governments' calculations of the 'political acceptability' of such measures is certainly the implication that, in effect, a state of virtual (in the sense of potential) war – the 'war on terror' – now obtains. The first casualty of this virtual war is not, in fact, the truth, nor civil liberties, but the time – and place – for proper political deliberation. Thus, alongside a culture of insecurity and generalized suspicion there emerges a culture of *preemption*.

Preemption in the simple sense of attacking the enemy first in order to prevent them from attacking you is of course nothing new: it is an available strategy in particular circumstances justified by the ancient vigilant philosophy of 'Si vis pacem, para bellum.'[24] But what is arguably new is an institutional culture in which preemptive action becomes a policy of first resort, where it is used by modern governments as a pretext for invasion motivated by other factors, or where the logic of preemption becomes a culturally accepted political precept overriding established principles of due deliberation, civil rights and policing protocols.

It is perhaps an exaggeration to say that we now inhabit such a culture, but there have certainly been instances in the recent political life of western societies of all of these features of a new preemptive security attitude. Most prominent amongst these is the so-called 'preemptive doctrine' which emerged in United States' defence policy in the wake of 9/11. This is enshrined in the 'National Security Strategy of the United States of America' published by the Bush administration on 17 September 2002. Section 5 of this document – 'Prevent Our Enemies from Threatening Us, Our Allies, and Our Friends with Weapons of Mass Destruction' – contains the key references to preemptive action:

> To forestall or prevent such hostile acts by our adversaries, the United States will, if necessary, act preemptively. The United States will not use force in all cases to preempt emerging threats, nor should nations use preemption as a pretext for aggression. Yet in an age where enemies of civilization openly and actively seek the world's most destructive technologies, the United States cannot remain idle while dangers gather. (www.whitehouse.gov/nsc/nsall (p. 10))

Despite the reassuring qualifications, it is difficult to see the political preparations for the invasion of Iraq in 2003 as anything other than a direct enactment of the preemptive doctrine.[25] The war was engaged specifically on the basis of the threat posed by the supposed stockpiling by the regime of Saddam Hussein of weapons of mass destruction.[26]

The case for British involvement in the conflict was famously made in a dossier, 'Iraq's Weapons of Mass Destruction: The Assessment of the British Government' on 24 September 2002. One of the key arguments of this document – now known to have been revised and edited to emphasize the risks posed to Britain – was the famous claim that, 'Military planning allows for some of the WMD to be ready within 45 minutes of an order to use them' (quoted in Hiro, 2004: 446). The issue of relevance here is not the blunt incorrectness of this claim – no weapons of mass destruction have been found in Iraq – nor, indeed, any alleged attempt to manipulate public opinion, but the way in which the speed of a possible attack by Saddam was a key issue used in making the case for war.

A more recent example, again from the United Kingdom, suggests the movement of security preemption into the civil sphere. This is the case of the shooting dead by police from Scotland Yard's SO19 firearms branch of the Brazilian Jean Charles de Menezes at the Stockwell Underground Station in London on 22 July 2005. Mr Menezes was killed as a result of his being mistaken for one of the suspects in the previous day's attempted bombings, by Islamic militants, of three Tube stations and a bus in London. His killing was violent – he was shot seven times in the head and once in the shoulder – and carried out with precipitate speed. No attempt was made to arrest Mr Menezes. The unambiguous intention was to kill, rather than to detain him.

On any consideration this is a shocking event and one that cannot be interpreted as simply a tragic accident. For, whatever the errors in police procedure that led to the killing of an entirely innocent person, there emerged from this incident an apparent shift in British policing policy, dating back to 2002, which has significant implications, not least of which is that they had not been publicly announced before the mistake forced their disclosure. This was that new guidelines on the rules of engagement of suspected suicide bombers had been implemented, advising shots to the head – effectively a 'shoot to kill' policy. The reason for this shift in policy is simple: it is intended to incapacitate a suspected bomber before they have any chance of detonating their charge – in the precise if gruesome words of an unnamed senior police officer quoted by *The Economist*, 'to destroy his brain instantly, utterly' (*The Economist*, Leader, 30 July 2005, p. 11).

Whatever one's opinion of the policy, or of the conduct of this particular case,[27] there is no easy answer to the moral dilemma posed by the example. Faced with the possibility that a suspect may indeed be about to commit a self-destructive act that could potentially kill members of the public (the previous bombings of 7 July had killed 52) it cannot be denied that police are placed in extremely difficult positions. And it is interesting to note that British public opinion – unlike that expressed in relation to the invasion of Iraq (Hiro, 2004: 432) – seems to support this particular preemptive policy. An opinion poll conducted by Yougov for *The Economist* (30 July 2005) found that more than 60 per cent of those interviewed believed that the police were right *at the time* to shoot Mr Menezes even though it transpired later that their intelligence was faulty.

It is difficult to interpret this definitively. It may reflect an increasingly risk-averse culture generating a 'What if?' moral expediency; but on the other hand it may simply reflect the general state of public nervousness of the time. But what does seem clear is that, where preemptive killing moves into the mainstream of law enforcement in mature democratic societies, a significant threshold has been crossed.

The publication of a book by the Harvard lawyer and constitutional scholar Alan Dershowitz is an indication of this. Dershowitz's book *Preemption: A Knife That Cuts Both Ways* (2006) has aroused controversy in so far as it *takes seriously* the possible moral and legal justification of a range of preemptive measures:

> ranging from targeted killing of terrorist to preemptive attacks against nuclear and other weapons of mass destruction, to preventive warfare . . . to racial ethnic and other forms of profiling, to inoculation or quarantine for infectious diseases (whether transmitted 'naturally' or by 'weaponisation'), to prior restraints on dangerous or offensive speech, to the use of torture (or other extraordinary measures) as a means to gathering intelligence deemed necessary to prevent imminent acts of terrorism. (Dershowitz, 2006: 2–3)

Dershowitz by no means concludes that all of these can be justified, but it is the fact that he initiates a serious discourse which brings such measures within the purview of moral sanction and jurisprudence that has been shocking to many people. His argument for doing so is that this is the only alternative to *ad hoc* action on the part of government.

Regardless of one's view of Dershowitz's actual arguments, his very attempt to bring preemption into the sphere of moral-legal deliberation is in itself significant. For what might be considered the underlying weakness is the assumption, implicit in this, that justice can ever be served in the context of preemptive speed. What Dershowitz does not confront – in a discourse which never probes the wider cultural politics and ethics of institutionalized acceleration – is the question of whether precipitate speed must *of itself* sacrifice justice in so far as it sacrifices the time–space of deliberation.

But we must now bring the discussion of the war-speed relationship to some sort of conclusion. We began by quoting Marinetti's attempt aesthetically to celebrate modern machine warfare. The most incisive critique of this is found in the Epilogue to Walter Benjamin's famous essay, 'The Work of Art in the Age of Mechanical Reproduction'. Writing in 1936, Benjamin understandably places Futurist aesthetics firmly within the purview of Fascism: '*Fiat Ars – pereat mundus*' ('Let there be art, though the world shall perish') says Fascism, and, as Marinetti admits, expects war to supply the artistic gratification of a sense perception that has been changed by technology. This is evidently the consummation of *l'art pour l'art*' (Benjamin, 1979b: 244). Benjamin's response to this 'self-alienation . . . that . . . can experience its own destruction as an aesthetic pleasure' deploys an historical-materialist analysis of technological change:

> If the natural utilization of productive forces is impeded by the property system, the increase in technical devices, in speed, and in the sources of energy will press for an unnatural utilization, and this is found in war. The destructiveness of war furnishes proof that society has not been mature enough

> to incorporate technology as its organ, that technology has not been sufficiently
> developed to cope with the elemental forces of society. (Benjamin, 1979b: 244)

Whatever one's opinion of the Marxist interpretation of war as the systemic consumer of surplus production, the historical record is without doubt with Benjamin and against Marinetti when it comes to the relation between technology and the 'elemental forces of society'. Marinetti had believed that war, 'establishes man's dominion over subjugated machinery', but the experience of the twentieth century that we have briefly reviewed here seems precisely to the contrary.

So perhaps the key point to stress in conclusion is that the 'rational' promise of a military strategy based on speed and the deployment of advanced technologies has proved one of the great illusions of our times. The imagery of the 'surgical strike' promoted in the 'televisualization' of the first Gulf War[28] seemed to offer a new sort of sanitized precision warfare – a swift and decisive campaign ensuring victory at an economic cost and with minimal casualties. Instead, technologies of speed in the context of a globalized warfare which has lost its traditional spatial and temporal delineations – a virtual war which reaches into the 'peace' of everyday civil life – has introduced new irrationalities and taken us into uncharted and perplexing moral-political terrain.

Conclusion: speed cameras – cultural contradictions of machine speed

In this chapter we have considered the different ways in which modern machine speed can be implicated in an 'unruly' culture: that is to say one that is at odds with the dominant modern discourse of reason, order, regulation and progress. In doing this we have focused on three main aspects: the sensual-aesthetic attractions of machine speed, the association of speed with a counter-cultural rejection of an ordered, bourgeois lifestyle, and the connection between speed and the violence of war.

However, this unruly speed cannot in any easy way be seen as an entirely independent cultural narrative. Much less can it be understood as a sort of dialectical antithesis of rational-progressive speed, nor, indeed, as a coherent discourse which has successfully challenged the dominant capitalist-modern order. With the notable exception of war, unruly speed has found its space within the interstices of a comprehensively organized institutional modernity. If we were forced to make the rather superficial judgement as to which narrative has had the most influence, there is no doubt that it would be the story of speed as the begetter of progress according to the model of regulated technological economic growth.

If this is so, how can we make sense of the relationship between these two divergent inclinations of modern speed culture? One short answer is that they simply co-exist in often contradictory ways. The continuing brutalities and horrors of war, executed with the development of accelerated military technologies might be seen as a paradigm case – as the prime example of the irrationality that co-exists with, and can be accommodated by, the ideology of reasoned modernity.

However, I think we can say rather more than this. We can see in the fate of some of the more individually transgressive elements of an unruly speed culture, as they have developed over the course of the twentieth century, an illustration of a central contradiction of institutionalized capitalist modernity. It is this: that the impulse to promote speed in one area of life begets the need to regulate, even to suppress it, in others. We can trace some of the tensions and frustrations of life in an accelerated culture to this contradiction, and we can also situate within it some of the less glorious instances of speed transgression.

The most obvious area of everyday life in which the regulation of speed is enforced is of course on the roads. It is on the roads (indeed in the area of physical mobility generally) that ordinary citizens are most likely to come into contact, and sometimes into conflict and confrontation, both with other citizens and with the police. Driving provides the most readily available opportunity for people to become the agents of their own independent speed and to experience the exhilaration of fast machines (Miller, 2001; Featherstone et al., 2004). Yet at the same time it is probably the most intensely regulated and, literally, policed area of everyday life. This context defines a fairly obvious source of tension, frustration and low-level transgressive behaviour.

The immediate rationality of the regulation of driving speed is plain: it is that driving fast is dangerous and much more so in the curiously haphazard arrangement – once one stops to think about it – whereby pedestrians in cities and suburbs routinely share a common unprotected space with car users. There is no doubt that road accidents are a hugely significant cause of avoidable death and injury in modern societies. Featherstone (2004) cites a World Health Organization report from 2004 which discloses some extraordinary statistics:

> [an estimated] 1.2 million people are now killed in road crashes every year and between 20 and 50 million injured. It is suggested that over the next 20 years the figures will increase by 65 percent making road traffic injuries the third leading contributor to the global burden of disease and injury.... The estimated cost of road crashes is currently $518 billion per year. (Featherstone, 2004: 3)[29]

Although speed is not necessarily the main cause of road accidents,[30] there is no disputing the relationship between speed and the potential fatality of accidents. Someone hit by a car travelling at 20 MPH has a 90 per cent chance of survival, at 40 MPH this is cut to 10 per cent. For these reasons it is entirely rational to limit the speed of vehicles, particularly in cities.

And the increasingly common use of surveillance technologies – speed cameras – seems to be justifiable on these grounds. The case for surveillance is strengthened by increasing evidence that speed cameras are an effective way of enforcing mandatory speed limits which have been routinely disregarded for years in many countries. The introduction of speed cameras in France in 2003, for example, reportedly coincided with a fall in road fatalities of 21 per cent.[31] The threat of detection seems to be a strong inhibitant of speeding, and this is understandable, given that penalties for repeated infringements include not merely fines but the much more significant consequence of driving bans (an instructive example of the social value of mobility as compared with the value of money within a speed economy).

Unsurprisingly, given the dramatic rise in speed penalties awarded – a ten-fold increase between 1995 and 2005 in Britain – the widening use of speed cameras has provoked controversy and resistance. Lobby groups in the UK like 'Safe Speed' have campaigned, with a moderate degree of success, on the grounds that cameras have been used for revenue raising rather than road safety purposes (Webster, 2005). The motoring journalist Jeremy Clarkson has been outspokenly critical of speed camera policies using the platform of the popular BBC programme *Top Gear*.[32] And more militant resistance has been seen in the systematic vandalizing of speed cameras.

Looked at purely in terms of a rights and responsibilities issue, the anti-regulation lobby has a very weak case. However, there is more to be considered if we frame this issue within the contradiction between the institutional promotion and inhibition of speed. As Mike Featherstone points out, the widely held 'traditional' view of road safety tends to displace responsibility on to individual road users, expecting and encouraging them to be 'error free' in their driving behaviour. An alternative approach – implicit in the WHO's report – would be to define road safety as a public health issue in which attention is shifted towards the *system* in which road accidents occur. As Featherstone says, 'From a systems point of view, a key obvious factor... is the vulnerability of the human body. ... the obvious solution would be to slow down the traffic, or design vehicles incapable of speeds in excess of the vulnerability limits of the human body' (Featherstone, 2004: 4).

The reasons why no government of a modern state would countenance this order of systemic solution are not difficult to come at: limiting traffic speeds to a maximum of, say, 30 kilometres per hour would have huge economic consequences – in the slowing down of the supply chain – which would be viewed as entirely unsustainable, and this is to say nothing of the political unacceptability of such a proposal amongst ordinary citizens. So, since slowing the speed of the social-economic system as a whole is not on the political agenda, the much less effective approach of regulation of individual behaviour is adopted. The situation in more general terms, as Ulrich Beck has put it, is that, 'how one lives becomes the biographical solution of systemic problems' (Beck, 1992: 137).

The systemic contradictions in respect of traffic speed can be seen not only in government policies, but in the design and marketing of automobiles, where power – that is the potential for acceleration and speed – is generally proportionally related to price and thus connoted with social status – as in the category of the 'executive' range.

But above all, it is the *context* of driving within a speedy, often time-pressured culture that is the key consideration. Speeding no doubt sometimes associates with the drive for exhilaration (and perhaps in some cases with high testosterone levels) or perhaps even with an opposite desire to lose the self in the experience.[33] But more frequently it seems to relate to a rather complex driver psychology, mixing compulsion and frustration with the ready availability of assertiveness via a simple machine-person gesture (Lupton, 1999), the pressure on the accelerator.

In this we can see the integration of 'buzz' speed with 'hurry' speed. This order of transgressive speed has little connection with speed-heroism; rather it suggests the mundane expectation and perceived necessity of uninterrupted goal-oriented progress. Speed here is frequently experienced as integrated with an itinerary or a schedule. In this sense it is not 'unruly', but, indeed, purposive, calculating and fully integrated with a rational, time-efficient life plan. And the sort of low-level aggression towards the driving behaviour of those who block progress (something which often correlates with habitually fast driving) similarly expresses itself as an affront to reason: for instance in the branding of perceived offenders as, at mildest, 'idiots'.[34]

Driving, then, invites interpretation in the context of a driven lifestyle. This line of thought can open up to the wider contradictions of modern 'mobile privatisation' (Williams, 1989). In this critical context, we might see the transgressive speed of the short fast life as having morphed into the banal impatience of high pressure, long-hours careers where success by the age of 30 (or at least, thirtysomething) becomes a life goal. Though this is not a line of critique that we have space to pursue at present, it consolidates the main point that I want to emphasize in relation to the fate of unruly speed. This is its general subordination to, and its frequent assimilation into, the dominant cultural discourse of speed as reason, effort and progress – where these ideals have themselves been generally translated into calculation, instrumentality, and the goal of private material acquisition.

With this chapter we conclude our exploration of the cultural implications of machine speed. Machine speed, we have seen, developed a distinct set of values, practices and experiences which lie near to the heart of modernity. As we move from the twentieth into the twenty-first century we continue in many ways to inhabit this culture. However, alongside, and to a certain extent developing from it, there are emerging various signs of something else. This is what I shall describe in the following chapter as the culture of 'immediacy'.

The main vehicles of the speed culture we have so far considered have been the 'hard' technologies of mechanical modernity which, producing so decisive an historical break with the constraints imposed on human culture by the natural order, have dominated the cultural imagination from the early part of the nineteenth up to the end of the twentieth century. By contrast, the emblematic carriers of immediacy are the 'softer' technologies of electronic information processing and of media and communications systems. It is not unreasonable – nor is it to fall towards a technological determinism – to suppose that new cultural experiences, imaginations and values are emerging out of our interaction with these emergent technologies, and it will be my purpose in the chapters which follow to explore these. But I want to end this chapter without, as it were, drawing a neat line under the discussion of the cultural world of machine-speed. In many ways the culture of immediacy *overlaps* with the culture of mechanical velocity in today's world. It is not as though one technology-culture displaces another, much less that the new resolves the problems and contradictions of the earlier formation. But as I shall argue, the condition of immediacy *does* alter the context of lived experience in significant ways which pose novel and indeed perplexing questions for cultural analysis.

Notes

1 Millar and Schwarz (1998: 19) see Futurism as 'arguably the most radical and influential artistic movement of the twentieth century'. But Apollonio's more detailed assessment, whilst evaluating them overall as 'true prophets', none the less points to the derivative nature of much of the work, particularly the way it draws on Symbolist and Art Nouveau themes and ideas (1973: 7–8). Lodder (2006: 32) also notes the way in which the Futurist artists' depiction of speed drew particularly on Cubist techniques.

2 Marinetti did actually write a more conventional political manifesto – an odd mixture of 'anarchistic, socialist and utopian demands' – for the Futurist Political Party which he founded in 1918. See Tisdall and Bozzolla's discussion of this in the context of the confused political climate in post-World War One Italy (1977: 203–9).

3 Inter alia: 'Manifesto of Futurist Painters' (Umberto Boccioni et al., 1910); 'Manifesto of Futurist Musicians' (Balilla Pratella, 1910); 'Technical Manifesto of Futurist Sculpture' (Umberto Boccioni, 1912); 'Manifesto of Futurist Architecture' (Antonio Sant'Elia, 1914); 'Futurist Manifesto of Men's Clothing' (Giacomo Balla, 1913); and 'Futurist Manifesto of Lust' (Valentine de Sainte-Pointe, 1913).

4 Marinetti was very wealthy and used his wealth to support the movement: for example he was able to afford to buy over two columns on the front page of *Le Figaro* – at the time probably the most influential newspaper in Europe – to publish the Futurist Manifesto.

5 Jeremy Clarkson is a British journalist best known as the lead presenter of the BBC's popular motoring programme *Top Gear*. He has a reputation for deliberately provocative 'politically incorrect' pronouncements, for example on the environmental movement or on the issue of speed cameras. He combines this with a disarming tendency towards self-irony.

6 See Giddens, 1990, 1994; Beck, 1994. The particular reflexivity involved here is in the importing of technical explanations into commonsense discourse, thus registering a general cultural awareness of biologically reductive explanations without commiting ourselves very deeply to them. It is interesting to compare a reverse case: the use of the term 'speed' to refer to amphetamines.

7 See Freud's (1953) *Three Essays on the Theory of Sexuality*.

8 As, for instance, in Benjamin's almost perversely incorporationist argument that, 'what the Fun Fair achieves with its Dodgem cars and other similar amusements is nothing but a taste of the drill to which the unskilled labourer is subjected in the factory . . . [demonstrating] . . . the true connection between wildness and discipline' (Benjamin, 1979a: 178).

9 An exception might be an elegant piece of reverse parking, though even here a certain level of speed enhances the experience.

10 Sheller's article provides an interesting account of the wider emotional entailments of automobility.

11 Dant is careful to distinguish his position both from notions of machine-human hybrids associated with cyborg culture and, more significantly, from the sort of human-object relationships posited in 'Actor Network Theory' – see the brief comments on this position in Chapter 1.

12 Tisdall and Bozzolla (1977: 18) note the formative influence of the late-nineteenth-century French Symbolist literary movement on Marinetti. Writers like Stephane Mallarmé, 'expressed their hatred of the mean, vulgar and money-grubbing life of the modern bourgeois through their elevation of the extra-ordinary, the gloriously immoral and the adventurous'.

13 There has been a tendency to associate Dean's role in 'Rebel' with his real life, and particularly his death, most obviously since a defining moment in the film is the famous cliff-top 'chicken run' hot-rod race. But it should be remembered that Dean's character, Jim, according to a much more mainstream heroic cinematic convention, survives, whilst it is his antagonist Buzz who quite accidentally perishes.

14 See, for example, Kristin Ross's discussion (1995: 46f.) of Dean's 'enormous resonance' in the youth and film cultures of, 'rapidly modernizing nations such as France and Japan' in the late 1950s and 1960s.

15 An egregious example of this is David Cronenberg's 1996 film adaptation of J.G. Ballard's cult novel *Crash* (Ballard, 1975). Amidst huge controversy, the film explores the erotic associations of injuries sustained in car crashes, and, in a key intertextual sequence, re-enacts James Dean's death crash.

16 This myth drew on an incident the night before in which Campbell, playing a game of Russian Patience drew consecutively the Ace and the Queen of Spades. Recognizing these as the deeply unlucky combination which Mary Queen of Scots had drawn on the night before her beheading, Campbell reportedly said, 'Someone's for the chop. I hope to God its not me'.

17 Marinetti is somewhat of a special case in that he retained his taste for war, volunteering at the age of 60 in Mussolini's invasion of Ethiopia in 1935 and even participating in the Italian campaign in Russia in 1942.

18 Giddens (1990: 9–10) observes that the deaths in war during just the first 80 years of the twentieth century, at over 100 million, are considerably higher than in either of the two preceding centuries.

19 But note here Kaldor's observation that the costs and logistical requirements of modern wars, make it 'almost prohibitive to mount a major operation except against a clearly inferior enemy' (Kaldor, 1999: 28). Kaldor cites as examples the 1982 Falklands/Malvinas war and the 1991 Gulf operation, to which we can add the post-9/11 war on Afghanistan and the 2003 war on Iraq. But these last two examples raise the other issue of the costs of victory and occupation. Sun Tzu's other famous dictum – that the superior strategy is not to go to war at all – seems apposite.

20 For good introductions to, and appreciations of, Virilio's work see Der Derian, 1998, 2000 and Armitage, 2000, 2001.

21 Douglas Kellner in noting how Virilio's texts, 'move along quickly ... catch[ing] their topics on the run' wonders, 'whether a critic of speed, war and technology should not occasionally slow down and more carefully and patiently delineate his theoretical position' (Kellner, 2000: 121–2). It's easy to agree. But see Der Derian's more sympathetic assessment of Virilio's speedy style and 'conceptual brio' (1998: 6f.).

22 The security staff at Chicago's O'Hare airport used to cheerfully tell you that though you are not obliged to do this, non-compliance with the 'request' will considerably lengthen the security scrutiny process. The irony is of course that security now reduces speed, imposing the anxiously slower time of the besieged nation-state on to the quick time of global travel.

23 Well, potentially everyone. But, should it appear as though some accidental democracy of suspicion had crept into the process, we must of course add, particularly those of a non-western appearance. And this has become more explicit with recent calls for 'selective' security screening and the black humour of the joke about the 'offence of travelling whilst Asian'.

24 'If you desire peace, prepare for war', attributed to Flavius Vegetius Renatus (*c.* 390 AD). A very similar quotation comes from George Washington, 'If we desire to secure peace, one of the most powerful instruments of our rising prosperity, it must be known that we are at all times ready for war'. This adds the significant equation between the defence of peace and the defence of wealth (what today we might call national interests). Interestingly the etymology of 'pre-emption' also connects with the economic sphere: from the Latin *praeemer*, 'to buy first'. See also Dershowitz (2006, 28ff.) for a short history of political and jurisprudential ideas of preemption and prevention.

25 Kofi Annan criticized the doctrine of preemption in a speech to the UN General Assembly in 2003:

> If [this doctrine] were to be adopted, it could set precedents that resulted in a proliferation of the unilateral and lawless use of force, with or without any credible justification. This logic represents a fundamental challenge to the principles on which, however imperfectly, world peace and stability have rested for the last 58 years. (quoted in Hiro, 2004: 390)

26 The moral, and indeed legal, justification for an attack based simply on the supposition of weapons stockpiling – even if this proved to be correct – has been widely disputed. The point was put with admirable clarity by the Republican Chair of the House International Relations Committee, Henry Hyde in 2002: 'You hit the other guy first, but only if you know he's going to hit you' (quoted in Rai, 2002: 150).

27 A subsequent inquiry cleared the Metropolitan police of any criminal responsibility for Mr Menezes's death, although charges of negligence, rather bizarrely under Health and Safety legislation, are, as I write, ongoing.

28 See for example, Kellner, 1992. If the surgical strike was the defining metaphor of the first Gulf War, more prosaic borrowings characterized the 2003 Iraq war: for example 'speed bumps': 'A speed bump is an obstacle on the way to capturing a strategic prize – like Baghdad – which does not stop you but slows you down' ('The language of War: Decoding the Military Jargon', *The Guardian*, 21 March 2003, p. 3).

29 Featherstone's discussion of the breakdown of these figures country-by-country also illustrates the fact that risk is unequally distributed globally, being highest in poorer countries. China's appalling figure of 104,000 deaths per year, for example, representing not merely its population base, but the fact that the Chinese government introduced its first traffic safety law only in 2004 (Featherstone, 2004: 19). Road accidents also display class and age differentials. According to an *Economist* report, in Britain whilst speeding drivers are likely to be 'young males aged 17–24 and those in higher income groups, earning over £30,000 per year', their victims are often children of school age. Moreover, 'The pedestrian death rate for children from families in the lowest social class is five times that for those in the highest social class' ('High on Speed' *The Economist*, 27 June 2002 (print edition) accessed via www.Economist.com). On the conceptual relationship between mobility and safety, see Beckman (2004) and for a discussion the relationship of road deaths to class relations see Kristin Ross's discussion (1995: 60f.) particularly of Luc Boltanski's work in France in the 1970s.

30 A report by the British Department of Transport in 2004 listed excessive speed as only the seventh most important contributory factor in accidents, the first being 'inattention'.

31 'Speed, Rules and Psychology': *The Economist*, 22 January 2004 (print edition) accessed via www.Economist.com (2005).

32 Clarkson could in fact claim to stand in a long libertarian tradition of opposition to speed restriction. As McCreery notes, the now eminently respectable British motoring association the Automobile Association (AA) 'was originally a radical direct action organization set up to frustrate police speed traps by positioning scouts to warn oncoming motorists' (McCreery, 2002: 358).

33 Kristin Ross (1995: 20–1) in an interesting comparison between the 'constrained time' (Lefebvre) of the commuter and the sublimely focused experience of speeding, cites François Sagan, 'even your sorrows are swept away; however madly in love you are, at 120 miles an hour you are less so' and Jean Baudrillard, 'it brings about a sublime immobility and a contemplative state. At more than a hundred miles an hour there is the presumption of eternity'.

34 But here see Jack Katz's subtle social-psychological analysis of driver anger and aggression in his evocatively titled chapter 'Pissed Off in L.A.'. In Katz's analysis the common perception of the 'dumb' behaviour of other drivers is interpreted, 'as an upshot of the exceptional and more literal inarticulateness of motorists in social interaction' – sealed as they are within their cars and communicating and interpreting in emotionally charged interactions via the restricted code of gestures (Katz, 1999: 25).

4

The Condition of Immediacy

The claim I want to establish in this chapter and to explore in the chapters which follow is that a new condition is coming to influence cultural practices, experiences and values in contemporary, that is to say early-twenty-first-century modernity. This condition, whilst in certain ways emerging out of the world of machine speed which so dominated nineteenth- and twentieth-century modernity in the industrialized West, differs from it in significant ways. This is what I propose to call the condition of immediacy.

The proliferation of analytical concepts and their associated neologisms is, of course, a practice to be added to only where entirely justified. But in this case, I believe it is. What prompts me to introduce the concept of immediacy is the difficulty I have of making sense of a cluster of new cultural phenomena. These are phenomena which appear to us as part of the modern world of increasing technology-driven velocity, but which at the same time refuse to fit into either of the cultural narratives – the ruly and the unruly – that we considered in the previous chapters

How are we possibly to understand, drawing on the cultural imaginary of mechanical speed, the following examples drawn from everyday life in developed societies worldwide?

- The shift in differentiation between work life and home life, indeed between work and leisure, introduced by the widespread distribution of domestic networked computers. And the way in which this complicates the shift between 'task orientation' to 'timed labour' which has been taken to typify modern industrial capitalist work relations.
- The truly astonishing informational resource that is the internet, and the commonplace assumption that the first and obvious place to go for information is not to a library but to a search engine. The rapidity with which the brand leader's name has extended from a noun to a verb – as in, 'to Google it'.
- The trajectory of shopping hours – which are, of course, for many also working hours – towards a 24/7 normalcy. Associated with this, the shift in the leisured use of urban spaces – exemplified in coffee bar culture – during what used to be thought of as the 'working day'. The curious co-existence of this with a culture of extended working hours in many modern societies.
- Twenty-four-hour news coverage and commentary in both broadcast and online forms, narrating in real time the social and political context of our lives as we live them.
- The migration of banking, insurance, utilities, travel and transport services and domestic service provision from local offices to remote telephone call centres, frequently on another continent. The consequent shift in routine

individual commercial interactions from a face-to-face to a hyper-mediated context involving abstract (and frequently frustrating) accessing protocols.

- Digital photography that no longer requires us to wait for the image to be developed and printed (and collected) – indeed in which printing becomes an option. The transformation this implies in our idea of what a photograph – one of the great emblematic artefacts of modernity – actually is.
- Computer-related pathologies, frustrations and anxieties: crashes, data loss, viruses ('worms', 'bots', 'diallers'), spam, downtime, 'URL unavailable', delays in data processing.
- The frequently cited statistic that workers today can expect to have on average 12 career moves during the course of a working life. The concepts of flexibility and transferable skills that have emerged to describe and justify this, and that have flowed from management into educational discourse.
- Speed dating.
- The defining, though environmentally unsustainable, assumption of the hugely expanding and globalizing sphere of consumption that the production of commodities can and will be matched to human demand and desire. Associated with this, the shift in consumer demand from mere possession towards speed in delivery. The connection between this and the logistics of supply, for example 'just-in-time' manufacturing and delivery systems.
- The generalization of the term 'multitasking' from the vocabulary of computer processing into a description of human activity. Perhaps related to this, the fact that psychological stress in the workplace is threatening to replace back pain as the major reported cause of long-term invalidity.
- A global youth culture in which mobile phones have become defining elements both in terms of style icons and as modalities of interpersonal relationship.
- The ubiquity of keypads and screens in our everyday environment and the indispensability of skills in their use as a basic competence of modern life.
- Finally, a widely distributed cultural outlook in which few ordinary people (and fewer intellectuals) appear to believe unproblematically in 'progress' in the sense of a general historical improvement in human well-being in the broadest terms, delivered through the application of science and technology linked with concerted human effort. Yet at the same time, a situation in which no more satisfying narratives of social purpose have arisen to replace the old ones. Consequently the continued, gestural, use of 'progress' in political or economic discourse in a sense restricted to short-term demands, agendas and goals. A public discourse which seems in fact – outside of the continuance of traditional religious beliefs – to have largely abandoned the attempt to define long-term collective purpose.

This is, admittedly, no more than a casually assembled set of observations, consciously and unconsciously selective, varying in terms of their level of significance, and no doubt bearing the traces of authorial predilection and prejudice. In citing them, I do not make any pretence to rigour in observation and they should certainly not be mistaken for the makings of an inductive analysis. But for all this, these examples can each of them make some claim, at a trivial or a more profound level, to typify commonplace modern life. And each of them is an historically novel cultural phenomenon. And each has at least an intuitive connection with a particular mode of the acceleration of social life. It is not implausible, then, to suppose that such examples, and others that could be added to the list, constellate into a more general intelligible pattern. This supposition is what prompts me to introduce the idea of immediacy.

So let's grasp the nettle of specification. Immediacy stands as a cultural principle in relation to the technological – and particularly the communicational – bases of our particular era of modernity as 'mechanical velocity' stands to those of the preceding era.

But what is immediacy? The concept has two relevant connected meanings. In connection with space: 'freedom from intermediate agency; direct relation or connection, ... proximate, nearest, next, close, near'. And in relation to time, 'pertaining to the time current or instant ... occurring without delay or lapse in time, done at once; instant'.[1] Although it is the relation to time that may seem most relevant to speed, as we shall see, both these senses are suggestive for an analysis of the transformations of speed culture in our era of modernity.

Indeed the term 'immediacy' is chosen, partly, *because* of its multivalence. For our purposes we can distinguish three core aspects.

It connotes, firstly, ideas of a culture of instantaneity – a culture accustomed to rapid delivery, ubiquitous availability and the instant gratification of desires. And of course underpinning this, an economy and an associated work culture geared not just to sustaining but to constantly increasing this tempo of life. This is the sense which is closest to the trajectory of mechanical speed, at least in so far as it seems to chime with the rhetoric of both the advocates and the critics of accelerated market capitalism.

Simultaneously however, immediacy can be taken to imply a sense of directness, of cultural *proximity*. Etymologically this is, indeed, the primary sense: from the late Latin 'immediatus', 'not separated'. In this second sense immediacy suggests not just an acceleration in culture, but a distinct *quality* to cultural experience. This may be variously grasped as a new kind of vibrancy in everyday life and perhaps (to use a rather pretentious term) a greater 'haecceity' to individual lived experience, as an increasing sense of connectedness with others, or as a prevailing sense of urgency and, perhaps, of compulsion and drivenness in our short-term preoccupations. What connects these is the sense of the general dissolution of mediation – of an intervening element, a middle term. We might put this in terms of an *ostensive* (important qualification) 'closure of the gap' that has historically separated now from later, here from elsewhere, desire from its satisfaction – the gap which, as we saw in Chapter 2, constituted the motivating challenge of speed-as-progress. In this sense, immediacy could be taken – again ostensibly – to signify the end of the era of mechanical speed in two senses of the term 'end' – as a goal and as a conclusion.

Finally, and on the surface in tension with this second sense, my deployment of the term involves a clear implication of the crucial significance of *the media* in modern culture. This is true both in the general sense of the increasing role which electronic communications and media systems play in the routines of everyday life, and in a more specific sense of a distinct, historically unprecedented *mode* of telemediated cultural experience typical of twenty-first-century global modernity. As I shall try to show in Chapter 5, a scrutiny of the nature of telemediated experience reveals a fecundity in the apparent tension between an increasing dependence on media technologies and systems and the idea of immediacy as the drive towards the abolition of distance and separation. The media of communications in this broadest sense are indispensable to any account of the condition of immediacy, as will be evident from their implication in the majority of the examples I have sketched.

But this should not be taken to imply that immediacy is a 'media centred' instrument of analysis, nor indeed that it is entirely bound up with a shift in technologies, from machinery to electronic processing. Rather, it is the integration of communications technologies into a modernity which is transforming in all its dimensions – globalizing, deterritorializing, shifting its methods and relations of production, delivery and consumption, producing new conveniences, excitements and delights but also new anxieties and pathologies – that is the broader context I want to grasp. The agenda for cultural analysis which this establishes is an extensive one, including implications for shifts in our emotional and aesthetic sensibilities and perhaps the transformation of our ethical dispositions and horizons. The ultimate challenge of such an analysis is to consider whether and how the condition of immediacy may be changing routine assumptions and expectations about how life is to be lived, and what we may reasonably expect it to deliver.

The chapters which follow will attempt some first steps in this direction. However the more immediate use of immediacy is as a category which will allow us to generate a more adequate vocabulary for understanding our common modern experience; a vocabulary which does not entirely break the intuitive link to older ideas of machine speed, but which recognizes some quite decisive shifts.

Fluidity and lightness

One way to begin this is to locate the concept of immediacy within other analyses which discriminate between different eras of modernity. A significant trope used here is that of 'fluidity' or 'liquidity' (Appadurai, 1990; Castells, 1996; Shields, 1997; Luke and Ó Tuathail, 1998; Bauman, 2000, 2003, 2005; Urry, 2000, 2003). In such analyses the metaphors of liquidity/fluidity[2] are deployed to grasp the social ontology of recent modernity. This analysis is applied to comprehend, variously: the permeable, protean nature of social space; the intrinsic mobility both of agents and of social processes and relations (as in the flows around a network); and the phenomenology of modern social existence. This latter, not only in terms of the common experience of mobility and deterritorialization, but also in terms of the constant dissolution of fixity in value, and of a different 'texture' of life.

As Zygmunt Bauman points out, the use of this sort of metaphor to capture modernity is not entirely new. Marx and Engels in *The Communist Manifesto*, for instance, famously employ the imagery of the 'melting' of, 'all fixed, fast-frozen relationships with their train of venerable ideas and opinions' in their depiction of bourgeois society (Marx and Engels, 1969; Berman, 1983).[3] However as Bauman says, the 'liquefaction' of the old social and cultural order described by Marx and others was one imagined as a necessary precursor to the establishment of *new solids*, 'much improved and preferably perfect, and for that reason no longer alterable' (Bauman, 2000: 3).

The key point of distinction which allows fluidity or liquidity to stand for a more recent experience of modernity is that these figures are now taken to represent neither a crisis nor the transitory stage in a progressive or a revolutionary process. Liquid modernity is not, then, a crucible; rather it is a continuing condition of mundane social existence, an existence experienced as plastic and evanescent, and predictable only in so far as it escapes prediction.

The metaphor of fluidity has been used by sociologists to explore this condition in different conceptual frameworks. John Urry employs it in what is one of the most original and penetrating social-theoretical analyses, drawing on the natural sciences and mathematics, and focusing on the inherent *complexity* of global-modern society. What he calls 'global fluids' are the entities that, as it were, 'inhabit' and thus give an inherently complex, dynamic and mobile quality to the network structure of global connectivity:

> Such fluids are partially structured by the various 'scapes' of the global order, the networks of machines, technologies, organizations, texts and actors that constitute various interconnected nodes along which flows can be relayed. Global fluids travel along these various scapes, but they may escape, rather like white blood corpuscles, through the 'wall' into surrounding matter and effect unpredictable consequences upon that matter.... Such fluids of diverse viscosity organize the messy power of complexity processes. (Urry, 2003: 60)

According to Urry, global fluids – amongst which he numbers global travel and population mobility, the internet, money, automobility, environmental hazards, and social movements – demonstrate a 'wave like' motion which shows 'no clear point of departure' and 'no necessary end state or purpose' (2003: 60). This, in part at least, accounts for the unpredictability, apparent instability and open-endedness of contemporary modernity, and its subsequent reluctance to yield to the rationalistic system building of earlier traditions of social analysis.[4] And it is this that allows Urry to claim that, 'linear accounts of the global, such as those that point to increasing wealth, or homogenization, or democracy, or violence, are wrong' (2003: 124).

The point I want to highlight is the distinction implicit in Urry's account between this sort of network fluidity and more 'solid' imaginations of modernity, particularly as they are associated with earlier mechanical technologies (Urry, 2003: 124f.; 2000: 56f.). Partly this is because it suits the broad distinction I want to draw between mechanical velocity and immediacy, but also because it is the most obvious point of contact between Urry's social-ontological deployment of fluidity and the more directly 'epochal' treatment of the theme by Zygmunt Bauman to whom I now turn.

In a series of texts which have gripped the imagination of thinkers across the humanities and social sciences – even extending to religious thought – Zygmunt Bauman (2000, 2003, 2005) invites us to understand our social condition as one of 'liquidity'. Bauman's choice of the term 'liquid modernity' as, 'the metaphor of the present-day state of modernity' originally arises from a dissatisfaction with terms like postmodernity or late modernity (Bauman, 2002: 2–3). Although the more substantial term is to be preferred to these problematic temporal qualifiers of the category of the modern, in a sense it performs, at base, much the same function. It allows us to reflect on our present condition by distinguishing it from a directly preceding one. The key to this is the contrast between what Bauman calls a 'heavy', 'solid' 'hardware-focussed' modernity and a new 'light', 'liquid', 'software-based' modernity.

Now, like all big general comparisons, this one is vulnerable to criticism in all sorts of ways, particularly from those worried about the precision of periodizations.[5] However there is little to be gained from picking away at the detail of the distinction because this misses the point: which is not to provide precise social-historical descriptions but to help us think creatively about processes happening around us. In this sense I consider Bauman's general approach to be *heuristic* in the pedagogical sense of encouraging us to find our own satisfying solutions to our social-existential condition.[6] I will disagree, later, with some of the ethical-cultural implications Bauman draws, but for the most part I want to take the contrast between solid and liquid, heavy and light modernity as a viable and an instructive one.

So, putting this rather briefly, according to Bauman we are currently witnessing the end of an era of heavy modernity, in which, 'size is power' and 'volume is success': 'the epoch of weighty and ever more cumbersome machines, of the ever longer factory walls enclosing ever wider floors and ingesting ever more populous factory crews, of ponderous rail engines and gigantic ocean liners' (2000: 114).

Apart from the obvious characterization in terms of heavy industrial and labour-intensive production, Bauman links heavy modernity with a relative fixity in time–space location – or at least a tendency in hardware to be, 'sluggish, unwieldy and awkward to move' (2000: 115). As a consequence, heavy modernity is a period in which both wealth and power is concentrated in physical locations: ' "embodied" and fixed, tied in steel and concrete and measured by their volume and weight' (2000: 115). Expanding power means expanding the ownership, occupation and control of these geographically fixed locations – which Bauman tellingly refers to as, 'simultaneously their hotbed, their fortress and their prison'. And so heavy modernity is associated with territorial expansion: the increasing possession of space and the related control of time. It is distinguished as both the era of territorial conquest, of imperialism and colonization, and of the institutional regulation of time, both in terms of the time-disciplining of the industrial labour force – as in Taylorism (Chapter 2) – and of the application of clock-time to the co-ordination – ultimately the global co-ordination – of time–space.[7] It is thus the era of the survey, the schedule, the timetable and the control plan.

By contrast, our emergence into 'light', 'liquid' modernity is into a world where solidity, fixity and sheer extension of possessed location is no longer automatically an asset, not at any rate for global capitalism. This is a world where capital is fluid and entrepreneurs travel light, where production methods are plastic, sourcing is variable, employment is temporary, planning is flexible and adaptable; where logics are fuzzy. Bauman points to the contrast in the realm of corporate culture between the looser and more 'flexible' organizational forms of companies like Microsoft as opposed to those of older heavy industrial giants like General Motors, Ford or Renault. From the position of employees, liquidity signals the end of the traditional notion of the lifetime 'career' as companies aim at organizational structures with ever greater 'adaptability'. And this flows over into the broader culture. The valuing of fixity, permanence and location – in everyday lifestyles, in attitudes and values – gives way to the valuing of mobility, flexibility and openness to change. Constructing, planning and regulating give way to coping with uncertainty, and 'going with the flow'; durability cedes to transience, the long term to the short term. Above all, in liquid modernity, distance becomes no object:

> In the software universe of light-speed travel, space may be traversed literally in 'no-time'; the difference between far away and down here is cancelled. Space no more sets limits to action and its effects, and counts for little, or does not count at all. (Bauman, 2000: 117)

The application of this contrast to an understanding of the career of speed is, at first glance, relatively straightforward. Despite Bauman's stress on the 'ponderous', gargantuan nature of heavy modernity, he understands how important speed – as the conquest of space – is to this era. Modernity, he says, 'is born under the stars of acceleration and land conquest.... The "conquest of space" came to mean faster machines. Accelerated movement meant larger space and accelerating the moves was the sole means of enlarging the space' (2000: 112–13). In heavy modernity what I have called mechanical velocity is crucial in overcoming the 'natural' resistance of physical space to the fulfilment of human desire: it is intimately tied into the early-modern narrative of scientific-technological progress. Bauman, citing Max Weber's concept of instrumental rationality,[8] says that much of it, 'focused on designing ways to perform tasks faster, while eliminating "unproductive", idle, empty and so wasted time' (2000: 113). The comparison between this and the quasi-moral association of speed – as opposed to lethargy and stasis – with visions of the human good will be apparent.

Bauman's analysis has, of course, no trace of nostalgia for this earlier manifestation of modernity. Indeed, it might even be argued that his stress on heaviness and solidity tends to lose sight of the intrinsic exuberance of this era's engagement with machines: as witnessed not only in the over-excitability of the Futurists, but in the many available contemporary accounts that mix fear with wonder and hope (see, for example, Jennings, 1995), and in the responses of nineteenth-century artists and intellectuals like Baudelaire, in Marshall Berman's words, 'simultaneously enthusiasts and enemies of modernity' (Berman, 1983: 24 – see also, Jervis, 1998: 204f.).

But, despite this, the contrast between heavy and light, solid and liquid modernity serves most forcefully as a hinge of criticism of present day capitalist modernity. Much of this criticism finds its target, and Bauman illuminates the vicissitudes of contemporary life – in the spheres of work, consumption, interpersonal relations and the fate of community – with his customary trenchancy. There is, however, something about the very pointedness to his account which does not quite grasp the range of issues that I want to address. Or rather it opens up to these issues yet seems reluctant to pursue them.

Let me broach this by way of the ambiguity that surrounds Bauman's deployment of the idea of 'lightness'. Despite a general association of liquidity with 'lightness', and indeed a key section headed, 'From heavy to light modernity', Bauman, apparently somewhat confusingly, then distances himself from the term. For example, in an interview in 2002 he says:

> I made a point...not to confuse 'liquidity' or 'fluidity' with 'lightness' – an error firmly entrenched in our linguistic usages. ... What sets liquids apart from the solids is the looseness and frailty of their bonds, *not* their specific gravity. (Bauman, 2002: 3)

There is of course a matter of precision in the metaphors at stake – the fact that volume-for-volume some liquids are heavier than some solids (Bauman, 2000: 2) – but Bauman is no pedant and there are, I think, other reasons for his uneasiness with the idea of lightness. What he doesn't want to suggest is that modern experience is 'light' in the sense of being easy, comfortable and anxiety-free – even for those who are, as it were, the economic winners in capitalist globalization. Capitalism has lightened its structures and processes, notably by shedding some of its older encumbrances – heavy plant, large, permanent (and powerfully unionized) workforces – but this has not made either the worker's or the consumer's yoke easier, nor their burthen lighter. Above all, I would suppose, Bauman wants to avoid confusing the lightness of liquidity with the sense of 'culture-lite' that we are increasingly offered in both marketing and political discourse.

The same sort of scruples emerge in a long footnote addressing Nigel Thrift's use of the term 'soft capitalism' (Thrift, 1997). Bauman applauds Thrift's exploration of the metaphors of 'dancing' and 'surfing', 'to approximate the nature of capitalism in its new avatar'. But he goes on:

> But there is nothing 'soft' about daily dancing and surfing. Dancers and surfers, and particularly those on the overcrowded ballroom floor and on a coast buffeted by a high tide, need to be tough not soft. And they are tough – as few of their predecessors, able to stand still or move along clearly marked and well-serviced tracks, ever needed to be. Software capitalism is no less hard and tough than its hardware ancestor used to be. (Bauman, 2000: 221)

The metaphors may be slightly laboured, but the point of principle is clear enough.

Now the reason I have myself rather laboured what might be considered a sidelight on Bauman's account is that I think it does turn out to have rather important implications for the way I want to connect general ideas of fluidity with the concept of immediacy. Indeed it is precisely the ideas of lightness and softness and ease that I want to accentuate in forming an analysis of the condition of immediacy.

What I want to get at here is that aspect of modern fluidity which presents itself as a displacement of effort and labour from the terms of the popularly imagined social contract. It seems to me that one of the most striking differences between the ideology of mechanical speed and that of immediacy is the conjuring away of *effort* – and particularly of concerted effort – from the imagination of the achievable good life. I say it's conjuring away, because it hardly needs to be added that effort in the labour process has not disappeared. It has been variously displaced: to the fields and factories of the developing world, to automated manufacturing processes, into various areas of discrete (and discreet) expertise, into fragmented packets of part-time work, into forms of service industry which absorb and disguise labour as an aspect of social and interpersonal competence, into the 'creative industries' a phrase which in so many of its actual manifestations turns out to be an oxymoron, and, as I shall presently argue, most deceptively, into practices of consumption.

None of this, of course, has resulted in the de-alienation of labour that Marx, in his philosophical anthropology, took to be the crux of praxis. Probably – almost certainly – there has been an increase in the opportunities for creative expression, and it must be said for fulfilment, in many areas of employment in contemporary modernity. But always this is qualified, hedged about and regulated by the contexts of profitability and market performance, which have been embraced, in the audit culture of 'performance indicators', in virtually every sphere of modern life.

But what *has* disappeared, at least from the mainstream of cultural representations is the overall *value* of effort which Marx, whilst criticizing its distorted appropriation by the ruling class into an ideology of wage-labour discipline, none the less subscribed to in a full-bloodedly progressive nineteenth-century spirit. If there is no longer in the social imaginary of fluid modernity a general enshrining of effort (and this is closely related to the failure of a widespread belief in progress) then we have to ask why.

Though there are surely multiple reasons for this, one is that the hard effortfulness of mechanical modernity has, in large areas of everyday life, been conjured away by both a literal and a figurative *legerdemain*. This 'sleight of hand' can be understood both as a lightness of touch and as a mystification.

In the first sense, it refers to bodily practices which are particularly underlined by the deftness of our interaction with new communications technologies: keyboards, keypads, screens, handsets and remote controls.

In the second, it refers to the apparent ease with which, in developed economies, and for larger sectors of the population within these economies, goods, and particularly technological advances, seem simply and continuously to be delivered, become affordable, morph from luxuries into necessities. This is not, of course, to say that wealth distribution overall becomes more equal. None the less there is a broad assumption underlying contemporary consumer culture that, whatever else may be taking place in our personal biographies and in the turbulence of global modernity, 'stuff arrives'. What unites these two senses – frequently in the same gesture, in the pressure on a keypad – is a *lightness of touch*.

Thus, a key theme that I will develop in the analysis of the condition of immediacy is a shift in association from an effortful speed to an effortless mediated delivery. This theme will run through both the discussion of media technologies in Chapter 5 and the discussion of consumer culture in Chapter 6. And to preface this, in the final part of this chapter, I will build this idea more firmly into the conceptualization of 'immediacy'.

But before this we need to look more closely at the acceleration of the recent career of capitalism.

Fast capitalism

Fast Capitalism is the name of an online journal. Its stated aim is to publish on, 'the impact of rapid information and communication technologies on self, society and culture in the twenty-first century' and to explore, 'how heretofore distinct social institutions, such as work and family, education and entertainment, have blurred to the point of near identity in an accelerated post-Fordist stage of capitalism' (Agger, 2005: 1). This is an important agenda which goes to the heart of our contemporary cultural condition. And though, as I write, only two issues have appeared, *Fast Capitalism* promises to be a significant forum for analysis and debate of what it calls, 'accelerated media culture', the more so since it aims to do this, 'dialectically, with nuance, avoiding sheer condemnation and ebullient celebration' (2005: 1).[9]

Well, it would be gauche simply to interpolate an endorsement into my discussion, and in fact I'm after something else here. It is that the appearance of this journal in 2005 raises the question of why the notion of fast capitalism is a particularly new one. Hasn't capitalism always been fast? Or to put it more precisely, hasn't speed in both production and in the circulation of capital (Chapter 2) been a defining feature of all modern industrial-capitalist economies? So what is it about contemporary capitalism that is fast in a new and distinctive way? This is a crucial question for us in locating the condition of immediacy in relation to contemporary capitalism. What I attempt in this section, then, is to identify some aspects of contemporary capitalism which make it 'fast' in ways distinguishing it from the capitalism of mechanical modernity.

The first and most general sense is of an increase in the intensity, energy and ruthlessness of the global capitalist order overall. Many commentators have recognized a step change in the pace of capitalism dating from around the last quarter of the twentieth century, and in the fact that, 'it has now a speed, inevitability and force that it has not had before' (Hutton and Giddens, 2000: vii). The economist Will Hutton describes it as follows:

> It's a capitalism that is much harder, more mobile, more ruthless and more certain about what it needs to make it tick. Edward Luttwak calls it turbo-capitalism, in contrast to the more controlled and regulated capitalism of the 1950s and 1960s. Its overriding objective is to serve the interests of property owners and shareholders, and it has a firm belief...that all obstacles to its capacity to do that – regulation, trade unions, taxation, public ownership, etc. are unjustified and should be removed. .... It's a very febrile capitalism, but for all that and its short-termism, it has been a very effective transmission agent for the new technologies and for creating the new global industries and markets. (Hutton, 2000: 9–11)

In some ways this change can be read as simply a quantitative one, as an acceleration of tendencies inherent in earlier forms of capitalism. Indeed, as Hutton describes it here, stressing the impatience with various forms of constraint and regulation, it might look like a recrudescence of the original impulses of nineteenth-century free-market liberalism (Gray, 1999). And this might be so. But what has enabled this to occur are some qualitative changes in the nature and indeed the culture of capitalism (Thrift, 2005; Goldman et al., 2005; Sennett, 2006).

Some of these are changes in the techniques of the production and exchange of actual commodities, particularly those attributable to the connectivity of globalization (Strange, 1996; Held et al., 1999). These include flexible, global sourcing of materials and components, a global distribution of labour, computer-controlled automation of production processes, web-based work flow systems, just-in-time delivery logistics and, overall, the integration of networked information and communication technologies into the essential operation of capitalism (Castells, 1996, 2001; Davis et al., 1997; Schiller, 1999). Others are essentially sophistications in the manipulation of the capitalist market, particularly in the sphere of finance capital. These latter allow, for example, speculation on the future value of commodities ('futures') and, through the increasing use of synthetic instruments collectively known as 'derivatives' (Pryke and Allen, 2000) financial trading at a high level of abstraction from the actual exchange of commodities. Or, as Manuel Castells puts it, 'the creation of market capitalisation value out of market capitalisation value'. The significance of derivatives trading becomes apparent if we consider an estimate cited by Castells, putting the global value of derivatives traded as far back as 1997 at US $360 trillion, that is, 'something in the vicinity of twelve times the size of the global domestic product (GDP)' (Castells, 2000: 54).

Derivatives, futures and the associated use of high-risk financing from outside the conventional bonds, equities and currency markets – so-called 'hedge funds' – are relatively novel features of capitalism, deeply implicated in both the frenetic speculative activity of the contemporary global market and in the turbulence, instability and constant threat of crisis that accompanies this (Soros, 1998). But in what ways is this abstract, mathematically complex, information-sensitive capitalism *fast*? The perceptive reader will realize that I am getting perilously close to the limits of my competence here. But, without paddling much deeper from the economic shallows, we can recognize a number of associations with speed. In the first place, it is the near-instantaneous speed of computerized, networked, fund-transfer systems combined with the speed of market intelligence via the internet which makes the whole business of this sort of high-risk, high-gain financial speculation possible. In the second place, and as a consequence of the first, these economic practices, though they are parasitic upon the slower pace of 'real' trade flows, and, in the case of futures actually *depend* on this slower pace, are necessarily short-term, super-fast deals, deals which generate their profits in anticipation of value fluctuations in the real world of trade. As Castells describes it, 'speculative investors looking for high financial rewards move swiftly from one market to another, trying to anticipate price movements of different products in different currencies, using forecasting models' (Castells, 2000: 55).

And so, in the third place, the influence of this speculation, which seems inherent to an information-based global economy without high levels of regulation, is to ratchet up the whole pace of the capitalist process, reaching back into the 'real world' of the production and the circulation of commodities. This is, in effect, the dynamic behind the 'market reality of increased global competitiveness' – a phrase which has become familiar in the mouths of politicians chastising liberal dissent from neo-liberal economic policy trends.

In Castells's analysis the new financial globalization is compared to an 'automaton'. This is, as he realizes, a slightly problematic way of putting things. He doesn't want to suggest that the whole process works automatically.[10] Rather it is a matter of an increasingly complex networked system of speculation, involving many more players with varying levels of market intelligence employed in, 'an endlessly variable geometry of value-seeking' (Castells, 2000: 53). This does not produce a system on 'automatic pilot' on the one hand, nor financial anarchy on the other. But it does introduce considerably more randomness and unpredictability into the system and in this sense puts it largely beyond the control of either governments, corporate capitalists, individual investors or indeed the market itself – at least the conventional wisdom of market regulation.

The worries of governments over global market volatility are often expressed in terms of concern over the differential speed of trade related to actual production, and the speed of finance capital. Teresa Brennan (2003) uses this worry to introduce a more radical critique of fast capitalism. Whilst recognizing the need to reconnect the speed of finance capital with the flow of 'real' trade, Brennan argues that there is a deeper disjuncture: that between the 'central speedy dynamic of capital' and the 'speed of the reproduction of people and natural resources' (Brennan, 2003: 13). Thus, couched in a re-working of Marx's labour theory of value, Brennan's critique of globalized capitalism rests on the argument that the tempo which it establishes races ahead of the tempos that are appropriate both to the natural re-constitution of biological resources and to a healthy, convivial human existence.

Brennan's is one of the most direct and wide-ranging critiques of the increasing speed of capitalism. Her argument that, 'environmental degradation and ill health are the *inevitable* consequences of global profit based on increasing speed' (2003: 16, emphasis in original) is elaborated to implicate fast capitalism in, inter alia: the pollution of the atmosphere and the oceans; global warming and the thinning of the ozone layer; the genetic manipulation of food crops and pathologies associated with this; a general reduction in the proportion of state spending on environmental protection as well as on social provision and education; increases in chronic ill health, particularly nervous and stress-related illnesses; indebtedness; depression; the breakdown in communities and personal isolation.

Brennan's work makes important links between the critique of environmentalism, the economic and developmental inequalities of globalization and the critical analysis of the quality of what she calls 'daily life in the West'. Yet, although these arguments are each coherently made and generally supported empirically, there are inevitably weaknesses in such an overwhelmingly totalizing critique – particularly when viewed from the perspective of cultural analysis.

One vulnerability, pointed out by Goldman, Papson and Kersey (2005) lies in the implicit naturalism of her stance, the assumption that there exists a constant 'natural time of organic life' against which the accelerations of capitalism may be indicted. These writers prefer to see 'organic time' as a cultural myth, 'one of our most important collective fantasies, a need to believe that we are part of some natural history. ... The myth of organic time beckons because it offers the prospect of achieving a form of spiritual salvation' (2005: 11). I suspect that Brennan might have responded to this by pointing to all the temporal constancies in human biology which govern our embodied existential condition: in the span of life and the aging process; diurnal rhythms and sleep patterns; heart and respiration rates; the menstrual cycle; the three trimesters of human pregnancy and so on. All these are of course variable within limits and all are subject to influence by social, technological and cultural practices and processes. But they none the less remain constants in a perfectly understandable and compelling sense which defines the human condition, at least in its present form.[11] Actuarial rates are changing with improvements in health care, but nearly all of us can (and do) still expect to die before we reach a hundred, that is within a span of time remarkably uniform across modern economically developed societies. And we can expect to die much sooner if we attempt to intervene in our 'natural' rate of breathing by more than a few minutes. And perhaps also, which is Brennan's point, if our bodies are subjected to variations from these 'relative constancies' which occur as the effects of work-related stress on the sympathetic nervous system.

It is these orders of empirical reality, inescapably part of human experience, which elicit incredulity (particularly in the eyes of that immense majority who are not social scientists) towards the claims of social constructivism, at least in its apparently more wilful expressions. But the social constructivist case in respect of human temporality is not a foolish one. There is an important aspect of social reality which is grasped, for example, in the apprehension that childhood is not a fixed stage in human maturation, but a constructed category, absent entirely from some cultures and periods of history; or that 'middle' and 'old' age are as much descriptions of cultural expectation and role ascription as they are of physical ageing – that (cheeringly) 50 *can* in fact be the new 30. Both Brennan and her critics are in this sense right, right that is in terms of representing equally credible perspectives. And these perspectives are not, so far as I can see, inevitably mutually exclusive if applied to a critique of fast capitalism. The issue at stake is not the rather tired debate between naturalism and culturalism as theoretical abstractions, but of economic practices in relation to the human existential condition, understood as socially and culturally mediated conscious embodiment.

However, it is also possible to launch a critique of fast capitalism without invoking biological quasi-constancies. To take the example of workplace tempo, this can be understood in other ways than simply a ratcheting up in demands of work rates, deadlines and so forth and their effects on health. It can be understood in terms of the increased *rate of change* of work institutions and practices that has become central to corporate culture both within capitalist enterprises and public sector institutions. 'Managing change' has indeed become the core mission of human resource teams. 'Change' in itself becomes installed as an institutional value beyond reproach, resistance to which signifies recalcitrance or at least human frailty. The ideology of change is a strange phenomenon. Regarded somewhat cynically it appears as a remnant of the ideology of progress admixed with a simplistic social Darwinism but curiously devoid of substance. Understood thus, it is one of the great mysteries of modern social existence how such a vacuous ideal has managed to achieve so much power within rational institutions from the state downward.

But its sources at least are evident in the shortening institutional lifespan of individual capitalist institutions – another core feature of fast capitalism – in the increasing incidence of mergers, take-overs and make-overs, re-branding, restructuring and so on. Richard Sennett, perhaps the most consistent and subtle interpreter of these processes (Sennett, 1998, 2000, 2006) points to the consequences, not in relation to bodily health, but to the viability of a sustaining 'work narrative' contributing to personal identity:

> Though the publicity for these institutional changes invokes an aura of precision as 're-engineering', the majority of company make-overs are chaotic: business plans appear and collapse, employees are fired only to be rehired, productivity falls as the company loses focus. Workers can hardly be expected to make more personal sense of this chaos than their bosses. . . . work itself is

shifting from the steady state repetition of tasks envisaged by Adam Smith to short term tasks performed by teams, the content in task-labour changing in flexible corporations in quick response to changes in global demand... all these material changes challenge the effort to forge a sustained work-narrative. (Sennett, 2000: 184)

What Sennett means by a 'work-narrative' is the story that has been available to people employed in stable long-term career structures by which what one does for a living is interpreted in a meaningful way as part of an overall biography. It is not a matter of finding one's work totally fulfilling (a rare enough occurrence) but of being able to regard work as sufficiently worthwhile and rewarding to justify the bargain of commitment of a life's labour time; of its having a forward developmental trajectory; and offering sufficient employment security to allow for planning for one's future and the future of one's family. Change regimes of fast capitalism are, as Sennett shows, inimical to this. And so nostrums of labour flexibility and adaptability can actually be read as instructions (increasingly issued by modern governments) to abandon a hard-won right not just of economic life but of culture.

It is puzzling that resistance to this trend towards employment insecurity is so weak – that it scarcely features on the political agenda of societies such as my own – particularly since the contradiction between this tolerance of structural employment instability and the common political rhetoric of individual providence, betterment via educational opportunity and family values is so starkly apparent.[12] This is the sort of contradiction which analysis of the culture of immediacy should, and might, be able to illuminate.

From what we have said so far, it is pretty clear that there is much to criticize in the combined acceleration and deregulation of contemporary capitalism. However, a cultural analysis needs to do more than this. It needs, if it is not to lose confidence in the human capacity for agency, to broach the attractions, comforts and satisfactions available from – or at least presented within the context of – contemporary capitalist modernity. This is necessary for two reasons.

Firstly because life under capitalism is not the whole of cultural experience. It is, of course, hugely influential in shaping cultural experience, but it is not co-extensive with it. The weakness of an account like Teresa Brennan's is that, in its relentless critique, it simply does not register the complex mixture of pleasures and frustrations, joys and fears, comforts and insecurities, that make up cultural experience in affluent societies in the West (and increasingly in the east).

And secondly it is important in order to recognize the terms of the 'bargain' people are implicitly offered within capitalism: a bargain it is possible to criticize for its rates of exchange and its mystifications, and a bargain, it is true, that few of us are in much of a position to refuse without consigning ourselves to hardship and marginality. But a situation that needs to be understood as a bargain nevertheless, in order to respect and render intelligible the rationality of everyday popular civil complicity with the capitalist order. It is this mixture and this bargain that contextualize capitalism's place within the condition of immediacy.

Having established this principle I don't actually want, at this point, to give much more than a brief outline of how it may be approached. This is because the most obvious place to recognize it is in the transformation of the sphere of consumption, to which I will return, at length, under the broader rubric of 'delivery' in Chapter 6.

But to conclude this section let me just flesh out a little more the idea that fast capitalism increasingly mixes and intertwines its woes and its satisfactions. An important contributory aspect of this is the subject of the claim by the editor of *Fast Capitalism* quoted at the beginning of this section, that we are witnessing a blurring of, 'heretofore distinct social institutions, such as work and family, education and entertainment'.

A prime example of the blurring of home and work life is in the creeping encroachment of work activities into home time, particularly via the use of networked computers. For example, the tendency to send or to pick up work-related emails outside of normal working hours is now widespread (not least amongst academics). There is a straightforward sense in which this is exploitative in simply extracting more labour time from employees than is contracted for. And of course, though this practice may be regarded, contractually, as voluntary, it is not cynical to see it as a tacit requirement of performance in competitive work environments – or perhaps better as 'image management'. Thus the sending off of emails time-stamped late in the evening or early in the morning may be regarded as the virtual equivalent of that emblem of 1980s corporatism, the ritual of the breakfast meeting. And yet, on the other hand, it would be uselessly cynical not to allow that for some – many – people and in many circumstances, this sort of practice represents a genuine exercise of autonomous time use and convenience. Where this sort of integration of work and home life occurs within *genuine* conditions of flexibility of employment we have to recognize that something else is occurring beyond the mere exploitation of labour.[13]

One way of approaching this is to compare this new integration of work and home life with the category of 'task orientation' which has been used to understand the apprehension of labour time in peasant societies – as contrasted with the 'time orientation' imposed within clock-regulated industrial capitalism, and particularly Taylorism (Chapter 2). Edward Thompson describes three salient aspects of task orientation:

> First, there is a sense in which it is more humanly comprehensible than timed labour. The peasant or labourer appears to attend upon what is an observed necessity. Second, a community in which task orientation is common appears to show least demarcation between 'work' and 'life'. Social interaction and labour are intermingled – the working day lengthens or contracts according to the task – and there is no great sense of conflict between labour and 'passing the time of day'. Third, to men accustomed to labour timed by the clock, this attitude to labour appears to be wasteful and lacking in urgency. (Thompson, 1991: 358)

Now clearly there are important ways in which the modern integration of work tasks into the sphere of home life differs from this: the practices involved rarely appear as wasteful and lacking in urgency and are unlikely to be confused with simply passing time. Indeed the awareness of an existence governed by clock time – by the multiple and competing itineraries of modern life – would seem to be uppermost in the motivation to fit parcels of work-time into gaps in these other routines.

Yet there are also similarities, most obviously the weak demarcation between 'work' and 'life' involved. Thus, what we could reasonably call a 'new task orientation' seems to grasp the experience of many people of the reach of capitalist (or capitalist-inflected) work relations into private life. And there is, to refer back to an earlier point, a 'softness' about this. It is the comparative softness of work schedules that demand more of us without imposing the harder-edged, clear-cut disciplines of the time clock and the factory whistle. The reach of work into home life, then, is not generally experienced as a colonization, but more subtly as a yielding, a give and take, a flexible arrangement with either a direct or an indirect *quid pro quo*. And it is the 'softness' of a labour which in some ways – in its actual exertions and manipulations – blends into those we also associate with leisure. For what really differentiates a work-oriented email from a message sent about, say, a sports fixture, or web-research for a work project as opposed to that done to help the children with their homework? Surely little other than, as Thompson puts it, 'a distinction between [the] employer's time and [the worker's] "own" time' (1991: 359). And this is a distinction that, with so little actual task differentiation involved, is often hard to maintain.

Which brings me finally and briefly to the sphere of consumption. There is a lot to be said about the immediacy of consumption, but most of this must wait until we have established the parameters of the concept more fully, and particularly its link with media technologies and systems. What I want to emphasize at this point is, again, the blurring of boundaries. Teresa Brennan offers a convincing argument here, to the effect that consumption in fast capitalism involves a significant element of unpaid labour, an element that is indeed necessary to offset the escalating costs of distribution needed to match an accelerating speed of production:

> To go online and buy products, or book airline tickets, is to perform delivery work. Such work is squeezed into the time once given to rest and revival. The turn of the century has witnessed a shift in the burden of service labour, from producer to consumer, that is impacting almost everybody. If you live in the so-called advanced West, you must have been spending more time doing telephone work, pressing '1' for this option and '6' for that option. When you do this, you are also making money (for someone else) insofar as you are saving labour and delivery costs. (Brennan, 2003: 133)

The point is well made and it adds economic precision to the intuition that many of us have that consumption is often a wearing and a time-consuming occupation. Often, but not, as a matter of perception, always – and certainly not to such a degree as to inhibit rational people from its diligent pursuit.

For the other point that needs stressing is that consumption is also probably the chief recreational activity of the modern world. This is a paradox which has fascinated and, it must be said, largely defeated critical cultural analysis at least since Herbert Marcuse's wonderfully elliptical description of the satisfactions of consumerism as 'euphoria in unhappiness' (Marcuse, 1964; Tomlinson, 1991: 122f.). Without adding much to this debate, it can at least be observed that consumption practices are intelligible as the first resort of a quest for satisfaction within capitalism, being, as it were, the imagined mirror opposite – and thus the most immediate reward – of wage labour. Thus, though Brennan is absolutely correct to point out how new modalities of consumption succeed in, 'sliding more of the residual labour of production and distribution under the door of exchange', this injustice conceals itself well since the labour it passes off inhabits the same world of leisure consumption and adopts cryptic colouring to hide within it. And, by and large, this is a soft, easeful and light world, continuously refining its efforts to anticipate our desires and speedily and effortlessly to meet them. 'Retail therapy' is an ironic coinage, but it neatly grasps these comfortable attendances.

This is not the whole story, and much more of a critical edge can be put on the analysis. But bear with me. All I want to emphasize for the moment is the increasingly porous texture of the boundaries between labour, leisure and acquisition, and the way that this builds towards a context of lightness and softness in the culture of immediacy.

Immediacy: speed without progress, arrival without departure

We need now to consolidate things somewhat and to firm up the concept of immediacy as a way of accounting for the transformations of speed culture in the contexts of fluidity and fast capitalism sketched above. In the first section I suggested that immediacy might be taken to mark the end of the era of mechanical speed in two senses of the term 'end'. And though this may sound like a bit of a rhetorical flourish, I'm going to stand by it. I don't, of course, mean that *all* the characteristics and the cultural preoccupations of mechanical speed have ended, have entirely disappeared. As I said at the conclusion of Chapter 3, in many ways the culture of mechanical velocity *overlaps* with the condition of immediacy in today's world, and there is no way of neatly and sequentially dividing the two. I take this shading and overlapping to be a general condition of cultural history.

However, I believe it *is* plausible to speak of the end (conclusion) of mechanical speed as a defining cultural preoccupation of a certain stage of modernity in the specific sense of its direct link with the early-modern ideology of rational-scientific and moral progress. In this sense of an implicit informing narrative – close to what Cornelius Castoriadis (1987a) called the 'imaginary significations' that lie beneath the surface of cultural phenomena – mechanical speed was, until quite recently, at the core of a robust and coherent set of modern social values, practices and individual imaginings.

This narrative wove the values of diligent application, effort, efficiency, planning and regulation into an imagination of personal biographical improvement tracking gradual but reliable social progress. This, as I argued through Chapter 2, was the dominant story of modern speed, the one to which the discourses of unruly speed (Chapter 3) reacted and rebelled, but were always in some sense subordinate to. Again, it is not as though all of these individual imaginations and ideals have disappeared. But what is clear is that they no longer hold together as an unshakeably resilient and confident story interpreting the acceleration of modern culture. This narrative has been displaced – but by what?

Answering this brings us to the second sense of an 'end' – as a goal. For what the imagination of immediacy suggests is that the goals of speed have now been somehow attained; that we have, as it were, surpassed the process – and particularly the need for concerted effort – that established speed as an independent value in the era of mechanical modernity. A difficult claim to redeem, perhaps. But there is a good deal in our everyday cultural practices, and particularly our interaction with new technologies, which might support this sort of imagination. Paul Virilio makes an apt observation here:

> Already, with the transport revolution of the nineteenth century, movement from one place to another had obviously undergone a mutation, since 'departure' and 'arrival' at a destination were peculiarly privileged to the detriment of the 'journey' properly so-called. Note in this connection the passivity, the somnolence of bullet train passengers and the screening of films on long-haul planes. With the instantaneous transmission revolution, it is now 'departure' that gets wiped out and 'arrival' that gets promoted, *the generalized arrival of data*. (Virilio, 1997: 56, emphasis in original)[14]

We should put this quotation in context. Virilio is discussing 'the law of proximity' or, as he also puts it, of, 'least effort or least action'. This is a story implicating technological developments in a decrease in physical effort and thus, more broadly, of deliberate action itself. According to Virilio this occurs as a function of an implacable logic of technological redundancy: 'where there is the choice between a lift or an escalator and a simple staircase to reach upper floors, no one takes the stairs' (1997: 55). In this context, Virilio's concern is, as always, with the emergent connections between a range of apparently discrete phenomena: 'teletechnologies', the characteristics of the built environment, and 'biotechnological miniaturization'.[15] The 'law of proximity' drives us towards technology-led cultural changes which may be dramatic in their implications – as for instance in the 'ingestion' of microprocessors within the human body – but which somehow steal upon us as inevitabilities, by-passing rational deliberation.

For our present purposes, however, the key distinction in the passage is the redundancy of 'departure' and the promotion of 'arrival'. In the most general sense we can take this to signal something suggested at the outset of this chapter as characteristic of the condition of immediacy: the apparent 'closure of the gap' separating human desire from its attainment.

If the function of mechanical speed, as Virilio suggests, was to reduce the significance of the journey, the way it did this was in the purposeful application of the ensemble of human will and mechanical power. Early modern speed was heroic – for Marinetti, for Le Corbusier – precisely because it displayed the will, the force and the effort involved in the overcoming of distance. But the crucial thing, in terms of the cultural imagination and the values it promoted, was that the gap between here and there, now and later, what we desire and what we can expect to receive, was *preserved* in the necessity of effort, in the application of will, and, for the most part, in the prudential deployment of planning and regulation.

The culture of immediacy, by contrast, involves as its core feature the imagination that *the gap is already closed*. This presses to the conceptual and etymological heart of the term: the sense of being without the intervening or the middle term. Immediacy – closure of the gap – is therefore most generally *the redundancy or the abolition of the middle term*. In the key areas of contemporary cultural life that I will consider in the next two chapters – in our interaction with communications technologies and media systems and in the sphere of consumption – this redundancy of mediation is offered to us in the form of a series of clues and indications about how life is and how it should best be lived. For example, in the lightness and comparative effortlessness of communicating with one another via mobile phones, we are offered the impression of both the instantaneity of contact and the closeness – indeed the ubiquitous presence – of others. And in consumption practices we are offered the impression that new comforts, conveniences and refinements will flow independently of our individual efforts: that little separates desire and its satisfaction, that, almost as a constant of modern existence, stuff arrives.

It hardly needs adding that these clues are in many ways unreliable indicators of what modern life as a whole involves – that there is, in the very lightness of these practices, an element of the sleight of hand that I mentioned earlier. Nor can we really say that they amount to a coherent cultural narrative in the same sense as the ones they have largely displaced. Immediacy in its several existence across a range of everyday practices and representations, and in the implicit meanings these constitute, is better understood as an essentially ambiguous condition rather than as a pellucid narrative.

But, having said this, immediacy is a condition with which we need to come more self-consciously to terms if we are to understand not only the recent-historical transformation of speed, but also of broader cultural attitudes and values. And one important aspect of this lies in not disposing the idea of immediacy too quickly to any one of its aspects. This is, I think, important to avoid what can be a rush to critical judgement. Zygmunt Bauman, for instance, tends to move quite quickly down one line of thought when he writes that, 'Instantaneity means immediate, on-the-spot fulfilment – but also immediate exhaustion and fading of interest.... Fluid modernity is the epoch of disengagement, elusiveness, facile escape and hopeless chase' (2000: 118, 120).

This is to think of immediacy particularly in its temporal mode: of closing the gap in *time* or more precisely, of abolishing *waiting* . And this can quickly refer us to some familiar current cultural anxieties: worries about diminishing attention spans, or a popular preoccupation with 'instant gratification', the 'three-minute culture', the 'now generation' and so on. Such worries invoke a critique of cultural acceleration focusing on the linked themes of compulsion, meretriciousness and impatience, and which can select from a list of ready exemplars: fast food restaurants; scratch-card gambling; compulsive shopping; channel hopping; serial infidelities; road rage.

These are genuine and significant anxieties of course, and Bauman does not exaggerate in saying that, 'the advent of instantaneity ushers human culture and ethics into unmapped and unexplored territory' (2000: 128).

But to begin to map this territory we need, I believe, to preserve as general an understanding of the condition of immediacy as possible and, as a first principle of cultural critique, to identify and consider both the positive and the negative moments: the cultural attractions in immediacy as well as its follies and dangers. Only by doing this can we avoid critique losing its essential anchoring in a hermeneutics of everyday lived experience, and sliding towards mere reaction.

Notes

1 *Oxford English Dictionary*: entries on 'Immediacy' and 'Immediate'.

2 Bauman begins his book *Liquid Modernity* by making the physical-theoretical point that fluidity is the quality of both liquids and gasses, both of which are to be distinguished from solids in terms of their characteristic property of undergoing 'a continuous change in shape when subjected to a stress' (2000: 1). Beyond this however he isn't much concerned to distinguish liquidity from fluidity and neither am I. 'Gaseous modernity' is of course, for all manner of reasons, an infelicitous term.

3 This is also a feature of Baudelaire's aesthetic imagination of *Modernité*. In 'The Painter of Modern Life' (1863) he stresses modernity's qualities as 'the transitory, the fleeting, the fortuitous' (Baudelaire, 1964; Frisby, 2001: 236f.).

4 It is interesting to compare a comment of Derrida's on the undulant character of mediated experience. Referring to the way in which historical events – the fall of the Berlin wall, the end of apartheid in South Africa – seem to 'break', unpredictably in terms of their timing, upon the world:

> For it is breaking, it is rolling up on itself like a wave, which accumulates strength and mass as it accelerates. . . . I think this acceleration in process is tied in an essential way . . . to telematic, teletechnical transformation . . . the crossing of borders by images, models etc. . . . The acceleration of all political, or economic processes thus seems indissociable from a new temporality of technics, from another rhythmics.
> (Derrida and Steigler, 2002: 71)

5 On the validity and limitations of epochal thinking see Therborn, 1995; Albrow, 1997; and Tomlinson, 1999: 35f.

6 And heuristic also perhaps in the application of the term to computer systems. An heuristic program – for example a spellchecker – is, according to the Microsoft Encarta Dictionary 'one that modifies itself in response to the user'. Not a bad description for reflexive sociology.

7 On the centrality of time–space co-ordination to modernity see, particularly, Giddens, 1984, 1990; Harvey, 1989; Lash and Urry, 1994; Urry, 2000 and in relation to conceptions of globalization: Held et al., 1999; Tomlinson, 1999.

8 See Weber (1970: 293f.). For discussions see Giddens, 1972; Morrison, 1995.

9 See also the editor, Ben Agger's, book *Fast Capitalism* (1989).

10 As might be inferred from the now notorious experiment in automated computer trading implicated in the 1987 New York Stock Market crash.

11 Of course I exclude here the possibilities opening up to us in the field of genetic engineering, for which perhaps new definitions of the human condition may have to be formulated. But, as Scarlet O'Hara sensibly said, 'I won't think about that today, I'll think about that tomorrow'.

12 The social compact in the employment field is stronger in some developed economies than others: as was instanced by the defeat by popular demonstration of the French government's controversial youth employment legislation proposals in 2006. Despite this, it is clear that the principle of 'a job for life' is under siege pretty much everywhere. The puzzle is not the economic reasons for this ('globalization pressures') but the fact that both centre-left and centre-right politicians seem to have abandoned this as a political principle.

13 Though this may be rare. See Sennett's critique of flexitime working patterns (Sennett, 1998: 57f.).

14 Virilio's observations about the somnolence of bullet train passengers could equally have cited nineteenth-century sources. Schivelbusch for instance suggests that, 'Dullness and boredom result from attempts to carry the perceptual apparatus of traditional travel, with its intense appreciation of landscape, over to the railway' (1980: 61). John Ruskin, whose antipathy to the railways we have already noted, was of the opinion that, 'all travelling becomes dull in exact proportion to its rapidity' and Flaubert, writing in 1864, says, 'I get so bored on the train that I am about to howl with tedium after five minutes of it' (both quoted in Schivelbusch, 1980: 60–1). In-flight movies seem to me to have rather different implications: both substituting a temporal for a spatial experience of distance (a long-haul flight can be measured in terms of the number of movies it is possible to watch) and diverting passengers from dwelling on the risks involved – see Tomlinson, 1999: 4–5.

15 We will return to some of these themes in the following chapter where we focus on the implications of communications technologies for routine experience, including the experiences of place and of embodiment that Virilio broaches. But unlike Virilio, who tends to associate 'the generalized arrival of data' (1997: 56) with an increase in sedentary existence, I will argue that it becomes much more interesting a phenomenon when understood as integrated into an increasingly *mobile* lifestyle.

5

Media

Foremost amongst the factors to be considered in the transition from a culture of speed to one of immediacy is the telemediatization of culture. By 'telemediatization' – an ungainly but relatively precise term – I understand the increasing implication of electronic communications and media systems in the constitution of everyday experience.

Telemediated activities – watching television; typing, scrolling, clicking and browsing at the computer screen; talking, texting or sending and receiving pictures on a mobile phone; tapping in PIN codes and conducting transactions on a keypad – can be regarded as unique cultural practices and ways in which experience is presented to consciousness. They occupy a space in the everyday flow of experience within the individual's lifeworld that is distinct, yet integrated with face-to-face interactions of physical proximity.

Perhaps the first step in understanding the increasing significance of communications and media technologies in our lives, however, is to recognize that they are, in fact, deserving of analysis. Telemediated practices and experiences are now so much a routine and taken-for-granted aspect of everyday life in developed societies[1] that they can appear almost transparent. This familiarity steals upon us unnoticed in the course of our lives, and so to appreciate their significance, we need to make these everyday mediations strange to us. One way to do this is to compare our current experience with a time in the near-history of telemediation.

In the opening scene of John Adams's opera *Nixon in China*,[2] Richard Nixon soliloquizes on the 'mystery' of the live broadcast, via satellite, of his historic handshake with Chou En-Lai in 1972 on the tarmac of a military airport outside Beijing. Nixon's thoughts go quickly from the world-historical to the provincial as his imagination conjures a picture of his domestic media audience watching the event during 'primetime in the USA'. He imagines a scene of middle-American domestic harmony, with the 'three main networks' casting their colour through the curtains on to the lawns of suburban houses. Though lyrical, the image is, of course, mythical. Yet the way in which the television audience is represented here as both the nuclear and the national family is plausible at least in terms of the technologies of the time. In 1972 broadcast television had no rival to its dominance in national media culture: the 'livid colour' was new enough to be worthy of comment and the 'big three' American national networks commanded virtually the whole of the prime time audience.[3] Since the time-shifting properties of the VCR were yet to come (Winston, 1998: 126) the image of the family circle assembled around the TV after the evening meal (Spigel, 1992) – an image emblematic of what might be called the broadcast nation – was not at all an unreasonable one.

The new media technologies and the associated practices that have been assimilated into the domestic sphere in the intervening time – a little over 30 years – have been sufficient entirely to undermine this media culture.[4] Personal computers, optical fibre cables, cellular phones, camcorders, video games, the internet, email, web sites, search engines, blogs, social networking sites, DVDs, digital television and radio, broadband, TiVo, MP3 players, pod-casts have fractured the temporal and the spatial frames of everyday media reception, fragmenting the media audience and undermining the rituals of collective viewing or listening. And they have introduced modes of experience for which we still have no adequate name: think for instance of the experience of the instant and infinite availability of the world's informational resources that is the defining phenomenology of the web browser.

So easily and so rapidly do media technologies become 'domesticated' (Silverstone and Hirsch, 1992; Morley, 2000; Berker et al., 2006), that we have to remind ourselves that few of the experiences of present day telemediation have any counterpart beyond the last few decades of world history.[5] And each of them helps to define what it is to exist as a social being in the modern world.

Proportion

It is this rather curious mixture of the familiar, the taken-for-granted, often the apparently trivial and banal, with the capacity to alter, radically and irrevocably, the terms of human intercourse which seems to characterize the telemediatization of culture and, in so doing, to pose a particular problem for cultural analysis. The problem is, I think, one of finding a sense of *proportion* in the way we approach telemediatization. Let me broach this anecdotally.

I recently bought a digital (DAB) radio. The main attraction was the consistency and quality of the signal, but there were also other features which looked appealing, a range of new stations not available on FM, and various clever functions: scrolling text, a memory function which allows you to 'pause and rewind' a live broadcast and so on. I'm pleased with the improvement in sound quality, but I find I rarely stray from my favourite two BBC channels and virtually never use any of the novel functions. Except one. This is the 'Sleep' button. Of course this is not really a new facility, I had one on my old bedside radio. And, indeed, when I come to think about it, it was pretty high on my list of priorities, since I generally fall asleep listening to the radio and having a function that will switch it off after 15 or 30 minutes is a great convenience.

There is however a difference that I've noticed with the new equipment. Instead of abruptly switching off the signal, this one gradually and subtly fades out over a period of, I would guess, four or five seconds. Now on those occasions that I am still awake when the sleep function cuts, or rather tiptoes, in, I find I take an odd pleasure in this fading to silence. Even if I am paying attention to the programme at the time, there is a certain satisfaction in yielding to this gentle contractual ending of the day's media experience. And I am never tempted to switch it back on.

This curious and, who knows?, maybe idiosyncratic little observation prompts a more general one about the nature of mediated experience. Reflecting on this I am led down two different paths of thought. In the first, what strikes me is the power of this small piece of everyday technology, the way it has insinuated itself into the rhythms of my life and the capacity it has even to mediate the transition from consciousness to unconsciousness. This thought even evokes a mildly McLuhanesque awe: media truly are 'the extensions of man'. It is not only the question of their ubiquity, their integration into pretty much every sphere of life in developed societies, it is their power to shape and perhaps even to *constitute* experience. For if I consider my pleasure in the fading from voices or music to silence, the particular experience of silence itself may be considered a product of this contrived transition. The influence of media is present therefore even in their absence.

But then the second thought asserts itself, rather like a stern self-corrective to all this rhapsodic techno-enthusiasm. Surely the main lesson is in the *dispensability* of media, the fact that, for all its ubiquity, we can and do routinely switch it off, or at least arrange for it to switch itself off. This dispensability makes itself apparent when we shift our focus from the admittedly increasingly wide range of mediated practices, to those which actually require or benefit from disengagement: sleeping, having a face-to-face conversation, reading, playing games, singing, practising yoga, making love, praying. We can of course do all these things in the presence of mediated technologies but, despite arguments that the rising generation is one constitutionally adapted to media multitasking,[6] most of us, most of the time, still prefer not to. Media technologies can in many contexts be a distraction and we often choose and are able, unlike the unfortunate Winston Smith, to switch them off. Even recognizing the growing instances of the incursion of media technologies into these other realms – television and radio as domestic 'wallpaper', telephone or computer sex, mobile phones interrupting face-to-face conversations, Karaoke, TV evangelism, text messages from the Vatican or from the muezzin calling the faithful to prayer – doesn't alter this case. The dispensability of media in the last analysis – disconnection – situates it more proportionately within human culture. The sleep function may mediate bodily rhythms but finally it is no more than a deferred 'off' button. The mistake is in seeing its use as a sort of contract between person and medium. It is not this: it is merely an act of programming. The real contract is with ourselves: how much we allow the media into our lives. The media remain under our control. The sleep function is a witness to human agency.

The sense of proportion that we need to apply in discussing the role of media technologies, processes and practices in contemporary culture really depends on reconciling these two thoughts: in getting this ambivalence between ubiquity and dispensability, determinism and agency, centrality and peripherality into proper focus. We live in a world in which media impinge on virtually everything we do and experience, even, arguably on what we are, or at least how we conceive ourselves to be.[7] But, even so, we risk delusion if we cannot view this influence in reasonable relation to other spheres of life, other aspects of lived experience. This involves something more than avoiding the 'hype' that tends to surround the media. It is a question of achieving perspective when we are *in medias res*. It is a matter of being proportionate.

I raise this caution because, in most of what follows, I shall necessarily focus on the influence of media technologies and systems and so neglect explicitly to renew scepticism as to their cultural centrality. But later in the chapter questions of the dispensability of these technologies will present themselves again, and here we shall have to avoid the opposite, reactive, position which recommends an abstemious attitude towards mediated experience as a moral or an aesthetic desideratum. So, again, proportion.

And, lastly, we have, as a practical matter, to find proportion in what aspects of telemediatization we can, realistically, broach within a single chapter. My solution to this one is to adopt, broadly and without particular rigour, a quasi-phenomenological stance. What is important is the way the media deliver experiences of immediacy to us. This suggests a focus on the 'point of delivery', that is, on the interface between the experiencing subject and the ensemble of media technology-system-institution. This focus should help us approach our key question: the mode in which the world is constituted, made present for us – made immediate – through telemediatization.

Now in the hinterland of this nexus of experience there lie all manner of other phenomena, concerns and associated ways of understandings – for example, the technical ramifications of communications systems and the political-economic context of media technologies and institutions – most obviously their relation to fast capitalism.[8] As a matter of necessity we shall have to pass lightly over many of these matters in this chapter. But this bracketing of other agendas has the virtue of keeping us to the point, and should hardly compromise the analysis. And, frankly, we shall have enough to occupy us.

Immediacy and the nature of mediation

So let's begin with the terminological felicity that places 'media' literally and exactly at the centre of 'immediacy'.

The way we conceived immediacy in the previous chapter emphasized the idea that a gap is closed – or is perceived to be closed – between certain separations that have historically defined the terms of human culture.

These include the spatial separation which establishes 'here' and 'elsewhere' as entities only to be joined by laborious effort, which consequently defines 'localities' and situates cultures within these localities, providing stable identity positions, but also keeping us, culturally and politically, 'in our place'. And they include the temporal gap between now and a future which may entail waiting and require patience, but which seems predictable and approachable as part of a deliberate, planned life strategy. The condition of immediacy – the closure of these intervals – therefore embraces the experience of the abolition of distance that is a central characteristic of globalization, and of a future which seems, in the rapidity of cultural-technological change, to rush upon us.

It is intuitively easy to see how media processes and technologies might contribute to this experience. And yet, once we begin to explore what 'media' are, there emerges a bit of a conceptual conundrum. Briefly put, it is that a 'medium' (the plural of which, 'media', we have adopted loosely to cover the whole range the modern communications practices, technologies and institutions) has two rather contradictory characteristics. It both connects and separates.

The idea of connection, particularly in spanning distance, is of course basic to communication and is given in many of the etymologies of electronic media forms, most obviously in the 'tele' root of 'television', 'telephone', 'telegraph' – from the Greek, 'far off, distant'. This is to understand media as agents of time–space bridging: bringing distant events into people's localities.[9] But the *way* in which this is achieved – through all the technical contrivances of electronic media, and in terms of the complex set of semiotic codes, conventions, genres, formats and modes of address that it employs – throws weight upon the notion of *separation*: of a medium as 'the intervening substance through which impressions are conveyed to the senses' (OED).

As Raymond Williams notes, the idea of the medium as an 'intervening substance' emerges early in the history of the term, in the first part of the seventeenth century:

> Thus, 'to the Sight three things are required, the Object, the Organ and the Medium'. Here a description of the practical activity of seeing, which is a whole and complex process of relationship between the developed organs of sight and the accessible properties of the things seen, is characteristically interrupted by the invention of a third term which is given its own properties, in abstraction from the practical relationship. (Williams, 1977: 159)

Williams notes this use of the term as the beginning of a process of reification. In this early usage there is clearly a simple mistake: of assuming an invisible, quasi-causal, entity – 'the Medium' – which is necessary to the process of sight. This, as he goes on to say, is rather like the imagination of entities like 'phlogiston' once thought to be the essential substance of combustion, invisibly and causally present in all combustible materials. But the reification of the medium persists, Williams argues, more subtly into our understanding of cultural practices.[10] In the visual arts, for example, the notion of the medium – 'the medium of oils', 'the medium of watercolour' – develops from a neutral technical sense – the carrier of a pigment – first into a specific category of practice – an artist working in oils or in watercolour – and, thence into the *definer* of artistic practice. It is here that:

> a familiar practice of reification occurred, reinforced by the influence of formalism. The properties of the medium were abstracted as if they defined the practice, rather than being its means. This interpretation then suppressed the full sense of practice, which is always to be defined as work on a material for a specific purpose within certain necessary social conditions. (Williams, 1977: 159–60)

Williams wants to remind us of the social relations contextualizing and expressed though all cultural practices and he is, of course, right to point to the mystification involved in this artistic reification of the medium. However in the case of the electronic media I think there is, in general, another, pretty much *opposite* form of 'obscuring' involved. This is that, in one way or another, electronic media tend to *hide* their mediation. Far from advertising it, they obscure the artifice of their practice and present their product or their access to communication as pristine, untouched, *immediate*.[11]

We can identify three senses in which this is so.

First there is the straightforward matter of technical improvements and innovations. One obvious theme that suggests itself here is the pretty universal assumption – defining a trajectory of increasing acceleration in media technologies, reaching back to the telegraph and forwards through computer-mediated convergences – that a progressive increase in the speed of communication is an undisputable good.[12] But, equally significant, is the technical goal of the delivery of improved 'quality', and what this essentially means is the elimination of 'noise' in all its forms, and of a nearer approximation to actual 'presence'. We may include here a number of recent innovations: the improvement of broadcast signal quality (particularly in the employment of digital technology); better image definitions and larger size screens provided by liquid crystal displays, plasma, and soon, polymer LEDs (and the consequential sudden collapse, *c.* 2006, in the wider market for the cathode-ray tube); and the speed of connection and downloading of material provided by broadband internet connections. All of these can be thought of as innovations which (amongst other benefits) reduce our awareness of the apparatus of mediation simply by making it more efficient, and so more discreet. Think, for instance, of telephones which once required the mediation of operators, of radios which needed delicate 'tuning' and time to 'warm up', of the television 'test card'.

Secondly, there is the goal of 'immediacy' as a professional media value. This embraces two fundamental informing assumptions of established media practice: that mediated material should be delivered both rapidly and with the rather illusive quality of 'liveness' (Feuer, 1983; Peters, 1999; Couldry, 2003; McPherson, 2006). These qualities are most evident, of course, in media coverage of 'live' events: news, sport, unique performances and so on (Dayan and Katz, 1992; Lee et al., 2002) where the obvious aim is to approximate the experience of actually being present. But the professional/institutional value of immediacy spreads out from this to inform a wider 'style' of media presentation, a style which favours informality, direct conversational modes of address, and a certain assumption of intimacy (sometimes even of ironic complicity) with the audience. The value of immediacy in this context tends to blur with other contemporary media values: for example, the idea that television programmes generally require 'pace' – forward movement, a relatively fast narrative tempo, background music and background visuals, activity and interactivity rather than simple 'to camera' monologue. This combination has generated some absurdities, such as the current trend for newsreaders to be obliged awkwardly to *stand* in order to deliver bulletins. The reasoning behind this however is perfectly consistent with the value of immediacy – the removal of symbolic barriers and conventions (the newsreader's desk) which signal the media *as mediators*, rather than as, say, everyday acquaintances and interlocutors.

It is thus only in the (still comparatively) rare context that we may ourselves become media actors (in both the sociological and the theatrical sense) – may, say, be interviewed on television – that the artifice reveals itself. Jacques Derrida spoke with characteristic subtlety of the difference in 'rhythm' experienced in speaking in front of a camera:

> I don't speak, I don't think, I don't respond in the same way anymore, at the same rhythm as when I'm alone, daydreaming or reflecting at the wheel of my car or in front of my computer or a blank page.... As soon as someone says, 'Roll tape!' a race begins, one starts not to speak, not to think in the same way anymore, almost not to think at all anymore.... This is in general part of the experience, shall we say, of 'intellectuals', of people who write or who teach, etc.: when they are in front of the camera or the microphone, the more they ask themselves questions about this situation, as I am doing here, the more they exhibit reticence, scruples, a shrinking or a retreat... the more they are removed from this experience, the less they are accustomed to it, the less they are able to forget the artifice of the scenario. (Derrida and Steigler, 2002: 70–1)

For Derrida, the question of technical mediation and of pace come together in a specific 'rhythm' which is second nature to professional broadcasters and is received as equally 'natural' by viewers, but which is nevertheless peculiar to mediated practice and experience. When we focus on the technical/semiotic/stylistic contrivance of this rhythm, we stall, we become 'inhibited, paralysed, arrested'.

Both these technological and professional/stylistic developments feed into the third and most general sense in which media obscure their mediation. This is that telemediated experience now inextricably intertwines with direct experience in the 'flow' of everyday life. This is not, of course, to say that we confuse the two, that we are becoming unable to distinguish between telemediated experience and 'real life'. Rather it is that the two modes of experience are presented to us, not merely intermingled, but, as it were, *on equal ontological terms*, so that a moment-by-moment discrimination is not generally required of us. Both the mediated and the non-mediated have such normalcy within our experience that we move between them with hardly any sense of changing gear. Think of the way in which we so easily switch between the mediated mode of listening to a news item and the 'non-mediated' one of discussing its implications with a partner; or of the complex modalities involved in holding a three-way conversation between a live partner and one on the end of a mobile phone. Or of that rather mysterious process by which, settling into a cinema seat, our conscious attention becomes absorbed *into* the screen – by which we seem to 'enter' the world of the film.

Indeed mediated experience has become so much 'second nature'[13] that it takes an act of deliberate subversion to draw its artifice to our attention. A good example of this is to be found in Michael Haneke's film *Caché* (Hidden) (2005). As part of a narrative built around the themes of surveillance and guilty secrecy, Haneke challenges the audience's assumptions about what they are watching. The extraordinarily long establishing shot consists of a view of the house in an affluent Paris neighbourhood which is to become the centre of the drama. In medium distance and from a fixed position, the camera dwells for minutes on this unremarkable scene, placing the viewer in the position of a surveillance camera, or possibly of someone watching the house. But then these assumptions are shattered in something of a *coup de cinema*, as the image becomes broken up by horizontal lines, instantly signalling that we have in fact been watching a videotape of the scene, now being rewound. Haneke deploys this sort of device throughout the film, concluding with an even more daringly extended shot of teenagers leaving a school, containing an ambiguous and 'hidden' clue to the film's mystery. But the fact that the 'media status' of this final image – is it another video? – is never disclosed, refuses closure of the narrative.

A subversion like this obviously plays on our routine assumptions about the reliability of cinematic narration, but what is perhaps more interesting is that the trick relies on our instantly recognizing the point at which 'video tape' is signalled and, just as instantly, understanding the implications of this deceit, not just for the particular narrative, but for the conventions of cinema. It works precisely because of our ability to shift effortlessly between different genres and modalities of mediated experience.

All the above can be thought of as aspects of the 'naturalization' of telemediated practice and experience within the modern lifeworld. And we can add to these a further point about the inherent *difficulty* of overtly conceptualizing the technical processes of mediation. How can we, for example, construct and retain a meaningful representation of the relationship between a digitalized signal and the voices and images that this brings to us as mediated 'presences'? This is a problem that has been broached within some areas of digital and internet art. For example, Rachel Greene describes an installation, *Live Wire*, by Natalie Jeremijenko of the group 'Bureau of Inverse Technology':

> *Live Wire* (1995–present) was an early internet-related project set up by Jeremijenko, which elided the standard activities of the internet (browsing web sites, sending an email), making use of a local network to visualise activity with a string that wiggled according to local computer usage. The dangling structure [a bright red cable] increased the peripheral reach of the formerly inaccessible and unarticulated network traffic.... In part because of its very banality...its wiggles claimed attention for neglected information. (Greene, 2004: 69–70)

Jeremijenko's work – placed in offices and cafés – has a political dimension, in drawing attention to the 'anonymous nature' of commercial trading activity that preoccupies the internet. But it also illustrates the inherent *obscurity* of the medium in which the internet artist works. This is where the contrast with Williams's critique of the dominance, the insistent foregrounding, of the medium in painting is most apparent. *Live Wire* may concretize invisible technical activity, but its primitive wriggling is surely also representative of the low level of sophistication that most of us can achieve in an appreciation of the technical medium which delivers so much of our everyday experience. It reveals what we might have suspected all along, that though the defining mode of telecommunication may be digital, the quintessential mode of apprehension of mediated experience remains analogue. That media disclose themselves to us most 'naturally' at the point of delivery and in increasingly close analogies with non-mediated reality.

In all these ways, then, we may justifiably say that the history of tele-mediatization has been one of the progressive obscuring of the evidences of mediation. This suggests clues for a general analysis of contemporary media culture, for the way it becomes second nature. But our interest is more specific: the implications for the mode of immediacy that telemediatization delivers. What I have tried to do in this section is to begin to sketch out some general features of telemediated culture that are relevant to this. In the next section we will start to explore these implications by considering how media technologies are integrating with patterns of physical mobility in the fluid, light modernity discussed in Chapter 4.

Changing terminals

Let us recall, from the previous chapter, Paul Virilio's comment about the successive technological revolutions in modern mobility: the transport revolution of the nineteenth century, and the twentieth century – and ongoing – revolution in communications and media technologies. Virilio argues that the second of these makes redundant the notion of 'departure' and promotes instead, 'the generalized arrival of data'. He goes on to say: 'The key notions of (radio, video, digital) signal input and output have overtaken those usually associated with the movement of people or objects traditionally distributed throughout the extension of space' (Virilio, 1997: 56).

What Virilio infers from these observations is that the nature of *proximity* is changing from a spatial into a temporal phenomenon. In a world where things are delivered to us via communications technologies, being 'close' is less a measure of distance than of time: 'the real time of immediacy (live coverage) dominates the real space of the building' (1997: 56). Here Virilio's architectural interests tend to colour his analysis, for he imagines the impact of communications technologies within the context of dwelling in buildings and the 'adoption of a sedentary life'. But this, I think, is a mistake.

The recent trajectory of the development of telemediatization has clearly been one integrating with the increasing mobility of people in 'fluid modernity' – the fact, as John Urry (2000: 49) puts it, 'that mobilities, as both metaphor and as process, are at the heart of social life'. This is instanced perhaps most obviously by the convergence of mobile phone technology with wireless internet access and the emphasis on this platform as a portable, multi-functional terminal for audio, text and picture messaging, TV, shopping, banking, digital photography and so on. More broadly, the cultural uses and connotations of the mobile phone (Katz and Aakhus, 2002; Agar, 2003; Crabtree et al., 2003; Rippin, 2005), particularly as they are exploited in advertising to the youth market, are predominantly those of a mobile sociability: the mobile phone is an icon of life in the twenty-first-century metropolis – imagined as integrated with all the vibrancy and stimulation of urban life (Maënpää, 2001). All of this suggests the busy, restless context of a culture on the move and on the streets, rather than the vision of isolated sedentary existences within the controlled, serviced environment of a wired dwelling.

Despite this, Virilio poses an important general question about the way in which new media technologies may be changing our lived and imagined relationship to the places we inhabit. But we can approach this in a way that recognizes the integration between mobility and telemediatization, rather than their stark opposition. Indeed interactions with these technologies have often been characterized precisely as peculiar forms of 'virtual mobility'. Thus, the use of the internet, and even to some degree of television, is sometimes understood as a form of 'virtual travel' (Benedikt, 1991; Rheingold, 1994; Moores, 1996) and popular expressions often employ metaphors of movement (surfing, channel hopping, navigating and so on). I want to develop this metaphorical use by thinking about a shift in our conceptualization of the *terminal*.

A terminal is both a place of departure and of arrival, of beginning and ending – but in either sense it implies a limit, a boundary, a set of fixed spatial co-ordinates for travel or for communication. During most of what I've called the era of mechanical modernity, a terminal was pretty much exclusively a feature of the built environment – typically, one of the great railway stations that were so much a feature of the modern metropolis from the middle of the nineteenth century.

The grandiosity of the architecture of these early-modern terminals is interesting. In the most general sense it is indicative of a broad cultural assurance about the power-geography of an era in which, as Zygmunt Bauman (2000) says, mechanical, 'heavy' technologies implied a certain reliable permanence in time–space location, a period in which power was perceptibly concentrated in physical locations. This cultural self-confidence is perhaps most completely expressed in the Victorian vogue for Neo-Gothic architecture (Clark, 1962), as instanced in Charles Barry's rebuilding of the Palace of Westminster in the 1840s (Wilson, 2002: 62f.) or in George Gilbert Scott's frontage for London's St Pancras Station (1868–1876).[14] Here the belief in mechanical progress is bound together with religion (in the ecclesiastical connotations of the Gothic style), with imperial power (for this style is mimicked in terminus stations across the British Empire)[15] and with commerce (Gilbert Scott's frontage incorporates the immense Midland Grand Hotel designed luxuriously to accommodate the rising business trade from the industrial Midlands).[16]

But the aesthetics of great railway terminals carried a further message about the triumphs of mechanical modernity: they were a demonstration of the way in which the pre-modern vicissitudes of travel – travel's etymological link with 'travail' – painful or laborious effort – were being swept away with locomotive power. The grandiosity of the terminals thus signified – and this is Virilio's point – the overcoming of the journey itself.

Walking the short half mile west of St Pancras along Euston Road brings us to Euston Station, site until 1962 of Philip Hardwick's great Doric portico (1839) for the terminus of the London and Birmingham Railway. Michael Freeman's discussion grasps the famous 'Euston Arch' both as the archetypal nineteenth-century metropolitan 'gateway' and, more significantly, as marking the 'victory of engineering' over nature:

> Critics of the time derided the vast scale of the entrance front, contrasting it with the meagre train sheds behind. But they were missing the point. The portico was a 'triumphal arch, bestriding the processional way of the first railway to march on London'. It also celebrated 'the victory of the engineers over the subterranean waters and quicksands of Kilsby and the great hewn defiles of Tring and Roade' (Freeman, 1999: 16)[17]

But the victory was won at a price: that of the industrialization of space. This is something that emerges in Wolfgang Schivelbusch's (1980: 161ff.) discussion of the terminal station as a metropolitan gateway. Schivelbusch stresses the 'two-facedness' of early station architecture like that of Euston: their function as a liminal point between two orders of spatiality emerging in the mid-nineteenth century. The departing traveller leaves the essentially pre-industrial city space of the 1830s, 'and enters the station's space which in turn prepares him for the actual industrial space of the railroad' (Schivelbusch, 1980: 164). The gateway function of these early terminals was, according to Schivelbusch, a way of easing the passage into the threatening space of the actual platforms with all the attendant industrial apparatus of locomotives. Thus a structure like Euston segregated passengers in reception areas that had no direct access to platforms: 'In these, the passengers (like air travellers in our day) have to congregate and wait until the doors of the midway are opened, shortly before the train's departure' (Schivelbusch, 1980: 167–8).

The development of station architecture is one of increasing integration of these segregated spaces. By the time St Pancras is completed in 1876 public sensibilities have become sufficiently robust to allow for reception areas and platforms to be directly linked. As Schivelbusch says, this is largely because cities themselves have now become as industrialized as the railway space. But rail terminals remain to this day both as emblems and as functional apparatuses of a certain *form* of industrialized mobility which was at the core of the early modern cultural narrative of speed. Central to this narrative, as I emphasized in the early part of this book, is the relationship between mobility as the hard-won conquest of nature, concerted 'heroic' effort, and, significantly here, the intrinsically hazardous *hardness* of the technology involved.

To understand how communications technologies might constitute a different form of mobility, we can make the comparison with contemporary electronic terminals – mobile phones, laptop computers, digital music players and so forth. There are obvious differences here – for instance of physical scale – which, at first glance, makes this seem an unlikely comparison. But don't let's be put off by that. In contrast with terminals in the built environment – precise points of departure and arrival – those that we now carry with us represent a quite different set of principles constellating around the imagined *transcendence* of space and place.

The key characteristics of these terminals seem to be their portability and personalization. If we carry our terminals with us – or maybe soon even *within* us[18] – they cease to be fixed points in physical space which organize our patterns of mobility. And so, in a certain sense, some of the constraints of human embodiment itself are overcome – at least to the extent that the 'presence' of the world now seems to move along with us – indeed, experientially, with us at its centre. This in turn comes to constellate a range of other assumptions, values, attitudes and postures which together make up the cultural style of telecommunicational immediacy: the apparent ubiquity of presence, the redundancy of effort, and a certain related *insouciance* in communicational style. As a shortcut to characterizing this, another anecdotal example.

I was on a train from Edinburgh to London and, most unusually for me, travelling, not only in First Class, but in a smoking carriage. At Newcastle a woman got on and sat in the seat opposite. She was elegantly dressed and poised. She was serenely oblivious to all the other occupants of the carriage. As she took her seat, in one assured and fluid motion she simultaneously slipped her expensive coat from her shoulders, with one hand lit a cigarette and with the other flipped open her tiny, latest model, mobile phone. For the three and a half hours that we journeyed south along the route of the Flying Scotsman, she chain smoked and held a virtually unbroken series of languid conversations, never once seeming to glance around her or outside the window. The condition of our physical motion appeared, in her case, to be almost irrelevant. She was, as the Spanish say, *en casa*.

What was striking was her combination of ease, elegance of movement, complacence, a certain discretion (for unlike the businessman or woman who regards the carriage as their open plan office, she spoke quietly, intimately), together with a curiously exaggerated inwardness and absorption, an absolute detachment from her immediate environment. And at the centre of this, the mobile phone, suggesting an aesthetic of miniaturization, discretion and personalization in such stark contrast to the grandiosity and public ostentation of the rail terminals that marked the limits of our physical motion. It was, I think, this that in some degree provoked my interest in the phenomenology of telemediated experience. For it seemed almost a perfectly constituted example of this historically unique mode of being.

Generalizing from this rather extreme instance we can say that the experience of using these new communication technologies – when they are working properly that is – is one of effortlessness and ubiquity. Things – and particularly people – do seem to be pretty much immediately available – to the extent that we may often feel an unreasonable resentment when occasionally someone's mobile is switched off, or the email response does not appear by return in our inbox. There is little effort in communicating; there seem to be few real obstacles to overcome: just scroll though your electronic address book and press the call button on your mobile, or click on 'Send' in your Outlook Express. These manipulations are light, deft and smoothly choreographed into our working rhythms: they almost seem less physical operations than gestures – *legerdemain*. And, by a similar sleight of hand, the discreet soft technology immediately responds: closing the gap – that was preserved in the era of heavy mechanical modernity – between here and elsewhere, now and later, desire and its fulfilment.

But now we must remember the principal of proportionality. This immediacy of contact is of course entirely limited to the modality of electronic communication. The constraints of place and embodiment and the concrete realities of physical distance are still of course with us, and their stubborn persistence is evident in the continuing, indeed the growing significance of old-fashioned fixed terminals – bus, rail and air terminals, taxi ranks, parking lots – and the vast associated economy and technology of the physical transport of people in twenty-first-century cultures. The experience of travel today is of course itself *relatively* easeful – compared at least with the exhausting and perilous processes that mechanical modernity liberated us from. But no one would claim that twenty-first-century mobility is without its own difficulties, frustrations and indeed dangers. These now divide between, on the one hand, the attenuated inconveniences of train and flight delays or traffic jams, and, on the other, the risk of death and injury in road accidents or in the more spectacular catastrophic system failures of plane crashes or passenger ferries sinking. And, since 9/11 – amongst all else, also a watershed in the social organization of transport – we have to add the mixture of inconvenience and threat introduced into the routines of travel by the possibility of deliberate sabotage.

In any of these forms, the vicissitudes of contemporary travel attest to the limits imposed by the fragility and sheer existential facticity of the embodied human condition. It is our *bodies* that mark the key difference between telemediated and other modalities of immediacy. If we want to encapsulate the prime cultural impact of new communications technologies, then, it might be fair to say that they have produced a kind of *false dawn* of expectations of the liberation of human beings from the constraints of both embodiment and place. And if we want an image – albeit a rather banal one – that grasps this overreaching expectation of immediacy, we need only think of the gesture of frustration with which a crowd of – let's say – train passengers simultaneously pull out their mobile phones in the instant that follows the announcement of a delay to their service. Here the true proportionality between the mediated and the 'real' discloses itself in the limitations of a technology which, while it can allow us to vent our spleen, and to re-organize our schedules, can do nothing to lift us out of a situation determined by our physical being-in-place. The existential worry, as we shall presently see, is that we begin to hope and expect that it can.

To summarize: in this section I have argued that the immediacy of telemediated culture is best understood as integrated into the generally high level of physical and cultural mobility of contemporary societies; that it contrasts with the cultural narrative of 'mechanical modernity' – and its associated celebration of speed – particularly in its assumptions of ubiquitous 'effortless' availability; that the use of mobile media technologies radically changes both our real and imagined relationship to place; but that this cannot alter the terms of our embodiment, though it might generate different attitudes to this condition. Thus – like most features of modernity – this transformation is neither complete, nor without its ambiguities. Telemediated immediacy perhaps generates as many cultural challenges, burdens and perplexities as it offers genuine emancipations. In the penultimate section of this chapter we will explore some aspects of this perplexity, and then go on to offer, in conclusion, a general assessment of the contribution of telemediatization to the condition of immediacy. But before this, a slight digression.

Keyboards: an excursus

When we think about our interface with media technologies, the tendency, naturally enough, is to dwell on sight and sound: on the way the world is delivered to us on the flat surface of a computer, television or cinema screen, in Dolby Stereo, through a mobile phone or the earpiece of an iPod. This in fact raises a much bigger question about shifts in the 'hierarchy' of the senses across the modern period, for instance in arguments about the coming to dominance of visual cultures. Without entering too much into the broader debate[19] we can see that this way of thinking about the media – in relation to only two of the five senses – emphasizes the impression of technologies directly impinging on human consciousness. That is to say, it invites us to regard the human–media interface as, in Freidrich Kittler's words, 'a short circuit between brain physiology and communications technologies' (Kittler, 1999: 216) – one in which the wider embodied condition of human being is largely ignored. And this in turn, as we shall see in the section which follows this, tends to colour expressions of anxiety about the physiological and cultural effects of media technologies.

But here I want to draw attention to another very common feature of everyday media practices: our habitual way of accessing and communicating via keyboards and keypads, practices which do obviously involve the body, particularly the hands and the sense of touch.

There are several reasons to do this. First, precisely because it has generally been ignored[20] and this, apart from throwing the great weight of media analysis on to the visual and the oral/aural, narrows the range of conception of telemediatization in other ways. Keyboards – or, perhaps more generally, the scaled down version, keypads – now saturate our environment. Increasingly, we must use them not just in more direct interactions with media and communications systems – on mobile phones, TV and Hi-Fi remote controls, computers, games consoles – but also to draw money from our banks, to cook food in microwave ovens, to open doors, to activate air conditioning, to park, wash (and in the more sophisticated models, actually to *drive*) our cars, to access commentaries in art galleries and museums and so on. What this suggests is that some features of the culture of telemediatization are, in fact, embedded in this wider cluster of keypad practices.

Another reason to pay attention to keyboards and keypads is that our obligation to use them has created a new set of cognitions, skills and accomplishments. These include not only the remarkable dexterities that young people seem to possess in text messaging, but more basic skills necessary to everyday social competence. Take for instance the *rhythm* of punching in a PIN code. Remembering the various codes we have to use (but must not write down) – to open doors, at automatic cash machines, at supermarket check-outs – seems rather subtly to relate to a rhythmic pattern of entering the code. This suggests an embodied form of memory. If we stall in this choreographed performance we may risk failing, or at least doubting our capacity, to recall the code, with all the resultant embarrassment and inconvenience this threatens. Even a simple miss-key can be disconcerting as we are momentarily denied access. For let us not forget that these numbers signal our 'personal identification'. Or consider the transferable skill of recognizing the 'key keys' – the menu, scroll, select and enter functions – as they appear in slightly different configurations on various keypads we may need to use – and the associated capacity, a type of 'negative capability', to ignore all the others. Generalized keypad competence – since no one reads the manual – seems to involve the development of intuitions of relevance. I have been calling these adaptations 'skills', but that is not quite accurate. For the most part they are not practised abilities requiring a regimen of training. They are much more typically casually acquired habits and sensory-bodily rhythms.

And so a third reason – and the one I shall focus on here – is that the typical *deftness* of manipulations of keypads, particularly as contrasted with the more muscular, energetic operations performed on mechanical objects, is suggestive of the experienced lightness and softness of these technologies.

Let's explore a comparison: the typewriter. The typewriter might seem to be the direct forerunner of the contemporary keyboard and keypad, but the two have less in common than at first glance it might appear. Friedrich Kittler, who has given us the most intriguing and provocative cultural history of the typewriter, begins by noting the term's ambiguity:

> The word meant both typing machine and female typist: in the United States, a source of countless cartoons. (Typed letter of a bankrupt businessman to his wife: 'Dear Blanche, I have sold all of my office furniture, chairs, desk, etc. etc., and I am writing this letter under difficulties with my typewriter on my lap'.) But the convergence of a profession, a machine and a sex speaks a truth. (Kittler, 1999: 183)

A good part of Kittler's analysis traces this convergence in particular instances such as the relationships between writers like Nietzsche or Henry James with their machines and their co-identified female amanuenses. But, more generally, he describes the beginning of the end, from around the 1880s, of the male monopoly on the clerical professions, in the displacement of exclusively male copy clerks by pretty much exclusively female 'typewriters'. Kittler tells a complex and ironic story of this gender inversion of writing, in which it was, 'precisely their marginal position in the power system of script that forced women to develop their manual dexterity, which surpassed the prideful handwriting aesthetics of male secretaries in the media system' (Kittler, 1999: 194). But this overturning of the systematic exclusion of women from the world of letters takes place within another revolution, that of the *industrialization* of (in the broadest sense) literary production and bureaucracy. The skills which women were acquiring, or perhaps adapting from other accomplishments,[21] were ones occupying a specific place in the changing labour market of mechanical modernity. And though these skills were not such as to open up the higher levels of professionalism to women, the important point is that they *were skills*. That is to say they were technical accomplishments which defined a specific independent artisanal role;[22] which in themselves constituted a job description. And the skill of the typist was a combination of dexterity, accuracy and *speed*: practised, examined and certificated in the all-important words-per-minute (wpm) score. Driven by an expanding capitalism, but developed within the organizational ethos of stable, regulated hierarchy – of messages passing up and down a command chain – the speed skill of the typist fits nicely into the cultural narrative of mechanical velocity.

Contrast the keyboard. Academics of my generation in particular are aware of how it has stolen upon them unawares, displacing the specialist typist role of the departmental secretary in a democratic division of labour against which only the crustiest dare complain. But when did we, or indeed our students, actually study keyboard skills: work on our speeds, practice our home key positions, or memorize QWERTY? The skill demands of the Remington and the Imperial 66 associate with their mechanical 'hardness' in making them the property of the specialist. Heavy, hard and cold to the touch, requiring determined, firm and clipped key-strokes, typewriters are quite obviously serious industrial machines. Indeed Kittler says they are 'like rapid fire weapons': 'A technology whose basic action not coincidentally consists of strikes and triggers proceeds in automated and discrete steps, as does ammunition transport in a revolver and a machine gun' (1999: 191).

In this and other regards, modern computer keyboards have only the faintest family resemblance to typewriters. The casual, 'undisciplined' way in which we approach them reflects their ubiquity and their user-friendly nature, their relative softness, particularly the way in which they are forgiving of error. Our touch on their plastic keys, unlike the decisive strike on the typewriter which engraves the letter, never really commits us. The words we process are always virtual, easily edited, erased, spell-checked. Little wonder then that the common conversational style of emails, tolerant of typos, betraying little anxiety over literary *amour propre*, has developed.

Our generally insouciant attitude to keyboards is attributable to the fact that they are, after all, only adjuncts of a larger, more powerful system, the computer, which not only takes care of the word processing in nanoseconds, but fits this menial task into all manner of other communicational virtuosity. This adjunct status also means that, unlike the typewriter, the keyboard has, in a sense, no integrity. Cheap, plastic, interchangeable, they sit, neglected, at untidy angles on desks, anyone's property. No one will treat them with the respect due to a tool of the trade; no one will place a neatly fitting cover over them at the close of a day's work. In one of the many ironies of the condition of immediacy, by making life too easy for us, the keyboard has forfeited our respect.

In a similar way, the amateur status that most of us enjoy in our relation to keyboards is not one that, in itself, gathers to it any particular pride in performance. There is certainly an experience of speed here, but how different – generally – from that of a skilled dextrous practice.[23] The bodily performance – always at a crushing disadvantage in relation to the speed of the processing chip that for the most part sits patiently twiddling its thumbs as we type – loses its significance. And so, curiously, what seems to colour our experience is a neurotic impatience with occasional glitches in the unimaginably fast pace of information processing – with slow start-up times, lengthy downloads, the appearance of the hourglass symbol. What these frustrations remind us of is the fact that, for the most part, we are not the dominant actor in our relations with computers. Keyboard speed has none of the skilled percussive exhilaration of typing speed, emblematic of direct mastery of a technology. Instead, it is subsumed into the ambient, anxious speed of modern telemediated life.

Only connect...

So far in this chapter we have been trying to grasp something of the peculiar nature of telemediated experience and action. I have argued that, as the mediations of electronic technologies of communication become increasingly discreet, calling less attention to themselves, so we find fewer reasons and occasions to discriminate in a self-conscious way between their modality and that of non-mediated experience. This normalizing of telemediation has its parallel in the way in which these technologies, *contra* fears over a drift towards sedentary isolation, have integrated into the mobility of contemporary modernity, transforming the significance of location and the experiences of presence and distance. But then, I have suggested that the very ease and 'lightness' of telemediated communication – not just in their concentration on the visual and aural senses, but also in the lightness of touch involved in their manipulation – throws into relief the embodied condition of human being. Telemediation has the potential to pose our embodiment as a limitation, even an encumbrance – at the very least, as an old existential question to be confronted in a new light.

Within this context I want, in this and the final section, to try to pin down more precisely the distinctive contribution of telemediatization to the condition of immediacy.

There seem to me to be two broad aspects of this, two sorts of 'closing of gaps'. One of these involves the implication of telemediated practices in the changing nature of *consumption* in fast capitalism: the way in which teletechnologies may be collapsing a clear distinction between the experience of desire for the objects of consumption (including information) and its satisfaction. We shall address this implication of telemediatization as part of the larger agenda of 'delivery' in the next chapter, and there the relationship of immediacy to an increasing pace of life will emerge more obviously.

But another type of closing the gap – not, to be sure, entirely separable from the context of consumption, but posing a distinct range of issues – is the role of telemediatization in the maintenance of constant and ubiquitous contact between modern people whose lives are lived, in various senses, at a distance. This is the aspect of immediacy that we have mostly been concerned with in this chapter, and I want to keep with it.

The argument I want to develop is that *telepresence* – which we can understand as the possibility, and increasingly for many, the *preference*, of 'keeping in touch' without actually, literally, being in touch – should not be considered as entirely a deficit condition. I mean by this that telepresence needs to be understood as a distinctive existential mode of presencing, existing alongside direct, embodied relations of presence, but *not* regarded and evaluated as a shortfall from the 'definitive' existential mode of embodiment.

To be sure, there are all manner of limitations and indeed potential dangers to telepresence, some of which we have already noticed. But it seems to me that we will make no great progress in understanding it, and particularly its attractions to young people, until we can grasp it on its own terms, rather than inevitably in a nostalgically comparative fashion. I say this as someone who, as the reader may have guessed, does not feel these attractions particularly strongly, and as a consequence is, like many of my generation, often puzzled by them.

My neighbour, a librarian, tells me of teenagers who come to the public library and sit side by side at rows of computers, silently emailing each other. Why, she wonders, do they prefer this to being outside in the fresh air, chatting live to each other? I have no adequate answer. And I don't think I will until I can grasp something of the way they intuitively feel at home in telepresence, and have developed an apparently comfortable relation between this and our older home of flesh-and-blood bodies and relationships.

But first let us look at some of the reasons why telepresence has been unfavourably compared with live presence. I'm going to ignore lots of straightforward anxieties over possible physical pathologies associated with new media technologies – from repetitive strain injury related to keyboarding (Hayes, 1995) to the increased risk of brain tumours in mobile phone use. And I'm also going to disregard the sort of educational concerns that have been expressed over the possible failure of computer-based learning regimes to develop a sufficiently broad range of cognitive skills in children (Neill, 1995; Millar, 2001). What cultural critics tend to worry about is an existential, rather than a physiological or psychological issue: whether cyber-culture and new forms of communicational prosthesis may be undermining our sense of embodiment as a grounding ontological state.

And they began worrying about this long before the technologies actually existed. E.M. Forster is often cited, for his short story *The Machine Stops*, as an early literary Cassandra of cyber-space. First published in 1909, two years before the Futurist Manifesto, and described by Forster as, 'a reaction to one of the earlier heavens of H.G. Wells',[24] *The Machine Stops* is scarcely Forster at his nuanced best, but it is remarkably prescient, certainly matching Wells in its predictive imagination of coming technologies.

The story, set in an unspecified future, imagines a world in which humans have so far given over their lives to technologies that they have retreated from life on the surface of the earth to dwell for the most part isolated from each other in individual underground modules, 'like the cells of a bee'. Here they live comfortable, sedentary, apparently highly cultured, yet entirely controlled lives, their every need catered for automatically by 'The Machine' – an all embracing technological system which has been elevated to a quasi-divine principle. The plot is a slender one, built around two characters, Vashti, a dry, cerebral intellectual concerned only with 'ideas', and her dissident, sensually inclined son Kuno. Kuno has lost faith in the Machine and has recklessly and illegally ventured on to the surface of the earth. Here, despite being unable properly to breathe the atmosphere, he briefly delights in the natural world (and, as we finally discover, experiences intimacy with one of its inhabitants) before being dragged back below the surface by the hideous white tentacles of the Machine's 'Mending Apparatus' and returned to his 'cell'. Vashti is shocked by Kuno's adventure and the 'blasphemy' against the Machine that this represents. She considers him mad and breaks off further contact. Some years pass before another message arrives from Kuno, tersely declaring, 'The Machine stops'. At first unable to comprehend this, Vashti soon experiences the first signs of systemic failure as the music to her cell begins to distort. Other malfunctions follow, culminating in the catastrophic failure of the entire Machine, confirming Kuno's prediction. The technological civilization of the Machine thus perishes, but the story ends on an optimistic note. As mother and son are briefly united before their death, Kuno tells Vashti of the people that have survived on the earth's surface, beyond the reach of the Machine, 'hiding in the mists and ferns until our civilization stops'. They will continue life on earth, now that, 'Humanity has learnt its lesson'.

Several things about this story seem to make it apt as a parable for our times. Most obviously Forster's technological predictions: he foresees instant global communication via videophones (a 'blue visioning plate') and something like the internet (through which Vashti, 'knew several thousand people'). And to some extent he also anticipates the social impact of these technologies: for example he suggests the constant implacable flow of communications to be dealt with, and there are constant references to Vashti's experience of time pressure resulting in a general state of impatience and irritability, 'a growing quality in that accelerated age': 'Be quick Kuno; here I am in the dark wasting my time' (Forster, 1954: 110).

But these observations are incidental to the story's two central dystopian themes. In the first of these, Forster is concerned with the hubris of a civilization that has placed so much confidence in scientific rationality to overcome nature that it has lost human control of the technological system itself, thus fatally allowing human beings to become utterly dependent on a machine (and a mechanistic reason divorced from intuition) which will inevitably prove fallible. In the second, the culture that has developed around this technological dependence has begun to disregard and even to despise its own embodied nature.

This latter is the aspect of the story with most resonance for contemporary anxieties about the implications of telepresence. The theme is presented partly in the form of an ironic commentary on the logic of technological progress. For example Vashti, in reluctantly making the journey to visit her son, reflects on the preceding civilization, 'that had mistaken the functions of the system, and had used it for bringing people to things, instead of for bringing things to people. Those funny old days when men went for a change of air instead of changing the air in their rooms!' (Forster, 1954: 115). But more significantly Forster emphasizes this culture's suppression of sensuality and physical contact: children are separated from mothers soon after birth, and those showing signs of athleticism are destroyed; touching other people – having become 'obsolete' – is now treated with repugnance; the natural world is ignored as containing 'no ideas'. On her journey, Vashti experiences 'the horror of direct experience' of other people and, more alarmingly, Kuno, it is implied, is emasculated by the Mending Apparatus as punishment for his illegitimate sexual congress with the surface dwellers.

We don't, of course, seriously judge science fiction on its predictive power, and the fact that Forster (at least so far) seems to have got some things quite wrong – particularly in the inference that telepresence will result in a sedentary lifestyle – is really neither here nor there. Equally, we should not expect science fiction to transcend the concerns of its own age. And so Forster's depiction of a culture which finds itself somewhere between embarrassment at, and the systematic repression of, the embodied condition of humanity can also be read as a comment on the particular mores of early-twentieth-century English society. I will return to this shortly. But if, however simplistically, we take the story at face value, it allows us to pose the question of how far we may be drifting towards a distorted attitude to embodiment in the way we routinely employ telepresence today.

To help to come at an answer we can turn to Hubert Dreyfus's incisive critique of telepresence in his short book *On the Internet* (2001). Dreyfus briefly cites Forster's story, and in a way that takes its dystopian themes seriously. His argument is particularly with those who are too enthusiastic about the virtues of the internet[25] but he also feels – and this is where he is closest to Forster – that we might generally be too sanguine about the long-term cultural consequences of technologies. His approach is, however, entirely different from Forster's. What chiefly distinguishes it, apart from its philosophical sophistication, is Dreyfus's determination not to rely on 'thin end of the wedge' style inferences, but to deal with the actual qualities of currently existing telepresencing technologies. He addresses a range of issues: the inherent difficulty of designing information retrieval systems that are able to search for specifically relevant information; the use of computers in distance-learning situations; the capacity of the internet to provide full meaningful relations with distant others; and arguments about the potential for establishing 'virtual communities'. In each case Dreyfus shows that there is a form of trade-off involved between what we gain from the internet and what we lose in the process. In the case of search engines, for example, the trade-off is a symmetrical one – we trade its scope in accessing information for its generally poor capacity – as compared with a human being – to discriminate in what is relevant to our purposes. However, in the other cases Dreyfus discusses, the trade-off is in various ways *asymmetrical*. We either lose more than we gain – for example the sense of mutual, risky engagement of the live classroom or the existential meaning that derives from making and taking real consequential choices and actions, rather than virtual ones that involve no real commitments. Or, in the case of distanciated interactions, he argues that 'telepresence can never give us a sense of the reality of far-off things, nor can it convey a sense of trust of distant human beings' (Dreyfus, 2001: 98).

In all these arguments it is the human embodied condition, as understood in the philosophies of Nietzsche, Merleau-Ponty and Kierkegaard, that is crucial for Dreyfus. There is not space here to explore the detail of Dreyfus's claims,[26] but his conclusion is unambiguous so far as the importance of embodiment is concerned:

> our body, including our emotions, plays a crucial role in being able to make sense of things, so as to see what is relevant, our ability to let things matter to us and so to acquire skills, our sense of the reality of things, our trust in other people, and finally, our capacity for making unconditional commitments that give meaning to our lives. It would be a serious mistake to think we could do without these embodied capacities – to rejoice that the World Wide Web offers us the chance to become more and more disembodied, detached ubiquitous minds leaving our situated bodies behind. (Dreyfus, 2001: 90)

Given this, a less judicious critic might conclude by either issuing dire warnings about regarding our bodies as biological encumbrances or simply dismissing telemediated technology for its specious promise. Dreyfus does neither of these. Instead he argues for the need 'to foster a symbiosis' between how we use our bodies with their unique capacities and the extraordinary new capacities – in information retrieval and storage and in distanciated connectivity – that the technologies provide. The key proviso is that, in doing this, 'we continue to affirm our bodies...not in spite of their finitude and vulnerability, but because, without our bodies, as Nietzsche saw, we would be literally nothing' (Dreyfus, 2001: 107).

This seems to me to be pretty much dead on. It precisely captures the attitude of proportionality with which this chapter began. And yet, maybe we need to go one step further in understanding how such a symbiosis would work.

Before we can promote a symbiosis we probably need to understand more of the intrinsic *character* of telepresence, at least something of how it is experienced, and not just its scope and limitations. To the extent that I differ from Dreyfus, then, it is in posing telemediated experience more directly as a 'way of being' deserving exploration, rather than simply as interaction with a practically useful set of devices.

As the epigraph to one of his much better works, *Howard's End*, E.M. Forster famously chose the cryptic phrase 'Only connect...'. It is probably only the relatively limited demographic of those likely to catch the allusion that has so far prevented its adoption as the snappy slogan of a mobile phone company. But the phrase is actually not directly aimed at the difficulties of interpersonal communication. It refers to the need to reconcile the various antitheses which the novel, structured around the interweaving lives of the Schlegel and the Wilcox families, addresses: commerce and culture, the urban and the rural, progress and tradition, intuition and intellect, the 'personal and the mechanical' and most significantly, body and 'spirit'.

The phrase actually appears three times on one page of the novel in a passage in which Margaret Schlegel dreams of redeeming Henry Wilcox, the reserved middle-aged businessman she has agreed to marry, following the death of his first wife:

> Whether as a boy, husband or widower, he had always the sneaking belief that bodily passion is bad.... The words that were read aloud on Sunday to him and to other respectable men were the words that had once kindled the souls of St Catherine and St Francis into a white-hot hatred of the carnal. He could not be as the saints and love the infinite with a Seraphic ardour, but he could be a little ashamed of loving a wife.... And it was here that Margaret hoped to help him.... She would only point out the salvation that was latent in his own soul, in the soul of every man. Only connect! That was the whole of her sermon. Only connect the prose and the passion, and both will be exalted.... Only connect and the beast and the monk, robbed of the isolation that is life to either, will die. (Forster, 1983: 188)

And if we are slow to connect this theme with the principles that separate Vashti and Kuno, Forster gives us some help in one of his diary entries for 1908, the year he wrote *The Machine Stops* and in which he began to plan *Howard's End*: 'No more fighting please between the soul and the body until they have beaten the common enemy, the machine'.

So there are two fights going on then. The older one is, as Dreyfus puts it, the 'Platonic/Christian' struggle against the flesh and the supposed sins that it makes us heir to. Dreyfus says that, 'our culture has already fallen twice' for this renunciation and that we had better avoid doing so again in our dealings with teletechnologies. But what about the new enemy – the machine? Well, regarding technology as an enemy was easy for Forster: he was deeply sceptical about the new technologies of his age – particularly the 'throbbing, stinking car' that recurs as a leitmotiv in *Howard's End*. He wrote: 'I have been born at the end of the age of peace and can't expect anything but despair. Science, instead of freeing man... is enslaving him to machines... God, what a prospect!'. But, despite this personal despair, Forster retains sufficient objectivity to add, 'Man may get a new and a greater soul for the new conditions'.[27]

And this brings me to the point about understanding telemediatization as a new common 'way of being'. As we can see now, Forster was right to suppose that the 'new conditions' may not, in fact, crush humanity. When so many blameless everyday activities involve telemediated interaction, when not only local councils and small businesses, but churches, charities, primary schools, gardening clubs, amateur dramatic societies and pigeon racing groups have their own web sites; when husbands call their wives on mobile phones from the supermarket to ask which sort of cheese to buy, it just seems perverse to think about the technologies involved as anything like 'enemies'. We need a more appropriate vocabulary for understanding how the terms of our embodied, but now otherwise ubiquitously connected cultural existence have changed.

Keeping in touch

To approach this, we can again make use of an example from the world that existed just before we became so used to teletechnologies – not in the spirit of, 'Well, we managed to get along just fine without them' – but to try to grasp that experience, vivid but fleeting, of a culture on the cusp of fundamental change. And an interesting source for this is the literary phenomenology of Marcel Proust.

In the second volume of *A la Recherche du Temps Perdu*, Proust writes vividly of the anxieties that attended the use of the telephone in the early years of the twentieth century. A key passage concerns the anxious attempt of the central character, Marcel, to receive a telephone call from his grandmother in Paris – such calls had to be booked and waited for at a telephone office. This is a particularly interesting description, since Proust begins, placing the narrative in retrospect, by observing how quickly telephony – first introduced during the 1870s – became taken-for-granted.[28]

> The telephone was not, at that date as commonly used as it is to-day. And yet habit requires so short a time to divest of their mystery the sacred forces with which we are in contact, that, not having had my call at once, my immediate thought was that it was all very long and inconvenient, and I almost decided to lodge a complaint. I found too slow for my liking...the admirable sorcery whereby a few moments are enough to bring before us, invisible but present, the person to whom we wish to speak. (Proust, 1981: 133–4)

Eventually Marcel is connected. But the process does not go well. What Proust goes on to describe is the perplexity caused by being able to hear the disembodied voice of his ailing grandmother whilst not being fully, physically, present with her. In a rather beautiful phrase, he describes first hearing his *grandmère*: 'A tiny sound, an abstract sound, the sound of distance overcome'. She is 'there', yet not there, he imagines her alone in her home in Paris, he can't reach out and touch or comfort her. Added to this, there are breaks in the connection and interruptions from the telephone operators. The telephone call finishes abruptly as the line is lost completely, leaving Marcel with that feeling of inconclusion, loss and wretchedness that is familiar to us even today when communication, at crucial moments, fails us. Being Proust, this leads to introspections about his relationship with his grandmother, her imminent death – the final separation – and, predictably, his own mortality:[29]

> I felt more clearly the illusoriness in the appearance of the most tender proximity.... A real presence, perhaps, that voice that seemed so near – in actual separation! But a premonition also of an eternal separation!...I longed to kiss her, but I had beside me only the voice, a phantom as impalpable as the one that would come back to visit me when my grandmother was dead. 'Speak to me!' But then suddenly, I ceased to hear the voice and was left even more alone. (Proust, 1981: 135, 137)

Proust's theme – the anxiety of human separation which provides the existential grounds of communication – is emphasized, rather than overcome, by the media technology of the day. Before the telephone, distance meant a more complete, unambiguous separation in which the distant other could not suddenly, phantasmagorically, enter our lifeworld for a few disconcerting moments. Separations had to be endured, but at least there was no troubling trespassing of the absent-mediated other into our presence to have to deal with.

The anxieties that Proust describes are not those of our world. We no more agonize over the occasional communicational glitch than we marvel at the sound of the distant other's voice. This is because ubiquitous connectivity has become a commonplace way of being for us, something we first need to 'make strange' in order to comprehend. But one question we can ask to disturb our familiarity is, why it is that maintaining more or less constant communicational contact with each other – something scarcely imagined in Proust's time[30] – has become so central a concern of twenty-first-century life?

The most straightforward, no nonsense, answer is that the technology is available and so we just fall into the way of using it. It adds to the convenience of life, answers needs posed by a more dynamic, faster-paced social and economic world, and generally extends our communicational options. We shouldn't discount such matter-of-fact, functional answers, but we should notice all the things they ignore. One such is that telecommunication is as much an *obligation* as it is a convenience. There is an increasing tacit assumption – structured into both the work process and wider social etiquette – that we have a social obligation to be both skilled users of the technology and, more importantly, to be almost constantly available to and for communication. That it is a mark of neglect, of irresponsibility, to be off-line, off-message, incommunicado. The denial of instant access to *ourselves* – not owning a mobile phone, or not keeping it switched on – has rather curiously become a breach of communicational 'duty', almost a token of cultural marginality. It is something that has to be owned up to, or defended as a rather defiant, eccentric circumscription of one's personal time and space. And this sense of obligation can also have a more directly exploitative aspect. We saw in the previous chapter that the sphere of employment encroaches more on personal time and space through the domestication of the networked computer. But fast capitalism also ensures that our very mobility is an opportunity for multitasking: those brief 'holidays' from the job that used to be a train journey 'on business', lost now to the panopticon of the mobile phone network.

Well, such obligations and incursions are reasons not to consider teletechnology an unmixed blessing. But they don't get us to the cultural-existential quick of ubiquitous, instant connectivity. For this we need to look for a moment beyond the genius of capitalism for turning things to account, and see that it works upon an already-established ground of practice which is concerned with the constant re-affirmation of our being-in-the-world and the relationships which stabilize this.

A constant danger attending critical interpretation in this area is that we come too quickly to regard the use of teletechnology as a condition of cultural pathology. Or at least, that we view it as symptomatic of a deficit condition, for example as a loss of the capacity to dwell comfortably at distance from others. This sort of interpretation is implicit in the way in which the use of mobile phones is frequently reported as a trend towards telecommunicational 'dependence' (Rippin, 2005). For example, a news report of a 2003 study of the social habits of teenagers in the UK stated that:

> 96% of 15–24-year-olds own a cell phone and most cannot function normally without one. Many of these felt isolated and deprived if they were prevented from using their mobile phones or accessing the internet for even a short period. Some were so dependent that they were convinced they could feel a phone vibrating in their pocket whenever they heard a cell phone ringing. (Uhlig, 2003: 11)

However, without succumbing to moral panic, I think we can trace some sort of thread linking the banal logistical discourses of mobile capitalism ('Claire? This is Richard. I'm just getting on the plane for Brussels. Can you call Alistair and get him to email the figures for the Frankfurt contract to Klaus in the next hour? I'm back in the office on Wednesday') with the remarkable rise in routine 'contact' communication ('Hello, it's me. I'm on the train . . .') and the opaque preferences of a rising generation for near-exclusive telemediated communion. Veiled by the instrumentality of busy, tightly integrated itineraries – which are always at hand to provide the rationale for our actions – we can glimpse needs for ontological re-affirmation: 'It's me, I'm here'.

The immediacy offered by teletechnology provides historically novel opportunities for such routine inscription of our presence – 'checking in' with significant others – and there is no reason to consider this as, in itself, indicative of a dependency, nor of an existential fragility in contemporary culture. We might regard it as simply a replacement for earlier forms of social 'binding'. The cultural geographer Yi-Fu Tuan offers a useful metaphor here in his discussion of the use of 'talk' in the maintenance of communal bonds. 'Talk' he argues, can be distinguished from the more modern communicational phenomenon of 'conversation' in that it is inwardly directed at the maintenance of existing relations, rather than outwardly directed at the probing of traditional boundaries and the exploration of the wider world. Conversation is 'an accomplishment of the cosmos' but talk is a practice of the 'hearth':

> People sit around a meal, a fire or just a patch of ground. Currents of words move back and forth, weaving individual speakers into a whole. What is being communicated? Nothing much. Social talk consists almost entirely of inconsequential gossip, brief accounts of the experiences and events of the day . . . . When, by chance, two people are drawn into a real conversation, the host considers it his duty to break it up so as to reintegrate them into the group. (Tuan, 1996: 175)

The essential function of talk as phatic communion places it closer, as Tuan nicely observes, to the almost lost practice of communal singing, than to discourse with a semiotic content. And I think this is a plausible way of interpreting a good deal of routine interaction via mobile phones. This is not to say, however, that there is not scope for critical suspicion of other manifestations of telemediated interaction.

The dramatic rise in popularity of social network sites like Friendster, Facebook, Bebo, and what seem to have emerged as the brand leaders, MySpace and YouTube, amongst adolescents and young adults raises a whole slew of perplexing issues (Dodson, 2006; Duffy, 2006; Ward, 2006). Whilst most of these lie beyond our present scope, it is perhaps worth registering, in conclusion, what appears to be the defining assumption of such practices: that viable forms of interpersonal relations can be established and maintained through the act of establishing and maintaining an easily accessible personal homepage. This is, in essence, what all social networking sites consist of: the free provision of web pages on which users may post photos or illustrations, describe themselves and their interests, list their cultural preferences – in music, movies and so on. This is combined with personalized email, chat and 'introduction' functions. The resultant user-base offers huge profitability to the operator as both a ready-made market research data base and a self-analysing site for targeted advertising.

There is no great mystery in the impulse to use these sites amongst adolescents struggling to establish their identity-belonging in a complex cultural environment. The question is rather one of the *status* of telemediated relations that can be established in this way. Clearly, a list of 200 or so instant 'friends' accessible in this mode of immediacy are not 'friends' in the conventional, embodied sense, implying, not least, time, effort and a level of existential commitment in their cultivation.[31] This is *not* to say, however, that social networking 'friendships' – existing via the proxies of web site content – are necessarily ersatz relationships. They are, as yet, indeterminate categories. What remains to be clarified is the new sense in which such forms of contact – what might be seen as an ideal of immediacy in the ease with which they are accessed, but which, in their intrinsic evanescence, carry little of the burden of existential anxiety that troubled Proust – can be understood as *personal* relations.

Conclusion

In considering the role of teletechnologies and the phenomenon of telepresence in the constitution of the condition of immediacy, we have focused particularly on the (apparent) closure of the gap between people that has been the historical telos of communication, and on the challenges this presents to our understanding of the deeper existential condition of embodiment. In doing this we have, necessarily, bracketed some important contextual issues, particularly the context of fast capitalism. But it is important, as McPherson (2006: 207) reminds us, 'to recognize that these emergent modes of experience are neither innocent nor neutral [but] can work all too neatly in the service of the shifting patterns of global capitalism'.

This context is, in one sense, almost a given of global-modern life. No one will be surprised, for example, to discover that MySpace was bought in 2005 by Rupert Murdoch's News Corporation for $580 Million (Duffy, 2006). And indeed, the fact that the experiences of telepresence seems *inevitably* to be appropriated and shaped towards market profitability – a fact of life almost to be shrugged at – is itself a dimension of the condition of immediacy.

And so, in accepting that our involvement with teletechnologies can hardly be disentangled from our involvement with consumption activities, we need to frame an analysis of immediacy in relation to the sphere of consumption. Here the focus will be on the collapsing of another fundamental cultural and temporal divide: that between material desire and its fulfilment.

Notes

1 Just to avoid misunderstandings at the outset, I want to stress that this discussion draws and reflects on cultural experience in those societies and amongst those socio-economic groups that have relatively easy access to these things, and does not broach issues – important though these are – of global or other inequalities in the distribution of such technologies (for discussions see Castells, 2001: 247f.; van Dijk, 2005). But even given this qualification, I believe it is still correct to think of these technologies as having global significance. Just to give one statistical example, the case of China. Recent figures show that China, the world's most populous country, currently has some 340 million mobile phone users – that is over a quarter of its population. What is more, this figure far exceeds the best estimate of China's new middle-class consumers at 200 million. What is even more, growth in ownership of communications technologies is faster in China and India than anywhere else in the world (Feuilherade, 2005).

2 *Nixon in China* Libretto by Alice Goodman (1987) Red Dawn Music.

3 As Bryan Winston notes, though in existence for nearly 20 years, sales of colour televisions did not really take off in America until the early 1970s. The 'big three' networks' share of 'prime time switched-on televisions was 93% in 1971' (Winston, 1998: 122, 316). See also, Briggs and Burke, 2002.

4 I don't want to make a categorical distinction between 'new' and 'old' media here. See Poster (1995) for the argument that we should distinguish between a first and a second media age, roughly paralleling the modern/postmodern divide, but Chun (2006: 9f.) for the argument that there are dangers of critical complacency in accepting the category of 'new media', 'firmly located within a technological progressivism that thrives on obsolescence'.

5 Some plausible lineages can be established for certain aspects of most media technologies: for instance, their time–space compressing properties as in the telegraph-telephone-internet progression (Standage, 1999). However there seem to me to be some genuinely unprecedented features of current everyday media culture. I am thinking here specifically of: routine interaction with screen-keypad interfaces in all sorts of everyday applications; the everyday practices of electronic data retrieval – particularly the use of search engines; conceptualizations of access to knowledge and information in terms of 'downloading' and 'uploading'; online visual-tactile combination skills such as pointing, clicking, scrolling and browsing; and the integration of mobile communications into the rhythms of everyday life

6 Maurice (Lord) Saatchi, executive director of the British advertising company M & C Saatchi wrote an article in the *Financial Times* (Saatchi, 2006) in which he suggested that the advertising industry faced fundamental problems stemming from dramatically different ways in which young people – whom he calls 'digital natives' – respond to television advertising:

> The digital native's brain is physically different as a result of the digital input it received growing up. It has rewired itself. It responds faster. It sifts out. It recalls less. This, apparently, is what makes it possible for a modern teenager, in the 30 seconds

of a normal television commercial, to take a telephone call, send a text, receive a photograph, play a game, download a music track, read a magazine and watch commercials at 6x speed....The result: day-after recall scores for television have collapsed, from 35 per cent in the 1960s to 10 per cent today'. (Saatchi, 2006) Although Saatchi's claims about ultra-short-term neurological adaptation have been, understandably, ridiculed, there is a significant *cultural* issue here in the distinctive ways in which young people use, manage and integrate a range of media: see Livingstone, 2003.

7 See John Durham Peters's insight that, 'Communication as a person-to-person activity became thinkable only in the shadow of mediated communication' (Peters, 1999: 6).

8 See, for example, McChesney et al., 1998; Schiller, 1999; Castells, 2001; Thrift, 2005.

9 For a more detailed discussion of this in the context of deterritorialization, see my *Globalization and Culture*, Tomlinson, 1999: 151ff. also Meyrowitz,1985; Morley and Robbins, 1995; Thompson, 1995; Morley, 2000.

10 See also Williams's explicit criticism of the technological determinism of Marshall McLuhan (McLuhan, 1964), 'in which the "medium" is (metaphysically) the master' (1964: 159). But, contra Williams's underlying position, see Scott Lash's argument, deployed against critical theories of the ideological function of the media, that we should not approach a medium as 'first and foremost a "means"' (Lash, 2002: 65f.).

11 Williams does elsewhere acknowledge that electronic media, in contrast with literature, possess, 'an apparent and often real immediacy'. This he says is, 'a change of dimension which appears to restore *presence* which, for the alternative advantages of record and durability, writing systems had moved away from' (Williams, 1981: 111). But he does not explore the idea that this immediacy is in any way contrived.

12 This assumption might be seen to lie at the heart of the concept of the 'news'. There is, however an interesting shift developing in the understanding of what news delivered by fast technologies might be. In a recent annual report, the BBC struggles with a dilemma of the status to afford 'user-generated' news content, that is, text messages, photo images and video clips sent in by members of the public from their mobile phones. The report raises the possibility that this sort of unconfirmed reporting may be more acceptable on its 24-hour news channel, 'where in the early stages of many breaking stories, it may be a more accurate reflection of reality to report uncertainty and competing explanations of events' (*BBC Annual Report 2005/6*: 48–9). This introduces the interesting idea of an epistemological distinction between slow and fast news.

13 In this respect, Walter Benjamin's famous contention that in film, 'perception in the form of shocks was established as a formal principle' (1979a: 177) and that films provide, 'a kind of rehearsal for the shock experience, a cultivated receptivity to shocks' (Jervis, 1998: 316) seems to have retained less persuasion as modern media culture has developed into an effortlessly and sophisticatedly integrated aspect of lived experience.

14 Of course other manifestations of metropolitan grandiosity are to be found in the various styles of nineteenth-century station architecture across Europe – for instance in Georg Eggert's monumental Frankfurt-am-Main terminus (1879–1888) or in François Duquesny's Paris Gare de L'Est (1847–1852).

15 For example in Mumbai's (then, Bombay's) Victoria terminus station, at the time of its building one of the largest railway stations in the world. Designed by F.W. Stevens in 1887, the station has been said to 'pay tribute' to St Pancras in its dominance of Gothic admixed with 'Saracen' features.

16 The robust commercial self-confidence of the Neo-Gothic, particularly as it is applied in secular architecture – at once, 'as new as paint...and...as old as the hills' (Wilson, 2002: 63) has another side in the anti-modern medievalism of architects like Pugin and critics like Carlyle and Ruskin (see Williams, 1963: 137f.).

17 Freeman is quoting L.T.C. Rolt's 'Lines of Character: A Steam Age Evocation' (1974). British Rail's highly controversial demolition of Hardwick's portico in 1962 and its replacement in a building of 'lavatory tile' (Carter, 2001: 229) was in the era before the debacle of railway privatization. However it seemed to prefigure this most dismal period in British transport history, particularly since Euston became headquarters between 1994 and 2001 to the justly vilified Railtrack.

18 See here Virilio's discussion of implant technology as the colonization of 'the last territory... the tragedy of the fusion of the "biological" and the "technological"' (1997: 57). This is no longer a science fiction scenario. According to Radford (2000), researchers at Roke Manor Research, a part of the Seimens technology group, have predicted the commercial development of a technique to embed microsensors in the optic nerves of television journalists – enabling them to 'transmit' what they see, live, to our television screens. The technology, it is claimed, already exists to do this. More generally, subcutaneous sensors are now employed in diverse commercial and security applications. Dance clubs in Spain and The Netherlands have also used implant sensors as fashion statement entry passes. The recent development of plastic as opposed to silicon-based semiconductors seems likely to accelerate the exploration of new ways of exploiting implant technology.

19 See the discussion by John Urry (2000: 77ff.), one of the few theorists to offer a detailed general social-theoretical analysis of the human senses. On visuality in culture see, inter alia, Jay, 1993; Mirzoeff, 2002; Howells, 2003.

20 Although see here Benjamin's insight into the significance of new abrupt movements such as 'switching, inserting, pressing and the like'. But the example he chooses as the most significant – 'the "snapping" of the photographer... [in which] a touch of the finger now sufficed to fix an event for an unlimited period of time' (1979a: 176–7), quickly returns the emphasis from haptic to optic experience.

21 Specifically, from piano playing. Kittler quotes a German source from 1895 discussing the typist as, 'the ruling queen in this domain': 'It may come as a surprise to find a practical use for what has become a veritable plague across the country, namely piano lessons for young girls: the resultant dexterity is very useful for the operation of the typewriter' (Kittler, 1999: 194–5). Early French terms for the typewriter – the 'clavecin à écrire' and the 'piano à écrire' – retain this connection (1999: 290).

22 In H.G.Wells's 1909 novel of women's emancipation, *Ann Veronica*, the eponymous heroine is given the following advice on achieving economic independence: 'make yourself worth a decent freedom... get a degree and make yourself good value. Or become a thorough-going stenographer and secretarial expert' (Wells, 1924: 129).

23 The thumb–eye coordination of the computer games player may be an exception.

24 In Forster's 1947 introduction to the *Collected Short Stories*. Specifically it was a response to Wells's novella *In the Days of the Comet* (1906) a utopian-moral fable in which, 'The world is gassed and cleaned up morally by the benevolent tail of a comet' (Wells, 1980a: 17).

25 Dreyfus cites, for example, 'computer-inspired futurists' such as Kurzweil (2000) but also over-excited business gurus.

26 The most relevant claim for the general phenomenology of telepresence is the idea, from Merleau-Ponty, that it is our embodiment that allows us to take, 'An optimal grip on the world' (1979: 55f.).

27 Diary entry for 27 January 1908. This and the previous diary entries are quoted in Oliver Stallybrass's excellent Introduction to the Penguin edition of *Howards End*, p. 10.

28 But see here, Stephen Kern's (2003: 214) comment that the French, with only 31,600 connections by 1898, were comparatively slow to take to the telephone, as compared with the British, the Germans and, by far the most enthusiastic, the United States, which had 10 million phones in operation by 1914.

29 Kern (2003: 215) points out that this episode builds on a real telephone conversation between Proust and his own mother, in which he describes her voice as, 'quite other than the one I had always known, all cracked and broken'.

30 As Winston notes (1998: 54) the telephone was, initially, 'a child of commerce' conceived as relatively restricted to business applications. Compare Standage's (1999: 120f.) account of the use of telegraphy for intimate communication in the nineteenth century.

31 It should be noted here that many social networking sites deliberately build, initially, upon 'real' relations. For example, Bebo, following the successful model of 'Friends Reunited', targets the networks established around schools and colleges.

6

Delivery

'We want the finest wines available to humanity; we want them here, and we want them now'. The eponymous hero of the film *Withnail and I*[1] makes these demands in the unpromising surroundings of the stiffly genteel 'Penrith Tea Shop'. As Withnail, an acerbic unemployed actor, delivers his order, with an hauteur fuelled by epic lunchtime boozing, we feel there exists in his beer-fuddled imagination at least a faint belief that it might be fulfilled. Instead the nervous proprietor calls the cops.

The humour of this situation is not just in the incongruity of the setting but in the juxtaposition of two dramatically divergent orientations to consumption. The tea shop is the epitome of petty-bourgeois complacence, restraint and regulation; a world in which modest requests are politely made and acceded to – in due time. Withnail's flamboyant demands, by contrast, though they affect the imperious style of the aristocracy, come from the *demi-monde*, and with the hot breath of urgent and untamed desire which unnervingly hints at a wider conflagration. They are not merely excessive, they are, in their very unreasonableness, a rebuke to a social class which has, at the same time so smugly and so undemandingly, come to comfortable terms with the capitalist order.

The film is set in 1969 and, though in parodic form, reflects something of the libertarian rebellion of the youth culture of the time. This culture, as Gilles Lipovetsky says, 'saw the immediate present turned into an absolute, glorifying subjective authenticity and the spontaneity of desire in a culture of "I want everything, now!" that made untrammelled pleasures a sacred right, without any worries about tomorrow' (Lipovetsky, 2005: 38). The counter-culture of the late 1960s, then, albeit briefly, threatened the status quo of a life organized around balanced but ultimately meaningless wage labour and consumption. And it did this in typically dramaturgic fashion, in a *reductio ad absurdem*. By demanding immediate fulfilment of desire, everything all at once, as of right, it exposed the existential absurdities of a social contract which offered a steady flow of consumer goods as the fair exchange for labour time, that is, for life itself.

There is a clear parallel here with the ethic of 'live fast, die young' as a challenge to the life project of slow, prudential, measured, accumulation (Chapter 3). And for similar reasons this was a gesture that could hardly succeed, but seemed doomed to be absorbed into lifestyles more congruent with the acceleration of capitalism.

The focus of this chapter is on the processes through which the anarchic, preposterous demands of Withnail have in a certain sense become the common sense both of individual consumers and of capitalist enterprise. It explores the integration of this immediacy – though in a much modified register – into the mainstream of consumer culture. What is primarily at stake here is the way in which capitalism, particularly via new technologies of consumption, has promoted a shift in the nature of consumer demand, from the simple amassing of possessions, to an emphasis on the *speed of appropriation* of commodities. But equally we will be concerned with the cultural contradictions of the condition of immediacy in the consumer sphere, and with how understanding these may entail re-thinking some conventional wisdom on the broad attitudes and expectations of contemporary consumer culture.

Immediacy in the sphere of consumption

Lipovetsky's comment on the immediacy of the generation of May '68 is made in the context of his analysis of the shift, since that time, towards what he sees as a 'hypermodernity', 'resting on three axiomatic elements…the market, technocratic efficiency and the individual' (Lipovetsky, 2005: 32). Hypermodernity is characterized by excess in all the spheres of life: 'hypercapitalism', 'hyperindividualism', 'hypersurveillance', 'hyperchoice' and 'hyperconsumption'.

His analysis is rather more subtle than these hyperbolisms suggest and, in particular, he offers insights into the relationship between consumption and immediacy in making a distinction between two senses of 'living in the present'. The counter-cultural celebration of *carpe diem*, he argues, began as a political project but soon shed its revolutionary impulse to become simply a rebellious hedonistic 'presentism': 'a Zeitgeist that was dominated by an absence of anxiety about the future…at once anti-establishment and consumerist' (Lipovetsky, 2005: 38). But this moment has also passed and we have entered, since the 1990s, a 'second generation presentism', much less optimistic, much more driven and obsessed with personal performance, and haunted by anxieties over health, employment prospects, environmental threats and the uncertainty of the future. Hyperconsumption, then, cannot be understood as mere hedonism, but as an intrinsic part of a modernity in which, 'the politics of a radiant future have been replaced by consumption as the promise of a euphoric present' (2005: 37). Lipovetsky's stress on the 'pre-eminence of the present' places consumption practices in the context of a shift in the overall character of a modernity in which its 'ideological and political heroism' have been defeated. That is to say, broadly in the context of the fluid modernity discussed in Chapter 4, and particularly the eclipse of, 'the mythology of continual and inevitable progress…the unstoppable march towards happiness and peace, the utopia of the new man, the redemptive class, a society without division' (2005: 42).

This contextualizing of consumerism in terms of shifts in the nature of cultural modernity puts us on a useful track of analysis and we can develop it further by turning now to Zygmunt Bauman's frequently overlapping position.

Bauman also asks us to think about consumerism as extending far beyond the simple act of consumption, as constituting a 'syndrome': 'a batch of variegated yet closely interconnected attitudes and strategies, cognitive dispositions, value judgements and...explicit and tacit assumptions about the ways of the world and the ways of treading it' (Bauman, 2005: 83). The implication of this is that consumer practices, quite apart from the many ways in which they have *themselves* been the focus of critique,[2] have achieved a grossly disproportionate place in modern culture, inflecting pretty much all else that we think, imagine or do. There is obviously a good deal of force in this argument, particularly if we take as evidence of this the commodification of many leisure activities (Rojek, 1987, 2000: 93f.; Tomlinson, 1999: 81f.). And yet, equally obviously, it may have the tendency to exaggerate the tightness of the grip that consumerism has on the modern cultural imagination. I will return to this point – not a criticism of Bauman's approach as such, but rather an occupational hazard of the business of critical cultural analysis – presently.

In common with Lipovetsky and others, Bauman (2005: 83) locates the 'consumerist syndrome' within a shift from a 'productivist' to a 'consumerist' moment in capitalism. It's worth pausing to reflect on the precise implications of this idea – for clearly it's not as though the significance of production has been entirely superseded by the significance of consumption. The circuit of commodities still requires production, exchange and consumption, although globalization has stretched these moments across time and space. But though this process has removed (and thereby sequestered) some of the harsher and more laborious aspects of production to the developing world, it remains true that we, most of us, are obliged to sustain ourselves through waged labour. Thus, particularly if we include the service and creative/cultural/educational sectors in the moment of production, we most of us live lives heavily influenced by the necessity of work, and an associated culture of production.

The key distinction implied in a shift from a 'productivist' to a 'consumerist' moment is the requirement that now more energy be put into the continual consumption of goods and services (Gorz, 1989; Smart, 2003, 53f.). Individuals thus come to have a system-related 'duty' to consume as well as to produce and this implies a shift in cultural experience and in the relative promotion and relegation of certain associated values. To put the matter rather baldly, whereas the dominance of a productivist culture involved promoting a belief in progress and betterment through industry, the dignity of labour, and the virtues of providence and accumulation, these have now largely given way to values consistent with the need for consumers to spend freely in the interests of avoiding systemic crises. This argument needs to be cautiously applied, since it can seem to assume a rather mechanistic relation between system demand and cultural change. But when regarded rather more loosely, as a way of connecting the various attempts by business and marketing enterprises, and increasingly by governments, to influence personal lifestyle in the direction of increased consumption, it makes good sense.

Bauman's key point of analysis of the consumerist syndrome concerns this shift in general value orientation and is worth quoting at some length:

> The consumerist syndrome consists above all in an emphatic denial of the virtue of procrastination and of the propriety and desirability of delay of satisfaction, those two axiological pillars of the society of producers ruled by the productivist syndrome.... [The] consumerist syndrome has degraded duration and elevated transience. It has put the value of novelty above that of lastingness. It has sharply shortened the timespan separating not just the wanting from the getting... but also the birth of wanting from its demise.... Amongst the objects of human desire, it has put appropriation, quickly followed by waste disposal, in the place of possessions and enjoyment that last..... *The 'consumerist syndrome' is all about speed, excess and waste.* (2005: 83–84, emphasis in original)

As a critical encapsulation of contemporary consumerism it is hard to disagree with many of these individual points. And clearly the general stress on a shift from the values of deferred gratification to immediate, though evanescent, satisfactions, chiming as it does with Lipovetsky's notion of the 'pre-eminence of the present', is particularly suggestive for an understanding of immediacy in the sphere of consumption.

But before we go further I want to return, briefly, to the point I raised earlier about the dangers of the all-incorporating nature of consumer culture being exaggerated. For there is something in the form of expression of both Bauman and Lipovetsky which seems to suggest this. For example, Bauman goes on to say, 'Whatever [the]market touches turns into a consumer commodity; including the things that try to escape its grip and even the ways and means deployed in their escape attempts' (2005: 89) and Lipovetsky speaks of a society, 'restructured from top to bottom by the technologies of ephemerality, novelty and permanent seduction' (Lipovetsky, 2005: 36).

The theme that both treat is excess in consumption and this seems to be carried over by a strange process of stylistic mimesis into the writing, which itself becomes hyperbolical. Yet I am fairly sure that neither writer wants to provoke in his readers a response along the lines of, 'My God, aren't things just desperate?'.[3] The tendency towards totalizing statements – which is surely not restricted to these two writers but is a fairly common occurrence in critical work in this area – is interesting. At least partly, it is a function of the very act of critical argument building: the result of the cataloguing of instances, the noticing of underlying trends, the forming from these of strong interpretations and generalizations – all the things that are the proper work of social and cultural analysis. But this risks a sort of premature critical closure in which the important *exceptions* to the trend are overlooked – in this context, all the many aspects of everyday life that are *not* in any significant way gripped by the consumerist syndrome (weeding the garden, amateur dramatics, charity work, teaching your children to swim, enjoying a joke, feeding your neighbour's cat). These and many, many other common practices are not negligible exceptions to a common iron rule: they are reminders that we must approach consumerism – however powerful it has become in inflecting contemporary culture – as but one aspect of a complex and often contradictory 'totality', not easily grasped in critical writing.

I don't suppose that this book is immune, overall, from these problems of over-generalization, but since I have noticed them here, I'm going to try to minimize them by keeping the focus on one key aspect of contemporary consumption. This is the point that Bauman makes about the increasing significance of the moment of *appropriation* as distinguished from the enjoyment of temporally extended possession. It seems to me that there is more to be said here. I want to understand both the institutional/technological contrivance and the phenomenology of this shift from productivism/duration to consumerism/transience in more detail because I have the feeling that this will add something to our general understanding of immediacy as a condition closely integrated with but, importantly, *not reducible to* the 'consumerist syndrome'.

To this end, in the following section I begin by locating some more precise aspects of the attempt by capitalist enterprise to maintain consumer demand by shifting the orientation of the consumer towards immediate 'consumption solutions'.[4] However, the sources of this new consumer expectation, I go on to argue, arise not only from the way they are laid before us as the enticements of marketing, but also from our interaction with various technologies of immediacy.

Concerted incitements to consumer immediacy

Although I don't believe that consumer practices can be uniquely inferred from a demonstration of the system needs of capitalism, I'm nevertheless going to take it as axiomatic that there *is* a systemic requirement of capitalism to ensure that consumer demand does not decline. It follows from this that a great deal of the human energy and creativity that is enlisted and deployed within capitalist enterprise is concentrated on maintaining and increasing consumer demand. But how is this achieved? For Bauman, it is a matter of the 'repeated frustration of desire', the endlessly created prospect of fulfilment through the purchase of new goods which inevitably fail to live up to their promise, thereby leaving desire fresh and urgent for new consumption. This explanation is of course familiar and, in part reflects a current of thinking on the necessity for social wants to be regulated, that can be traced back at least to Durkheim's writings. Thus in *Suicide* (1897) Durkheim wrote that: 'irrespective of any regulatory force, our capacity for social wants became insatiable and a bottomless abyss; the more one has, the more one wants, since satisfactions received only stimulate [further wants]' (Durkheim, quoted in Morrison, 1995: 186). But in Bauman's account, this is a vicious cycle not on account of some tragic dimension of the human condition, nor even, as in Durkheim, of the waning of a culture of moral or religious constraint, but rather on account of the cynical manipulation of desire by marketing. It involves the deliberate deception of the consumer: 'Each single promise *must* be deceitful, or at least exaggerated, if the search is to go on' (Bauman, 2005: 81).

Bauman is obviously right in seeing the business of marketing and advertising as essentially cynical in so far as it does not – cannot – sincerely believe in its own endlessly fugitive *promesse de bonheure*. However I am not altogether convinced by his stress on *deception* in so far as this implies that consumer desire is, as it were, blindly ineducable. After all, twenty-first-century consumers have had getting on for a century of experience of living with developed and sophisticated strategies of marketing. For example, Alfred P. Sloan Jnr introduced the annual model change, along with the system of trade-in, at General Motors in the early 1920s in response to the decline in demand for affordable standardized cars like the Model 'T' Ford. Both of these were purely marketing innovations involving no fundamental engineering changes in the product (Setright, 2002: 63). It would be surprising if, in the intervening time, consumers had not built up stocks of commonsense understanding of marketing strategies and perhaps themselves developed a matching 'cynicism' about the consumption process. This is a point I will come back to in the final part of the chapter.

Aside from this issue, though, it seems quite clear that the maintenance of consumer demand involves the continual search for the commodification of new areas of life. This is received wisdom not just amongst the critics of capitalism, but amongst its proponents. In his book *The Future of Success*, Robert Reich, Bill Clinton's former employment secretary, argues that, 'The future of economic success... lies in selling those goods that we can never have enough of, such as health, beauty and sexual gratification' (quoted in Davies, 2006: 3). These marketing trends are evident, and it is clear to see how they conform to the general pattern of the exploitation of the existential grounds of desire. But what is not quite so clear is precisely how the issues of speed and immediacy fit into this scenario. In Bauman's argument, speed appears as essentially an increase in the frequency of the vicious cycle of stimulation, consumption, frustration. But this seems to me too stark a conclusion and, more importantly, one that tends to cast too much of everyday consumption practice as obsessive-compulsive. Endless stimulation of consumer demand indicates irrationality in the *system*, but it does not follow that consumer behaviour is equally irrational. So I want to explore other ways of approaching the implication of immediacy within consumption practices. And we can begin by exploring the increasing consumer market for immediacy itself.

The market for convenience

What I want to get at here are various ways in which the value of immediacy – here in the simple sense of instant, ready-made solutions – is structured into certain consumer goods, becoming, as it were, their 'unique selling point'. Perhaps the most obvious examples of this are so-called 'convenience goods' such as prepared 'ready meals' and their associated technologies: fridges, freezers and microwave ovens.[5] The prime notion of convenience here is as 'time saving' (though as we shall see there are other relevant meanings) and this has led to the general understanding of these products as solutions to the 'problem' of cooking and eating in the context of a busy time-pressured lifestyle.

This of course raises the whole issue of 'time poverty', particularly amongst the relatively affluent professional classes. Explanations of this phenomenon have often been proposed within the general framework of the idea of the intensifying pressure both to produce and to consume more, as for example in Staffan Linder's early study, *The Harried Leisure Class* (1970). More recently Juliet Schor's *The Overworked American* (1992) has proposed an influential version of a vicious cycle thesis in which people invest more hours at work in order to support a high consumption lifestyle which in turn involves them in more time spent in spending. Free time is thus eaten into from both ends of the work-consumption relation. In another version of the time squeeze argument Hochschild (1997) describes the way in which domestic life can come to resemble a workplace culture, ordered to cope efficiently with time scarcity, while workplaces, somewhat ironically, take on some of the emotional and affiliative characteristics of the home.

Elizabeth Shove makes an interesting intervention in these arguments by focusing on the *normalizing* of technologies of immediacy. She explains the recourse to convenience goods not so much in terms of a general decline in free time in modern societies – for which, as she points out, the evidence is inconclusive – but rather as ways of coping in a society characterized by, 'the weakening of a shared sociotemporal order' and a corresponding 'fragmenting of activity and the personalization of scheduling' (Shove, 2003: 180, 184). What is important for her account is the transference of responsibility for constructing and maintaining personal and domestic schedules on to the individual,[6] in a world in which collective institutionalized time conventions (like nine-to-five working, restricted shop opening hours, washing day, regular fixed family mealtimes and (pre VCR) TV viewing times – all features of a more regulated modernity which tended to co-ordinate individual schedules) are disappearing. Shove sees the use of convenience goods as strategies for making complex individualized schedules work, for coordinating them with the itineraries of others, for 'keeping on top of things' and maintaining a sense of meeting social obligations. She concludes that:

> The resulting dynamic has a life of its own: each solution adding to the menu of problems that future solutions seek to resolve. . . . the cumulative effect is to

engender and legitimize new, typically more resource-intensive, conventions and expectations built around the successive appropriation of convenient solution. (Shove, 2003: 183)

This is an escalatory spiral, but importantly one which understands the consumer not as a dupe, but as engaged in the rational, if ultimately vain, attempt to use technologies to control events: 'as a self-evidently sensible response to the unending problems of organizing life in a do-it-yourself society of the schedule' (2003: 183).

One virtue of this sort of approach to the issue of immediacy in the sphere of consumption is that it steers us away from an emphasis on obsessive-compulsive consumer behaviour. In doing so it draws attention not only to the social economy of time, but also to the characteristics of the convenience goods themselves, how they are used and the ways in which they interact with other consumer goods (for example, time-shifting technologies like answerphones and DVD recorders (Silverstone and Hirsch, 1992)) in shaping life routines. However there are many other types of 'immediacy goods' on offer which don't easily fit into this sort of 'time juggling' analysis, and looking briefly at some of these discloses another aspect of the shift from possession to instant appropriation.

Impatient and immoderate media technologies

Microwave ovens and ready meals may be salient features of complexly scheduled, time-scarce modern lifestyles, but it is within the new technologies of media and cultural consumption that we find perhaps the truest emblems of consumer immediacy. Devices like MP3 players, digital cameras, multi-function mobile phones (and the various ways of accessing internet search engines) afford conveniences that are quite different from the time-saving properties of the more utilitarian consumer goods just described. They promise convenience not only in the sense of being functional solutions, but in the broader definition of the term, of 'serving one's comfort', and being 'easily accessible' (OED). Specifically, these personal media technologies offer the 'light' qualities of being always ready-to-hand, of ease of operation, and of delivering an instant response to commands. In connection with this category of consumer goods, these qualities are best regarded as having a *sensuous* rather than a rational-functional appeal. If one were to imagine a spectrum of the various orders of commodity desirability, they would cluster towards the voluptuous rather than the serviceable end. And they correspond, quite precisely, to the three key features of the condition of immediacy: ubiquity, effortlessness and speed.

In describing these media technologies as 'impatient' and 'immoderate' – descriptions that are in a certain tension with their appearance as 'effortless' – I am suggesting that there is something in their very nature which is an incitement to consumer immediacy. This sounds, on several counts, a rather controversial idea, so let me clarify the claim. I don't mean to suggest, applying some version of technological determinism, that these technologies have the power directly to produce or shape behaviour. However I *do* mean to say that, contrary to some social constructivist arguments, technologies do have distinct and discernible inherent properties, and that these, as it were, *invite us* to respond to them in particular ways. This is to see technologies, as Elizabeth Shove describes them, as bringing with them particular 'scripts' or as it is sometimes put, that they offer certain 'affordances'.[7] My argument is that human responses, in daily use, to the scripts of these technologies feeds into a wider imagination of the nature and value of consumption, and indeed, into more general ways of seeing the world.

One important reason to think about technologies in this way is to identify aspects of consumer culture that are analytically independent of the contrivances and attempted manipulations of marketeers. And so I'm going to take for granted all these strategies: the fact that inbuilt redundancy and high-frequency model updating is peculiarly marked in this sector;[8] that fashion appeal is ruthlessly exploited; and that there are deliberate attempts to 'lock in' consumers to more consumption. These strategies are not only cynical, they are objectionable in other ways, particularly in regard to their wastefulness, something we will consider later. But for the present purposes I'm going to disregard them all. And for the same purpose of focus, I'm also going to bracket several other considerations relevant to consumer practices in this area, for instance the sort of informed discriminations consumers often make about various qualities of design and format.[9]

To get to the point then, these are *impatient* media technologies because they bring with them the script of instant delivery. MP3 devices deliver music in the minimal time it takes to download audio files from a computer; digital cameras deliver images instantly without the mediation of a chemical process; search engines deliver information that might have taken days, if not weeks of research in a library, as fast as the speed of your broadband connection. And they are *immoderate* technologies because they deliver this in extravagant super-abundance. Here are some examples. The current 60 GB iPod has the capacity to store around 15,000 4-minute songs, which would take over 1000 hours to listen to.[10] It is estimated that the global total of digitally captured images in any one year now exceeds the whole of those made in the previous 160 years of photography, a situation described by Ang (2005) as 'image pollution'. A not-untypical results list for a Google search runs into the thousands or even tens of thousands, though most users stop at the first five results (Ward, 2006).

These capacities are in one sense just characteristics of the technologies, but the scripts they carry with them go quite beyond this. They 'write out' the expectation of a gap between demand and delivery: for example, of the time taken in photochemical photography for the picture to 'develop', or (more typically) to arrive back from the processors.[11] And they invite us to see super-abundance as the norm. They may be reasonably said to delete the typical early-modern experiences of scarcity, waiting and anticipation, at least in this area of consumption. And the important point is that this writing out is a function of the technology's *script*, independent of any attempted manipulation of human desire.

It may be objected that we are dealing here with only a relatively small area of consumer culture, and an even smaller proportion of daily life. But, without exaggerating their significance, it's not difficult to see how the routine integration of these technologies into mundane cultural experience contributes towards a more general shift in cultural dispositions and values. This is particularly evident in the case of blasé attitudes towards technological developments in general: the commonplace assumption (Chapter 4) that new waves of innovation will inevitably arrive and that current ones will become redundant.

It is, admittedly, a bigger step from this to the implication that more general culturally embedded values and attitudes related to temporality may in consequence be eroding. But it's not an implausible one. Take for example the value afforded to the *anticipation* of satisfaction. The value of anticipation has always been a subtle and an ambiguous one, somewhere at the border between a piquant pleasure and a virtue made of necessity. And so it's not unreasonable to think that it may quietly slip away if not reinforced by conditions of general scarcity, let alone being routinely undermined in our interfaces with impatient and immoderate technologies.

To summarize then, the argument of this section has been that new media technologies have characteristic scripts which incite expectations and attitudes of immediacy, providing the model for broader assumptions of instant delivery and effortlessly achieved abundance. Although I have been concerned to argue that this sort of incitement is distinct from the strategies of marketing, I don't want to suggest that it has explanatory priority, rather that it acts in concert with – is echoed and amplified in – other areas of cultural experience.[12] And so for my last example I want to return to a more central aspect of the process of consumption within capitalism.

New technologies of spending

The last source of incitement to consumer immediacy that I want to consider is another aspect of mundane interaction with new technologies, in this case those by which we enact the pivotal point of consumption, the actual moment of exchange, of spending.

When people shop, increasingly they use methods of electronic purchase – plastic debit, credit or charge cards – for the transaction.[13] This is true both for really large transactions such as buying a car or for very small ones like paying for a few groceries. Democratic technologies, levelling the distinctions that once existed between working-, middle- and upper-class modes of paying, plastic cards have, during the last 20 years or so, become ubiquitous in all societies with sufficiently developed banking systems to support them.[14] They have largely displaced personal cheques and, for the most part, have driven cash spending into particular niche locales: in pubs and bars, but not so usually in restaurants; in greengrocers and newsagents, but not so usually in clothes or shoe shops.

What is the difference between using a plastic card rather than cash or cheques to make a purchase? All are of course in a broad sense forms of money, and so at a certain level of abstraction have the same characteristics of being a common medium of exchange and a store of value, guaranteed, ultimately, by the state. However, beyond this they exhibit some differences. Cash – coins and banknotes – are in a sense relatively concrete and 'substantial' stores of value (at least in stable economic conditions) in so far as they can be directly, literally, *exchanged* for goods. Cheques are rather more abstract representations of the 'debt' implied in purchase, principally since they involve a deferral in time. But they share with cash the quality of being physical objects which can be directly exchanged for commodities. But both credit and debit cards are different from cash or cheques in that they are not actually exchanged in the transaction. If we wanted to be pedantic, we might say that they are not really money at all in the sense of being the store of value, but merely instruments of *access* to money either stored in the account of the holder (debit cards) or of a lender (credit cards). To this degree they are the characteristic spending technology of a contemporary economy in which money, as Anthony Giddens puts it, 'is independent of the means whereby it is represented, taking the form of pure information lodged as figures in a computer printout' (Giddens, 1990: 25).

It is of course not accidental that money used in purchasing has taken on progressively abstract forms throughout the modern period. For despite the expense of developing, installing, maintaining and providing security for systems of electronic purchase, it is hugely to the benefit of producers, retailers and banks to employ these technologies. This is because their use reduces labour costs (for instance in the processing of cheques) and above all because it speeds up the overall circulation of capital by cutting down intermediary stages in the debiting and crediting of computerized accounts, so benefiting profitability in all the sectors of capitalist enterprise. There are also certain obvious – though not unmitigated – advantages of speed and convenience for the consumer which have made these systems relatively easy to introduce. There is an obvious sense, then, in which electronic purchase is integral to the trajectory of fast capitalism.

But I want to focus on something slightly different from the bottom line strategies of parting the consumer from their money as swiftly and efficiently as possible. This is the way in which the use of plastic cards may alter the *experience* of paying for goods. This is not so much a matter of making transactions universally more convenient or, indeed, always quicker. Electronic purchase is not generally quicker than cash purchase and sometimes can be much slower – particularly at times of high demand on computerized banking systems, as on Saturday afternoons, or when randomized computer security checks interrupt the transaction. It is more a question of an aura of lightness and effortlessness that surrounds the act of electronic purchase in its normally efficient mode of operation.

We can begin with the material lightness of the card itself. This is of course part of its attraction: a plastic sheet of a uniform $85 \times 55 \times 1.0$ mm, its weight and bulk is negligible in relation to its potential cash equivalence. The card is of course valuable and must be taken care of, but it does not reflect this (potential) value in its substance. Plastic is, after all, a cheap material in most contexts; in its adjectival form it is the antithesis of luxurious or 'quality' products: 'plasticky'. In this sense the plastic card embodies its nature as a tool of access[15] rather than, as in the case of cash, as the intrinsic holder of value. (Limitation of liability means that losing your card is generally less of a disaster than losing a roll of banknotes, something closer to losing your keys.) And this combination of virtual value and physical, material lightness and 'negligibility' sets the tone for its use in transactions.

The use of a card is, thus, typically a *casual* affair in comparison with the use of cash or cheques. Cheques involve a number of actions at the point of sale: writing, dating, signing and normally offering some form of guarantee – a cheque guarantee card or the address written on the back. This activity also has a certain ritual element: inscribing the identity of the purchaser in the transaction and so formally recognizing the 'seriousness' of the event. In cash transactions the seriousness of the exchange – even in the case of small purchases – is signalled in the rituals of checking the amount tendered and counting out the change to the last penny. In the case of large cash sums, the ritual becomes more marked and the importance and dignity of the exchange is proportionately recognized. During an earlier era of consumer modernity these point-of-sale encounters were given further weight by the techniques used to handle cash and cheques – for example the common practice of separating the duties of the sales assistant from the cashier. This was often accompanied, particularly in department stores, by elaborate paraphernalia for moving cash between sales desks and a centralized cash desk. Such 'cash railway systems' employing either overhead ropeways and shuttles or, later, pneumatic tube systems added a certain connotation of early-modern mechanical heaviness to the ritual.[16]

Compare with this a typical card purchase. It has often been observed that this is a socially sterile operation. The customer is invited to insert the card into a terminal and prompted to key in their PIN number. The online electronic verification and debiting process which follows, culminating in the generation of a printed receipt, can be achieved with minimal interpersonal exchange, indeed, as Marc Augé (1995) observes, in principle wordlessly. But a point I think more significant is the *insouciant* nature of the routine of purchase. One element of this is in the literal effortlessness of the physical operation – something soon to be brought to its apogee with the introduction of 'contactless' card technology, requiring nothing more than the waving of the card before a sensor.[17] Even short of this reduction to the gestural, there is little in card purchase routines that signifies the seriousness of parting with even rather large sums of money. The effect, on the contrary, is to make light of the process. It is as though the actual act of payment is contrived as almost incidental to the overall business of shopping – which may involve concentrated activities of selection and, in some contexts, extended and elaborate interactions with sales staff. Spending is thus both speeded up and casualized within the more prolonged, intense and engaging activity of shopping.

Does this casualizing of the moment of spending have any deeper consequences? Well if we regard it properly, not as an independent effect of a shift in technologies, but in concert with broader changes in the culture of consumption, the answer is that it does. It results in a weakening of the experienced link between the sphere of production and of consumption; between work and earning on the one hand, and spending on the other.

Marx famously regarded money itself as having an alienating effect, that is of separating human beings from a true relation to their own productivity. In his *Economic and Philosophical Manuscripts* of 1844, he describes money as, 'the *pander* between need and object, between human life and the means of subsistence'. A 'pander' is a sexual procurer or a 'go-between' in illicit affairs: further on he uses the expression, glossed from Shakespeare, 'the universal whore' (Marx, 1963: 180–1). In using these unflattering analogies, Marx tries to express the role of money as not just an innocent intermediary, but one which separates us from our essential 'species being': it is, 'the alienated and exteriorized species-life of men'. In *Capital* he relates money to the fetishism of commodities, the idea that the products of human labour come to be regarded as independent entities, having a mysterious life and power of their own. The theme of all these ideas is that money involves a distortion in human relations, centred on the mystifying separation of creative labour from exchange and consumption.

It is not necessary to subscribe to Marx's view of the essential species nature of human beings in order to see the general force of his argument about the role of money in separating and obscuring the social link between the spheres of production and consumption.[18] And I think we can plausibly read in contemporary consumer culture a further development of this process, as the act of spending becomes, in a sense, further alienated from the lifeworld of labour and earnings. In the working-class world of the weekly wage packet, money may have been, as Marx says, a mystifying form of the value inherent in the labour process, but its material presence on the table on a Friday night and the contiguity of this event with the pleasures of Saturday consumption reinforced the connection between the two worlds. In the condition of consumer immediacy, the practice of spending is not just made light and effortless; contexts of consumption come to dominate overwhelmingly. Shops become the prime location in which personal economics are enacted and experienced. 'Cashback' facilities (themselves a function of the acceleration of capital circulation) have the effect of integrating a banking act with a spending act. In effect, shops become banks. And banks, where they have not withdrawn from the high street into the world of pure information – web sites and call centres – become shops, offering financial 'products'. Or the older, grander, ones, their large lobbies and massive architectural inscriptions as the solid and sober depositories of value now (like their counter staff) redundant, become bars and restaurants.

All of the above – to repeat the caution I made earlier – requires the qualification that it be seen in the light of other relevant processes and trends: for example the increasing inducements towards personal credit (Ritzer, 1995; Manning, 2000) and the associated confused and contradictory cultural attitudes towards debt that are typical of many modern societies. But what I have tried to stress, both here and in the other examples of incitements towards consumer immediacy, is the importance of *material* practices of consumption.

Louis Althusser, now a rather unfashionable theorist, tried to argue that ideology had an existence in a material form: as repeated rituals. And to make this point he quoted an earlier French philosopher, Blaise Pascal: 'Pascal says more or less: "Kneel down, move your lips in prayer, and you will believe"' (Althusser, 1971: 168). Moderately interpreted, there is a lot in this ambiguous formulation. It can, as Althusser tried, be invoked to support the rather odd idea that actions somehow embody ideology. But on the other hand, on a more ironic reading, it can mean that the formal actions stand in place of a deeper conviction. In this sense, it can be taken as a recognition that much of what we do in everyday culture is a matter of simple iterated practical activity, shaped, to be sure, by institutional pressures, but giving, as it were, no more than lip service to a dominant ideology.

Following this second interpretation, consumer culture does not need to be regarded as either a state of systematic ideological deception or indeed (a more dispiriting thought) a condition of deep existential commitment. It can, instead, be understood as the nexus of the concerted efforts by capitalist-inflected modern institutions towards expanding consumption, the scripts offered by associated technologies, and the attitudes, expectations and stocks of knowledge that people bring to their interaction with these various incitements. And so, I want to turn, albeit briefly, to the question of general cultural attitudes and expectations.

Delivery: low horizons in consumer expectation

If there has been a broad shift in the character of consumption practices from an emphasis on steady accumulation and the enjoyment of continued possession, to one on the immediate and repeated appropriation of new goods, what does this imply in terms of a shift in cultural attitudes?

In most of the discussion I have tried to resist the idea that it implies a driven attitude, a compulsion towards buying, the futile pursuit of fugitive satisfactions, orchestrated by marketing. I do not, of course, deny that there is a concerted and, indeed, an *experienced* pressure – which comes not only from marketing, but also from the other sources I have described, to increase the amount and the frequency of consumption. What I'm unhappy with is the assumption that this experienced pressure translates, at least in the general case, into attitudes symmetrically obedient to the system needs of fast capitalism. There are two main reasons why I distrust this implication.

The first is an objection which is commonly made in relation to critiques of consumerism. It is that human beings, in their role of consumers as elsewhere, are knowledgeable agents. This means they are likely to possess a broad reflexive understanding of the nature of consumption: of its increasing centrality in everyday life, of the strategies of marketing and advertising, (at various levels of sophistication) of the importance of consumption in the overall system of capitalism, and, importantly, of the potential and limitations of consumer goods to bring different levels and orders of satisfaction. This sort of everyday understanding arises from a variety of sources. It comes from accumulated stocks of knowledge produced in previous consumer activity, it is inculcated in both formal and informal socialization practices which stress, at a minimum, a practical attitude of 'caveat emptor', it is familiarized through media representations, and of course it derives from the roles many consumers *themselves* occupy within the marketing and retailing sectors. If modern culture is saturated with advertising imagery and marketing discourse, it is also replete with common-sense understandings and popular interpretations of consumer culture. This does not, of course, imply that average consumers have a developed critical attitude to consumerism, but it does suggest that they are, in various ways, 'less deceived'.

The second reason relates more specifically to the idea of consumers being caught up in an endlessly repeated cycle of stimulation and frustration. This is the key idea in Zygmunt Bauman's association of consumption with speed: not only are consumers routinely deceived by the promises of consumer goods, but in an almost comically heroic triumph of hope over experience, they keep coming back for more, thereby increasing the frequency of the cycle. This just seems to me to be implausible. It is not merely that hardly anyone, outside of a very small number of genuine compulsives, would recognize their routine consumption behaviour in this pattern (always a useful rule of thumb in making claims involving cultural experience). It is that it is very difficult to *imagine* a cultural attitude that would actually correspond to this state of affairs.

If we reject ideas of repetition-compulsion, sustained and comprehensive deception or some version of general human incorrigibility this does not mean we have exhausted ways of interpreting the perplexing phenomenon of consumer immediacy. Indeed it may be interpretable by considering an almost *opposite* general informing attitude. This is that, far from having consistently high expectations of the capacity of consumer goods to provide satisfaction – expectations that are routinely (indeed, systematically) dashed – the great majority of people actually have rather *low* expectations of what consumer goods can and should provide.

One way of putting this is to say that contemporary consumption is characterized by the expectation of *delivery* rather than of satisfaction.

What I mean by this is that there is probably a widespread *disbelief* in the capacity of consumer goods to provide ultimate satisfaction; but that there is, none the less, an expectation that the capitalist system will – and should – continue to deliver the goods. 'Delivery' thus in a sense becomes the *telos* of consumption; it is the termination of the implicit social contract between consumer and consumer capitalism, the point at which (both economic and cultural) liability ceases. We expect consumer goods to be functional or novel or amusing; to be stylish, fashionable of good value and of good quality; we increasingly expect them to provide the 'lifestyle semiotic' function that marketing strategies so intensely focus upon. We expect warranties and after-sales service. But in the vast majority of cases these expectations stop short of a conviction that they will, in any profound sense, satisfy our deepest desires. This is not however an obstacle to continued consumption, particularly since it is combined with the happy expectation that something new is always on the way and so it is not necessary – nor does it do – to invest too much into the thing of the moment.

How can we best characterize this situation? It's pretty much the opposite of the idea that consumers are open-endedly hopeful of fulfilment, and in this sense deeply emotionally invested in the system. However it's not a condition characterized by a blasé attitude, either in the general sense of over-familiarity breeding a relative indifference to the pleasures and novelties of consumer goods, or in Simmel's more diagnostic sense of, 'an incapacity to react to new sensations with the appropriate energy' (Simmel, 1997b: 178). It is quite too vigorous, energetic and 'well-adapted' for this. Neither is it quite right to think of consumers as precisely cynical in their attitudes, although an unattractive level of cynicism does enter into some areas of consumer interaction, for example, those that have developed around call centres.[19] Perhaps the best way of thinking about it is as a condition of reciprocally low horizons of expectation. The intrinsically prosaic nature of consumer goods and the transparently disingenuous nature of the claims made for them are matched by a low level of what we could call 'fulfilment demand' by consumers on the system itself. This pattern has, moreover, become so naturalized that its existential poverty can only be revealed by acts of theatrical absurdity – as in the wilfully insatiable, system-corrosive desire of a Withnail.

How does this view of a low threshold of consumer expectation square with the acceleration of consumerism? In fact, rather well. Making delivery, as distinct from satisfaction, the key term offers to render intelligible some puzzling aspects of the shift from possession to appropriation.

For example, it helps to explain why the trend towards a rather blatant contrivance of redundancy in consumer goods has become acceptable. Why, to take an instance already noted, the average shelf-life for a mobile phone is now a little over six months. Understanding why consumers tolerate this situation of high frequency obsolescence is made easier if we focus on delivery rather than satisfaction. To value goods for their qualities of endurance, where this is more than simple economy, is to integrate them into an imagination of satisfaction as a settled state of being, of contentment. In contrast with this, to expect ongoing 'delivery' is to imagine consumption as a 'life process', as linear rather than as punctual, as something strung out across a biography. Imagined in this way, inbuilt redundancy in a product may seem less unreasonable. Not that it loses its exploitative character, but that this seems, viewed in the light of the expected flow of new goods in the future, something less worth our outrage.

The tolerance of contrived redundancy is close to another crux of consumer immediacy, the human delight in novelty. This is something which is often overlooked in the critique of consumerism, mostly being absorbed into the more negatively marked categories of capriciousness, faddism and whims, and thence into the general idea of the manipulation of desires. But thinking about consumerism in terms of delivery recovers some of the innocence of the attraction of novelty.[20] For this is a desire which is, of its nature, matched to the repeated events of consumer delivery, and which cannot be understood in terms of enduring satisfactions. It is, of course, immensely convenient to the system demands of capitalism that such a desire exists, and there is ample scope for its exploitation. But the point to note is that recognizing the legitimacy of the desire for novelty casts a different light on the open-ended nature of consumer demand. The delight in the newness of things or experiences seems to be pretty much a general feature of the human condition, and as such it is an aspect of desire which we should not allow, in the process of cultural criticism, to slip into being regarded as a pathology. On the contrary, it should remind us that the model of a rational, proportionate culture of consumption against which we can criticize the irrationality of fast capitalism cannot be one that imagines satisfaction as some punctual endstate, as the terminus of aspiration. To consume rationally does not mean to extinguish the restlessness that is inherent in desire.

The critique of delivery

It might be objected that this account, in emphasizing human knowledge-ability and avoiding the exaggeration of the susceptibility of consumers to manipulation, passes too lightly over the negative consequences of immediacy in the sphere of consumption. So finally I want to raise, albeit briefly, some grounds for a critique of a culture of delivery.

This is not difficult: a good many social problems can reasonably be laid at the door of accelerated consumerism, particularly in its association with the promotion of consumer credit (Ritzer, 1995; Smart, 2003). The problem of personal indebtedness for example has become a major one in many western societies, particularly in the United States and the United Kingdom. In 2005 the personal savings rate in the United States was negative over the whole year, the first time this has occurred since the Great Depression of 1929–1934 (Elliott, 2006). A report published in 2005 disclosed that credit card debt in the United States rose by 31 per cent over five years to reach a total of $800 billion, with an average credit card debt amongst low-to-middle income families of $8650 (Draut et al., 2005). The situation in the United Kingdom follows a similar trend, with the Governor of the Bank of England warning in May 2006 about the problem of rising indebtedness. A YouGov survey in the same month revealed that one in five British adults, some 8 million people, have unsecured debt of over £10,000, with around 100,000 people likely to declare themselves bankrupt over the year (Seager, 2006).

The causes of personal indebtedness are not simply reducible to prodigality in spending, but, as the American survey shows, can be the result of 'bad luck, bad health and hard times'. In a society in which the deregulation of the credit card industry combines with generally low levels of public welfare provision, the credit card takes on the function of a 'plastic safety net', the first recourse for meeting unanticipated expenses such as medical bills or the immediate financial impact of redundancy. What this illustrates is how the critique of consumerism implies a wider critique of the accelerating and deregulating drive of fast capitalism: in the insecure conditions of 'labour flexibility' of the culture of production (Chapter 4), as well as in the overall systemic drive to increased rates of personal consumption. Long-term indebtedness[21] can be the hopeless and miserable consequence of becoming vulnerable to these two dynamics, and its apparent rise in high consumption societies must indicate a fundamental problem in deregulated capitalism.

At the other pole of socio-economic problems from the question of debt is the issue of waste, something which Bauman rightly highlights as being central to the critique of consumer culture. The issue of waste has generally been understood as either a moral one – as the immorality of squandering valuable resources, particularly where there are shortages elsewhere – or as an environmental issue – for instance in the difficulties involved in the safe disposal of unwanted goods and of packaging materials.

An example which brings these two aspects close together is the case of so-called 'E-waste', that produced specifically by the inbuilt redundancy of goods like computers and mobile phones. Such products typically contain high levels of toxic waste such as lead, arsenic, antimony trioxide, chromium and cadmium, which makes their safe disposal a specialized and an expensive undertaking. The result is that much of this waste finds its way to dismantling sites in countries like India and China. Here impoverished workers in small unregulated businesses with no health and safety protection dismantle the goods by hand to recycle second-hand electronic components as well as metals like copper, and very small amounts of gold and silver. The practice is immensely damaging to the health of the workers and disastrously polluting of the local environment. It is also illegal under international conventions. The 'Basel Convention on the Transboundary Movements of Hazardous Wastes and their Disposal' introduced in 1992 and ratified by 139 countries (but not by the United States) is intended to restrict the export of this waste. However this regulation is difficult to police and is routinely circumvented (Black, 2004; Twist, 2005).

This problem of the displacement of responsibility for hazardous waste is generally invisible in the immediate sphere of consumption and so it might appear as only tenuously connected as a moral issue, belonging more closely to the general institutional trend of the globalization of risk (Beck, 1999). However there is an inescapable moral connection here. But it is not one that is presented as a direct challenge to the consumer as a moral agent. The same consumer who has a relaxed and complacent attitude towards the rapid obsolescence of technology may, at the same time, be an assiduous re-cycler of newspapers, bottles and packaging material. The moral issue, then, is one reasonably raised in relation to the *system* rather than the individual: as the systematic obscuring of the true costs of contrived material redundancy.

The issues of debt and waste are just two examples from several that could be cited as objectionable social consequences of immediacy in the sphere of consumption. Beyond these specific issues however we can also point to a more general cultural criticism. This is that, though it may not be as compulsive, as driven or as or ideologically manipulated as it is sometimes characterized, consumer culture based in the limited expectations of delivery remains fundamentally complicit with the impetus of fast capitalism. Because of this it is unlikely to generate much in the way of progressive reform. A culture of delivery is one which has come to an uneasy accommodation with the status quo; one in which, though the inadequacies of consumer goods alone to human fulfilment are widely recognized, their energetic pursuit continues almost as a cultural default position. Perhaps the most serious criticism of contemporary consumer culture, then, is that it seems incapable of generating within itself new imaginations of the good life. There are of course external challenges to the dominance of consumer culture, on the one hand from new social movements like the anti-globalization movement or 'neo-tribal' youth cultures (McKay, 1996; Maffesoli, 1996; Shepard and Hayduk, 2002) and on the other from traditional religious cultures (Brennan, 2003: 165f.). But none of these have made a serious impact on the central position which consumerism continues to hold throughout global modern cultures.

Like most people who address these problems I can think of no easy set of solutions. It may indeed be that the problem of accelerating consumption within the global capitalist system as it is currently constituted is simply an intractable one: a condition in which modern cultures, short of a major crisis in capitalism or of an environmental catastrophe, will remain locked. However, this chapter has not been directed towards the analysis of contemporary consumer culture *per se*; it has been concerned with the inflections of a broader culture of immediacy within the consumer sphere. Here other possibilities and imaginations have recently begun to assert themselves.

Supposing we were able to slow down not just the cycle of consumption, but the whole process of the enactment and experience of everyday life? Would this be possible? Would it be beneficial? In the concluding chapter we will examine some of these aspirations and arguments.

Notes

1 *Withnail and I* written and directed by Bruce Robinson and starring Richard E. Grant, Paul McGann and Richard Griffiths is a *rites of passage* comedy centring on the 'accidental holiday' of two dissolute actors in the Lake District. The film's sharp observation of the hippie lifestyle of the late 1960s has given it a cult status.

2 The wider debates in the extensive literature on consumer culture lie beyond the scope of this discussion. For appraisals of the trajectory of these debates see, inter alia: Featherstone, 1991; Slater, 1997; Miller et al., 1998; Ritzer, 2002; and Warde, 2002. Of particular interest for situating Bauman's position is his own analysis, in an interview with Chris Rojek, of the history of sociological approaches to consumer society (Rojek, 2004). It is perhaps worth registering one point about my discussion here in relation to these wider debates. Although I take issue with that form of the critique of consumer culture, represented here particularly in Bauman's position, that stresses the manipulation of the consumer, I none the less situate the discussion broadly within the critical rather than the 'celebratory' analysis of consumerism. Overall I subscribe to the view of Warde (2002) that, notwithstanding the virtues of broadening the analysis of consumer culture beyond the adamantly censorious, the trend towards 'diluted critique' that has accompanied this is for several reasons to be regretted.

3 Indeed Lipovetsky explicitly distances himself from determinist-pessimistic positions: 'I am radically opposed to the arguments that see in our temporal regime nothing more than "impoverishing traps", "a whirlwind flight", "the mutilation of duration" that make any distance and mediation impossible, as well as any "reversibility of thought"' (2005: 70, note 17).

4 I adopt this functional sounding formulation here in order to avoid 'satisfactions' – a term which I will presently cast some doubt upon.

5 See Warde, 1997 on the general idea of 'convenience' in relation to food. Convenience food can be argued to have a long history, the tin can being invented by a British merchant, Peter Durant, in 1810 (Dowling, 2006, see also Goody, 1997). However the 'ready meal' is a more recent conception, having its roots in the 'TV Dinner' of 1950s America. The apotheosis of convenience food might seem to be the announcement by Heinz in 2006 of an 'instant baked beans on toast' product (a frozen fused sandwich which is inserted directly into a toaster). This, however, promises, like other oddities such as instant granulated tea, to have only limited appeal. It is the more labour intensive dishes such as curries and casseroles and the key technologies of food chilling and microwave re-heating that are the most significant innovations.

6 On the wider context of institutionalized individualism see Beck and Beck-Gernsheim, 2002.

7 I have outlined in Chapter 1 the general stance of this book in relation to sociological approaches to technology and particularly the issue of 'technological determinism'. Although I'm not much interested here in the intricacies of these debates, it is worthwhile expanding a little on the concept of 'affordances'. Ian Hutchby gives an admirably clear account of the idea, first introduced, as he says, in the work of Gibson (1979) in the psychology of perception. The key point is that the affordances of objects (including technologies as well as features of the environment) are not to be regarded as simply and solely the intentional constructions of agents in their interaction with them – broadly, the core social-constructionist argument. An object's affordances – the possibilities they offer for use – should be regarded as properly belonging to the object, in a sense separable from human intentionality:

> In this sense, the uses and the 'values' of things are not attached to them by interpretive procedures or internal representations, but are a material aspect of the thing as it is encountered in the course of action. We are able to perceive things in terms of their affordances, which in turn are properties of things; yet those properties are not determinate . . . since they only emerge in the context of material encounters between actors and objects. (Hutchby, 2001: 27)

As Hutchby goes on to say, the focus on affordances *is* to take a stand against the social constructivist understanding of the nature of artefacts, but one that does not commit us, in understanding technologies, to a determinist reading.

8 The iPod has gone through five generations of basic model between its introduction in 2001 and 2006, alongside occasional cosmetic changes designed to cash in on particular fashions – the 'U2 Special Edition' and the 'Harry Potter Special Edition'. During this time Apple also launched a number of spin-offs: the iPod 'mini' which went through two generations (2004, 2005) only to be replaced in September 2005 by the iPod 'nano', and the iPod 'shuffle' also introduced in 2005. (Details from the highly informative Wikipedia entry on the iPod: en.wikipedia.org/wiki/Ipod.) These model changes are in no way out of line with the general trend towards contrived redundancy in this sector. Most models of MP3 player, digital camera and mobile phone are discontinued within nine months of their introduction (Duff, 2006).

9 Contributions to online message boards and 'weblogs' are rich sources of evidence of such informed consumer interest. An example is the 'Guardian Unlimited Culture Vulture' blog on the issue of digital downloading of music and its relationship to other technologies and formats like the CD (blogs.guardian.co.uk/culturevulture/archives /2006/03/30). Comments posted on this issue included, for instance, fine discriminations about the quality of the sound from digitally compressed music downloads on MP3 players – typically described as 'lossy' as compared with the fuller sound spectrum available on CDs. Along with these technical discriminations there were exchanges between bloggers on the demographics of taste, the hyping of the iPod as compared with other MP3 devices, the history of recording technologies and so forth. All of which indicate that the appropriation of technologies is frequently active, informed and intelligent, and so suggest the inadequacy of what we might call 'bottom line functionality' characterizations – 'they only play music', 'they just take pictures' – as critical ways of understanding the nature of consumption practices.

10 Richard Sennett's most recent analysis of consumption and politics in the new capitalism offers a different insight into the excessive capacity of the iPod: that it offers the associative attraction of 'consumer potency'.

> [T]he iPod's phenomenal commercial appeal consists precisely in having more than a person could ever use. Part of the appeal lies in a connection between material potency and one's own potential ability…. Buying a little iPod… promises to expand one's capabilities; all machines of this sort trade on the buyer's identification with the overloaded capacity built into the machines. (Sennett, 2006: 153–4)

11 One curious consequence of this is the tendency not even to bother printing up digital photographs, but just to view then on the camera screen or, less commonly, as a slideshow on the computer screen. This practice raises interesting issues about the changing nature of a 'photograph' as a cultural artefact.

12 One such area worth mentioning is the question of the styles and genres of contemporary television. Here representations of immediacy abound, for example in the vogue for 'makeover' programmes exploring and promoting the possibilities for instant transformations: change your interior decoration; create an instant garden (a particularly contradictory idea); change your job; get a new image; pay off your mortgage and so on. But more interesting than these, it seems to me, are instances in which there appears to be a direct link between technologies and styles. 'Rolling' news channels, for example, not only feature as standard a moving 'strapline' – a continuous ribbon of news underlaying whatever story is being described or discussed – they also commonly utilize a split screen technique in which pictures of a new 'upcoming' story are shown while the 'old' story is still being featured. This sort of restless, fickle presentation technique and the multitasking it demands of viewers seems to be driven by the capabilities of the broadcast technology rather than any significant level of consumer demand.

13 They also, of course, increasingly enact transactions, in certain contexts, at a distance, either online, on the telephone or using mobile phones. So called 'M-shopping' – a form of catalogue shopping via online sites accessed through mobile phones – has become particularly popular in Japan, where there is already a strong tradition of conventional catalogue shopping and where ownership of 3G handsets, at 43 million, is particularly high (McCurry, 2006). In choosing to focus on more conventional spending in the physical locales of 'real' shops I risk being behind the curve. However, despite some predictions of the coming shift to 'immaterial

means of consumption' via the internet (Ritzer, 2001: 146f.) and though high-end retail outlets may be shifting, under pressure from online retailing, towards becoming places of entertainment (Abrams, 2006) there does not seem to be evidence of a general decline in the popularity of physical shopping, and my approach conforms to the argument made in Chapter 5, that media technologies are, in general, integrated into a mobile rather than a sedentary lifestyle.

14 Credit and debit cards have different histories, different roles in the sphere of consumption and different attractions for banks, retailers and consumers. For example, debit cards were introduced by banks (in the UK at least) in the 1980s with the specific aim of reducing the use of cheques at the point of sale because of the costs involved in processing them. Whereas credit cards, though they may serve the same function, have evolved out of various token credit systems having a much longer history. For the purposes of the present argument, however, both have the same key physical characteristics, as specified in the ISO 7810 standard (see: en.wikipedia.org/wiki (/Credit_card and /Debit_card)).

15 It could, of course, be objected that in modern 'smart' cards the key component is the embedded microprocessor, which is not only intrinsically more valuable than the plastic carrier, but is the real tool of access. But this would be to miss the phenomenological issue: it is the card itself that is the material proxy of money in the ritual of spending.

16 These contraptions, which people of my generation may just remember as intriguing features of childhood shopping trips were still in isolated use in stores in the UK up to the 1980s. Their history is overall poorly documented, but see the enthusiastic 'Cash Railway Website' (ids.u-net.com/cash/).

17 Prepaid (offline) contactless card payment systems utilize what is called 'near field communication technology' and are already in operation in transport applications that require fast flows: for example London Transport's Oyster Card or Hong Kong's Octopus card. These are now being integrated with mobile phone handsets to produce so-called 'wallet phones', seen by some as the viable route to the so far illusive cashless economy. See *The Economist*: Technology Quarterly, 10 December 2005, pp. 21–2.

18 For a different approach to the idea of money as 'alienated' see George Ritzer's interesting reading of Simmel's *Philosophy of Money* (1907/1978) on the way in which money existing as credit, 'seems more distant from us than cash in our wallets' (Ritzer, 2001: 76).

19 Call centres have been the subject of a good deal of exploration in terms of their workplace culture – sometimes described as a combination of Taylorism and Panoptical surveillance. What has not been so much studied, so far as I know, is the rather curiously debased interaction between consumers and call centre operatives working to scripts. For an interesting journalistic account, see Ronson (2006).

20 Although I've not stressed it much, it is probably important not to overlook the fact that some phenomena of consumer immediacy are comparatively innocent of any deeper significance – for instance the novelty involved in having something delivered rapidly simply because it can be done. A good example of this is the recent practice of having downloads or even CDs of a live music performance available for sale at the end of the concert.

21 See here Appadurai's observations on the effects of modern credit practices on the temporal-cultural imagination:

> They have created an open-ended rather than a cyclical climate for consumer borrowing: they have thereby linked borrowing to the long, linear sense of a lifetime of potential earnings and the equally open-ended sense of the growth values of assets such as houses, rather than to the short and inherently restrictive cycles of monthly and annual income. (1996: 81)

7

Deceleration?

The significance of the 'slow movement'

Some organized signs of dissatisfaction with the pace of life in developed industrial societies are to be found in the so-called 'slow movement'. For the sake of style, I shall drop the scare quotes hereafter, but it's going to be necessary to keep them conceptually in place.

Of the various initiatives that make up the movement, the most well-established and high-profile ones are the slow food and slow cities movements. These are both international organizations with all the usual institutional infrastructural features: co-ordinating committees, income streams, permanent administrative staff, annual general meetings, mission statements, press offices and so forth. Slow Food was established in Paris in 1989, but has its roots in Italy, in the reaction of the food writer Carlo Petrini to plans, in 1986, to open a McDonald's in Piazza di Spania in Rome. Out of this has developed an extensive organization of some 80,000 members across 100 countries, with offices in Italy, France, Switzerland, Germany, the USA and Japan. The aims of the movement are essentially to oppose the spread of standardized fast food, promoting instead the local, sustainable, environmentally friendly production of high quality food, and to defend both traditional regional cuisine and (implicitly, slower) patterns of conviviality and enjoyment in food culture (www.slowfood.com).

The slow cities movement ('*CittàSlow*') was originally an outgrowth of Slow Food and extends the stress on the relation between slow pace, locality and conviviality to the broader sphere of urban policy. It was established at a meeting between the leaders of four small Italian towns held in the Umbrian city of Orvieto in 1999, with the aim of defining and promoting the distinctive qualities of traditional, slow paced, small town life – *città lente*. Its principles now embrace the preservation of local traditional economic and cultural practices, policies to maintain conviviality and hospitality in the slow rhythms of small urban settings, and the protection of the urban environment from noise, visual and traffic pollution. Like Slow Food, *CittàSlow* has grown to an international movement having, by 2005, 44 registered member municipalities – mostly in Italy, but also in Germany, Norway and the United Kingdom – and applications for membership from many other countries (www.cittaslow.net).

Both of these organizations have their base in broad cultural principles opposed to the cultural drift of global modernity. However to call them 'grassroots' oppositional movements is rather problematic. This is not just because both arise from well-established institutional bases within developed capitalist societies (the food industry; local municipal development) but more significantly because both have found their niche within the material and cultural economy of western modernity. Slow Food, though it presses broadly for preserving locality and biodiversity against the globalized food business is effectively a large commercial organization linked to its own specific upper-end gastronomic industry and market.

In a similar way *CittàSlow*, in promoting the development of small towns (of 50,000 inhabitants or less) represents the interests of a particular spatial-cultural constituency and a related localized form of capital. In a sense then, and without being unduly cynical, both movements could be seen as defending enclaves of interest, rather than offering plausible models for more general social transformation.

For the rest, the slow movement is an interestingly mixed bag of (generally local) initiatives across mostly western societies. These range from groups exploring or advocating general lifestyle change (for example, the Austrian-based *Society for the Deceleration of Time* or *slowlondon*, or the US-based *Simple Living Network*), to art and design-oriented initiatives like *SlowLab* in New York, and to narrowly focused groups like *Tempo Giusto* – a group of German musicians dedicated to the performance of classical music at much slower – in their opinion, authentic – speeds. Most of these initiatives are to be distinguished from the more institutionally organized movements like *Slow Food* and *CittàSlow* in terms of their independence from particular political economic constituencies of interest. They represent an interesting and, for the most part, serious and committed groundswell of thought, dialogue and action on the issue of the pace of contemporary life which deserves more attention from academic research than it has so far received.[1]

But my interest here is not with the details of these initiatives but with how to understand their collective significance within the culture of immediacy. To this end it will be useful, briefly, to clarify their status in relation to the idea of a social movement. This is a variously interpreted concept (Touraine, 1965, 1978; Melucci, 1989; Eder, 1993), but Manuel Castells (1997: 3) offers a useful basic definition as, 'purposive collective actions whose outcome, in victory as in defeat, transforms the values and institutions of society'. This applies well in the case of, for example, the women's movement, the environmental movement, the peace movement, the civil rights movement and the anti-globalization movement. But to appreciate its problematic applicability to the slow movement we should consider the typology of 'identity, adversary, and societal goal' which Castells, following Alain Touraine's analysis, deploys:

> *identity* refers to the self-definition of the movement of what it is, on behalf of whom it speaks. *Adversary* refers to the movement's principal enemy, as explicitly identified by the movement. *Societal goal* refers to the movement's

> vision of a kind of social order ... it would wish to attain in the historical
> horizon of its collective action. (Castells, 1997: 71)

The attempt to apply this categorization to the slow movement pretty quickly justifies maintaining the imagined scare quotes. Unlike other social movements – in particular the civil rights movement, the women's movement, or the gay movement – there is no strong sense of cultural identity attaching to slow initiatives. They don't express the situation of oppressed or culturally dissident groupings in society, nor articulate a struggle for recognition or emancipation. Nor do they demonstrate the sort of 'identity-building' character of movements like the environmental-activism movement or the anti-globalization movement, in which a sense of belonging is often constituted in opposition to the cultural values of global capitalism.

Similarly it is generally difficult to point to the sort of sharply defined 'adversary' that is found in other movements: institutional racism, patriarchy, homophobia, corporate capitalism and so forth. Though there is sometimes an *implied* critique of the forces – particularly globalization – that produce the increasing pace of life, this generally remains vague and politically muted. Compared with the sort of bilious conservative critique of early mechanical speed that we noticed in Chapter 2, the contemporary slow movement in the main deploys a politely dissenting discourse, oriented more towards exploring change in personal practices, and generally avoids picking a fight with large social forces. The word capitalism is rarely encountered on the web sites of the slow movement. And in pretty much all cases there is an insistence that the movement is not anti-modern. For example, one of the most reflective and articulate groups, *slowlondon*, insists, 'Slow is certainly not a rebellion against technology or modernity. It is not anti-speed nor anti-anything really (except people who chuck chewing gum on the street)' (slowlondon.com/whatisslow.php).

This diffidence is reflected in the articulation of a general 'societal goal'. The obvious, unambiguous one of slowing the pace of life is in fact hardly ever set forth without hedging and qualification. Carl Honoré's *In Praise of Slow* website is typical: 'Despite the name, it is not about slowing the whole world down to a crawl. The aim is to do everything at the right speed: Sometimes fast. Sometimes slow. Sometimes in between' (www.inpraiseofslow.com/slow/faq.php). Of course all this hedging risks banality. But it also expresses one of the key features of the slow movement: that, unlike politically focused, emancipatory social movements, it is a response to a complex and value-ambiguous cultural condition rather than to an obvious situation of social injustice or oppression. Thus, typically, the aims of the movement are articulated in terms of a complicated lifestyle *problem* to be confronted, rather than as a goal to be achieved:

> This is not working. Just look around. There are many wonderful advantages to living and working in a city. Despite this, we see faces that are restless and anxious ... We see people who are falling victim to ... our obsession with speed. ... Where in our lives are we rushing and why? What advantages does

this fast pace give you? How does the way we live affect both ourselves and the people around us?
... This is not working. (slowlondon.com/problem.php)

These are fundamental questions for contemporary cultural modernity and their public expression is in itself useful. But what, beyond this, is the significance of the slow movement?

I think, in the first place, that it is important not to dismiss the movement as merely an expression of (otherwise comfortable) middle-class cultural anxieties and an apolitical, quasi-therapeutic response to these. The dominant stress on self-help – though it is, in both analytical and political terms, a weakness – can be understood as expressing the broader experience of immersion in a complex cultural condition which is most easily grasped, not in institutional abstractions, but in the data of individual experience. And it is an easy slide from this subjective interface with speed to the perception – at least partly justified – that the problem resides within individual practices. In this sense, the slow movement is congruent with the condition of immediacy, matching both its mood of fluid complexity and over-determination, and the individualizing effects of both telemediatization and the shaping of consumption towards delivery.

It seems unlikely that the slow movement can in any direct way challenge the institutional grip of the condition of immediacy. However the focus on the experienced problems of pace of life that it provides should not be discounted. For it is possible to discern within this discourse certain emergent values – the other aspect of Castells's stipulation of the impact of a social movement – which might in the longer term be consequential. And if we, as we surely should, reject inevitabilism, then exploring such values, and the conditions for their cultivation, seems worthwhile.

Slow values

Cultural values, as I understand them, are not precise critical instruments. They are not programmable devices to screen out moral viciousness or ideological delusion. Much less are they scalpels with which we can dissect a body of cultural practice and discourse and remove malignant tissue. Values are not sharp entities. Shading and softening at their edges and – importantly – subject to wear and tear and ageing, values are best understood as the malleable constituents of cultural narratives. Under analysis, and in contestation, values need to be defined as clearly as possible; but they remain inert and useless in abstraction. It is when they are woven into stories of how life may best be lived that they gather sway and even compulsion.

This is how I want to approach slow values: on the basis of their prospects for building into a narrative that can give us some cultural grip on contemporary speed. The main implication of my analysis of the condition of immediacy is that, compared with the bold collective stories of mechanical speed, it lacks such a compelling narrative. It would be quite absurd to pretend to offer one here. But what we can do, in a rough and schematic fashion, is to explore some of the implicit values that inform the discourse of the slow movement and try, as it were, to assess their cultural-imaginary promise. This is, it needs to be noted, a quite different, more modest, undertaking from that of judging their merits. I will organize the discussion around two pairs of values: the first pair, for various reasons with dim, and the second with rather brighter, prospects.

Abstention and patience

The idea of 'downshifting' has sufficient currency to have made it into the Microsoft Encarta English Dictionary: 'To change a highly paid but stressful job for one that makes it possible to improve quality of life in other respects'. This is in many ways an appealing thought, but not a practice that has made more than minor inroads into contemporary culture. And it's not difficult to see why. For, though it is generally played down because of connotations with asceticism and self-denial, the challenging idea of *abstention* is at the core of philosophies of downshifting.

Thus, for example, the *Simple Living Network* describes its goal as, 'to present alternatives to the standard American dream of more ... faster ... bigger ... better ...'. This is elaborated in various understandings of the idea of 'simplicity'. For example, 'frugal simplicity' – 'cutting back on spending that is not truly serving our lives' or 'uncluttered simplicity' which, 'means cutting back on trivial distractions, both material and non-material, and focusing on the essentials – whatever these may be for each of our unique lives' (www.simpleliving.net/content/custom_garden_of_simplicity.asp). To be fair, not all of these versions of voluntary simplicity directly advocate abstention, but it is difficult to avoid its general implication as the price to be paid for alternative living.

Let me repeat. I'm not criticizing any of these values and attitudes. As they shade into other moral and political positions – for example those of the Green agenda, or of positions of solidarity with the developing world – they seem to me to have some clear enough virtues. But we are not judging merits here, but cultural-imaginary appeal.

Abstention means the deliberate choice not to do something. It derives from the Latin verb *abstinere*, to 'hold yourself away' and this is a clue to its limitations. The problem with the value of abstention lies in this sense of disengagement. To hold oneself away from the cultural mainstream – as a protest, as a route to spiritual fulfilment or as a personal contribution towards environmental preservation – are marks of a sense of individual moral responsibility. But the problem is with how to build abstention into a *positive* collective narrative of the good life. Given not only various pressures towards immediate consumption, but an underlying drive in modern cultures towards expanding experience rather than contracting it, 'simple life' advocacy and downshifting don't look too promising as constituents of a robust story of a full and satisfying engaged modern existence. In order to have this compulsion, they need the support of other values and imaginations such as those that have been traditionally supplied in religious thought. And it has to be doubted that the constellation of quasi-spiritual, conscientious and socially responsible attitudes sponsored in this sort of group has the same degree of cultural force as religion. Without doubt, voluntary simplicity has its constituency, but, though it may be growing in some western societies, it is an appeal which seems likely to remain quite limited. And these limitations emerge even more clearly when we consider abstention's time-inflected cousin, patience.

Patience is a complicated idea with a number of different aspects. It implies, for example, a sense of emotional self-control: the sort of patience that is pretty uncontroversially deemed a good thing in relation to driving behaviour, or a necessary quality in handling tense and difficult negotiations or in working professionally with various contexts of challenging behaviour. However, beyond this, the claim of patience to be a virtue is less absolute. There is, for example, what we might call a *calculating* aspect to patience, expressed in a comment in Disraeli's novel *Tacred* (1900), that, 'Everything will come if a man will only wait'. Leaving aside all the cases in which this does not actually occur, it is difficult to see why such calculation should anyway be in itself virtuous. I have always had a wry regard for the old proverb that says, 'Sit by the river long enough and you will see the bodies of your enemies float past you'. But I don't consider this to be a particularly virtuous thought.

No, if patience is held to be a virtue it is mostly on account of its links with abstention. Virtuous patience is the temporal manifestation of restraint. Patience understood as the deliberate deferral of satisfaction, and the contentment in waiting, is the antithesis of the driving spirit of immediacy. Patience means deliberately leaving the gap open. It is plain to see the attractions of this sort of attitude in the face of the critique of the culture of delivery. Cultivating patience as a value implies the inhibition of constant impulsive consumer desire and perhaps even shifting the temporal horizons of cultural value from the immediate towards the *longue durée*.

Despite these attractions, patience is clearly a value in broad retreat across modern societies. To understand this we have to look not just at the technological and institutional forces and pressures discussed in the previous two chapters, but to the contexts in which it has been invoked, and the connotations that have accrued to it.

'Sad patience, too near neighbour to despair'[2]. The thought is a reminder that, in its core definitions as, 'calm endurance of hardship, pain, delay', or as 'tolerant perseverance', patience has its roots in a cultural response to suffering. The Latin root 'patiens' also gives us the term 'patient' for someone undergoing medical treatment. This is perhaps the prime example of a virtue made out of necessity. 'What cannot be cured must be endured' and so patience valorizes the dignified endurance of pain, illness and hardship. But it is not difficult to see why such a cultural value loses its force with the development of modernity, in which expectations of technological solutions to an increasing number of life's vicissitudes are constantly growing and, more significantly, are deeply structured into the legitimating discourses of social institutions. In this context, ideas of the toleration of hardship or deprivation have scarcely any moral-political purchase – *vide* the public attention given to waiting times for surgical procedures, or the immediate moral appeal of emergency relief-aid appeals.

The pale appeal of patience in these contexts cannot be easily detached from the weakness of purchase it has in the context of consumption practices. This is particularly so given the democratizing tendencies that are also deeply structured into modernity. For the appeal to patience cannot be cleared of an ideological suspicion: as the counsel of the powerful to the subordinate to tolerate their lot. Since the unwillingness of modern political subjects to settle for pie in the sky when they die is (rightly) upheld in democratic societies, the impetus towards enjoying more pie today thereby receives legitimation in the name of equality.

As in the case of abstention, none of this is to decry the merits of the concomitant values of tolerance, forbearance, or respect for the long term. But to avoid these becoming the casualties of the condition of immediacy, we need to give attention to more imaginatively promising elements of slow value.

Focus and balance

A recurrent theme within the discourse of slow is the need to draw breath in order to take stock and examine our lives. 'Slow asks us to step back just a little and create a bit of space...only then can we get a better view of what is going on' (*slowlondon*); 'Simple living...is about living an examined life – one in which you have determined what is important' (*Simple Living Network*); 'Slowness...describes the individual's elevated state of awareness in the process of creation [and] the tangible quality of its outcomes' (*slowlab*). The core idea can be described as aiming for 'existential focus': sharpening the resolution of our present experience of being-in-the-world rather than allowing the speed and flux of life to carry us away. But this thought can take us in two different directions. In one, what is valued is an experience of 'sheer being' without becoming:

> *Rien faire comme une bête*, lying on water and looking peacefully at the sky, 'being, nothing else, without any further definition and fulfilment', might take the place of process, act, satisfaction.... None of the abstract concepts comes closer to fulfilled utopia than that of eternal peace. (Adorno, 'Sur L'Eau', 1978: 157)

To appreciate Adorno's vision of passive bliss we need to understand that he poses it dialectically against the distortion of philosophies of becoming. There was altogether too much productivity in modern culture for Adorno. What appears in Marxian philosophical anthropology as the realization of human potential in creative labour becomes, in the 'repressive totality', a 'conception of unfettered activity, of uninterrupted procreation, of chubby insatiability, of freedom as frantic bustle' (Adorno, 1978: 156). For Adorno, capitalist modernity had installed, both in the sphere of production and consumption, 'the collective as a blind fury of activity' – against which sensual passivity becomes a radical recourse.

The astringency of Adorno's critical theory – this was written in 1945 – remains remarkably impressive. But with the coming of immediacy, the object of critique has shifted. The ideology of productivism has waned and consumption practices inflected by the assurances of eternal, ubiquitous delivery, whilst expanding and accelerating, have become lighter, softer and more effortless. So we may have to conceive an antithesis in which focus implies existential *effort*. What could this involve? One example could be more searching self-scrutiny in terms of the satisfactions of consumption, which might lead to the stimulation of higher levels of 'fulfilment-demand' on the system (Chapter 6). But more generally it is a question of experiencing moral agency at the core of social existence. The ever-perceptive *slowlondon* site emphasizes this point: 'The irony is that in a way it is lazy to live a fast life. Everyone else is doing it so why should I be any different? ... Slowness is activity. A positive activity with a quality of *balance and measuredness*' (slowlondon.com/whatisslow.php, emphasis added).

Balance is perhaps the most commonly encountered word in the slow movement. Usually it refers to finding a sense of personal equilibrium within the disorienting hurry of life, of locating one's emotional and experiential 'centre'. But there is more to the idea than vague notions of spiritual harmony. As it connects with the theme of active existential focus, personal balance implies the reflexive monitoring of practices and experience. That is to say, it depends on assuming an ongoing control of one's life by choosing and deciding what is appropriate, what is sufficient, what is excessive, and acting to achieve these ends.

These are distinctly modern ideas. There is no sense here of either retrospection or renunciation, and balance, unlike patience, is not linked to a philosophy of consolation. Living a balanced life implies taking a grip of the speed that surrounds us in ways that reflect the energy of modernity. Balance in this sense has all sorts of connotations that are attractive to modern ideals of identity: for example the idea of *poise*. To possess poise is to have style, composure and calm self-assurance in social situations. It is a positive, dynamic characteristic: to be ready to act or respond. In such associations, the idea of cultivating balance in response to the pace of life engages with modern vitality and looks much more promising for telling a compelling story about how life might best be lived in accelerating times.

And perhaps it has more significance. The attractive idea of taking control of one's existence by exercising autonomous, proportionate judgement has obvious relevance for the values embedded within the institutions of modernity. These institutions were, in the main, formed out of the rational-progressive discourse of mechanical modernity, in which speed was recognized as both vital and emancipatory and – in all its directly experienced shape-edged, noisy, brutish, metallic materiality – as intrinsically dangerous. This was the key perception that inaugurated the discourse of simultaneous acceleration and regulation.

Many of the features of life in the condition of immediacy that we have considered begin to build a case for saying that contemporary institutional modernity has lost its sense of balance and proportion. We can observe this in the qualitatively aimless trajectory of fast capitalism; in the (possibly disastrous) failure of governments locked into high-growth economic policies to confront environmental threats; but most dramatically in strategic and security policies caught up in ever-shorter response times which marginalize deliberation and trigger the dangerous logic of preemption (Chapter 3).

The implication is that the sheer power and drive of the modern dynamic – particularly as expressed in and through new technologies – has overtaken the deliberative-regulative principle. And this has been exacerbated by the associated problem of getting a grip, phenomenologically, on the speed of the electronic processing that now permeates modern institutions. How do we regulate that which we do not fully grasp?

In such a context, ideas of balance, measure and proportion become crucial to the governance of modernity. Whilst there are no guarantees that these values will prevail, the hope must be that the attractions of personal balance may resonate in the political cultures of democracies. Thus, in establishing a cultural politics of immediacy, it may be the value of balance that provides a bridge between the personal-existential and the political realms.

But the key here is to separate out the idea of balance-as-control from a more total reactive politics of deceleration. What is at stake is the possibility for institutionally conducting modernity rather than being swept along by it. The very idea of a 'cultural politics' in a certain sense rests on this assumption. As Derrida puts it, 'If there is negotiation, this presupposes the possibility of braking, of putting things back in gear and of accelerating. If something has a rhythm, this is because speed or acceleration is not homogeneous, because there can be deceleration' (Derrida and Stiegler, 2002: 77).

Not uniform deceleration then, but the scope to intervene, to apply deliberate pressure to either pedal. This prompts the final thought of this discussion. It is that proportion also has to be applied to our critical understanding of acceleration itself: that there may be *intrinsic value* in speed which should be preserved within any potential intervention in the rhythms of modernity.

Conclusion: finding virtue in speed

Acceleration does not find too many serious advocates amongst contemporary intellectuals, but it has a powerful one in the political theorist William Connolly. In his book *Neuropolitics: Thinking, Culture, Speed* (2002)

Connolly offers an original and in many ways compelling defence of contemporary acceleration in terms of the cultural political virtues it brings with it. This is both a bold and a subtle analysis which embraces a very wide compass of issues, from the re-evaluation of key aspects of Nietzschian thought within a democratic frame, through a critique of universalism and Kantian sources of contemporary cosmopolitan political positions, towards the construction of an original 'deep pluralist' conception of the possibility of cosmopolitanism. There is a lot here and all of it important. So I apologise in advance for the way I'm going to have to pare it down to the 'essentials' dictated by my own discourse.

The thread that runs through all of this is that acceleration – 'a constitutive dimension of late-modernity' – is essentially ambiguous, and that responses to it need to grasp both its dangers and its promises. More than this, in fact. Connolly takes a stance against powerful arguments that connect deceleration with the necessary conditions for democratic cultural life and argues to the contrary: that wider forms of pluralist democracy actually depend on fast processes and are threatened by some versions of slow reaction.

Connolly's argument is spread across the concluding two chapters of his book and he begins each with an appreciation of the work of theorists – Sheldon Wolin (1997) and Paul Virilio respectively – who stress the corrosive effects of speed on democratic deliberation. We explored Virilio's position in Chapter 3. Wolin, though with a very different discursive style, similarly implicates speed in overwhelming politics and argues broadly for a deceleration which will allow democratic deliberation within a localized political context. Whilst being to a certain extent sympathetic with both positions – at least to the extent of sharing the sense of potential danger and violence inherent in the compression of time – Connolly nevertheless resists the idea of deceleration:

> The acceleration of pace carries danger, then. But it also sets a condition of possibility for achievements that democrats and pluralists prize. The question for me, then, is not how to slow the world down, but how to work with and against a world moving faster than heretofore to promote a positive ethos of pluralism. (Connolly, 2002: 143)

So what is it precisely that he finds (potentially) virtuous in speed? There are really two answers.

One finds virtue in the opposition to some vicious associations of slow culture. Connolly argues, for example, that there is a danger in nostalgia for the 'long slow time' as expressed in some retrenching versions of localism and communitarianism that fail to confront the larger social forces – particularly fast capitalism – that underlie it:

> These devotees of community act as if locality, community, family, neighbour-hood and church could be blocked off from the mobilities of capital, labour, travel, fashion and communication. Such a selective hostility to speed pulls its proponents towards an ugly politics of cultural war against those who both lack

institutional power and challenge through their mode of being the claims of traditional constituencies to embody final moral authority. (Connolly, 2002: 162)

The result is the scapegoating of, ' "Gypsies", "Jews", "women", "homosexuals", "Indians", "prostitutes", "welfare freeloaders", "Blacks", "atheists" and "postmodernists". ... The resentment against speed and the refusal to challenge its most salient institutional sources combine to foster an accusatory culture' (2002: 162). And the most virulent form of this tendency is to be found in, 'national and religious fundamentalisms that deploy media sound bites and military campaigns of ethnic cleansing to return to a slow, centred world.... Fundamentalism is the shape the desire for a slow, centred world takes when its temporal conditions of possibility are absent' (2002: 179).

One can readily see the dangers of this regressive drift. But why should embracing speed positively oppose these vicious tendencies in the imagination of deceleration? Connolly offers two lines of possibility.

The first – which proceeds from his attempt to democratize some themes in Nietzschian philosophy – is the possibility of developing an 'experimental', 'improvisatory' attitude to the contingency of existence. This sort of attitude is necessary because of all the accidents and surprises the flow of time has in store for us if, as Connolly maintains, time is neither linear-progressive not cyclical in character, but constituted by profound 'rifts' and 'forks'. Thus:

> it becomes wise to fold the expectation of surprise and the unexpected into the very fabric of our explanatory theories, interpretive schemes, religious identities, territorial conceptions of politics and ethical sensibilities. And to work on ourselves subtly to overcome existential resentment of these expectations. (Connolly, 2002: 145)

The acceleration in the pace of modern life makes us more aware of these constitutive 'rifts in time', forcing its contingencies upon us in daily life. And so, while speed creates existential anxiety, it can also shock us into developing a vigorous, courageous and affirmative disposition. By denying us, in everyday experience, the comforting delusions that a sanctified past may be clung to, or that a pre-ordained future might be rolled out before us, speed makes us face up to both material and moral contingency. It can thus force us to find within ourselves appropriate attitudes and life-techniques: to resist cultural *ressentiment*, to experiment with our beliefs and identities, and to improvise in our moral stance towards the world. Overall, to become morally more agile, quicker on our feet and so, perhaps more generous in our regard for the challenging 'worlding' of the cultural other.

And so the second possibility. That speed can be the catalyst in the production of cultural-political pluralism. As speed pulls the rug from under traditional assumptions of cultural certainty, so it obliges us to attend to other voices and imaginations and to give up on the idea of any possible monopoly of wisdom. Speed's intrinsic iconoclasm can thus find positive issue in the virtue of a deep-pluralist cosmopolitanism. Connolly makes this argument in a brilliant critique of Kant's cosmopolitanism, and those which – like Martha Nussbaum's (Nussbaum, 1996) – have followed broadly in its wake. Connolly lifts Kant's cosmopolitan vision out of its historical embeddedness in the slow pace of late-eighteenth-century culture – in which, 'clocks did not have second hands; it took a week to set the print for a newspaper run, [and] months to sail across the Atlantic' – to see how it fares in the context of modern globalizing speed. And his answer is, not at all well. The 'concentric' moral universe which Kant inhabited and which allowed him to found his cosmopolitanism ultimately in the European experience and in Christian dogma simply do not answer in the contemporary global-modern condition:

> Today the specific terms of that cosmopolitanism have not only become even more contestable, they continue to carry within them elements of a dogmatic Western imperialism still in need of reconstruction. One key, in my judgement, is to relinquish the demand that all cultures must actually or implicitly recognize the logic of morality in the same way Kant did.... Once this pivot of Kantian morality is transfigured into a contestable act of faith finding its most active expression in states shaped by the history of Christianity on the European continent and the settler societies it spawned, it becomes more feasible to engage a late-modern world of speed and dense interdependencies. Kantianism can provide one noble moral faith within a plural matrix of cosmopolitanism. But this cultural particularism can no longer pretend to set the universal matrix of cosmopolitanism itself. (Connolly, 2002: 183–4)

Modern speed, in Connolly's view, pushes us down a different, radically pluralist route to cosmopolitanism by kicking out the residual supports which the hope of variously grounded universalisms provides. I wish I could wholeheartedly agree with this. But, like many others, I remain ambivalent, divided between the claims of universalism and difference, even as I see the need to reconcile them (Walzer, 1994; Tomlinson, 2001, 2002). But this is not the place, nor is there the time, to pursue these questions. Instead I want to move towards my conclusion by exploring an issue closer to our overall concerns.

This is the question of how Connolly's general 'cautiously affirmative' attitude towards speed – which overall I find attractive – can be reconciled with the 'slow value' of balance-as-control, which in a different way is equally attractive to both of us. How, whilst rejecting uniform deceleration, can we preserve deliberative time–space in both personal-existential and institutional terms? Or to pose the question in a broader way, what sort of culturally regulative principles can be appropriate to acceleration?

At a practical level the problem is not intractable. Since speed, as we know, is not homogeneous, it should be possible to build slow zones into our cultural-institutional practices as a selective form of applying the brakes. In this spirit, Connolly recommends the general provision of, 'structural opportunities for periodic escape and retreat from a fast-paced life' in the form of sabbatical programmes and increased opportunities for midlife education. 'Such retreats enable us to revisit from time to time selective assumptions and dispositions that have gripped us and to refresh our energies to re-enter the rat race' (2002: 144). Good practical – and, given imagination, practicable – proposals, but as Connolly recognizes, not sufficient in themselves.

For there remains the deeper problem that we have been struggling with throughout this chapter: to what story of the good and fulfilling life can this periodic personal deliberation be referred? And, at the institutional level, what collective understandings of this good life can legitimate cultural or political-economic regulation? What we can't do, if we accept Connolly's analysis, is try simply to re-vivify the old progressive-regulative narrative of mechanical-modern speed with its linear model of time, its sense of mastery, and its faith in planning. This would be as nostalgic in its way as misty-eyed dreams of return to the 'long slow time'.

For what we have to confront – something which Connolly does not broach in his analysis – is not just zones of acceleration, but a broad condition of immediacy which, whilst providing no coherent narrative, none the less offers many prompts, cues and incitements. The attractions of immediacy are strong because they *do* deliver the comforts, conveniences and pleasures that have been long promised in the cultural imagination of modernity. But in moral terms, it is the cultural assumptions and expectations of effortlessness, ubiquity and endless delivery in a fast-paced, technologically-replete and telemediated world that now need to be challenged. The intrinsic complacency of immediacy needs to be disturbed because it provides no existential resources with which to respond to the contingency of modern existence and to meet the surprises that await us.

In this sense, the ideal subject of immediacy is as dull-witted and morally inert as the belief-fundamentalist: locked into low horizons of existential fulfilment by consumer culture and into security-oriented and risk-averse sensibilities aimed at preserving the limited comforts of this condition. There does not seem much here to incline people towards the sort of reflective cosmopolitanism that Connolly and I favour. So the potential moral dynamism that Connolly detects in fast culture needs to be released from the grip immediacy holds over speed.

We all agree that the problem is deep and that there are no guarantees here. My contribution towards a way forward is appropriately modest and tentative. It is, borrowing one of Connolly's formulations, to 'fold in' the value of existential balance to an affirmative attitude towards acceleration. Balance, as I have defined it actively – as taking positive control of life – fits Connolly's pluralist specifications. It is not a regressive or nostalgic 'slow value'. It does not imply self-scrutiny or self-control according to any traditional or fixed precepts. It does not look for life formulas or try to achieve settled states of inner harmony. Balance-as-control is not about coming to rest. It's more or less the opposite: a process of constant reflexive *re-balancing* in the face of contingency.

The thought of applying this hard discipline of balance to modern life – both personally and in social institutions – is deeply disturbing not only to the ideals of nostalgic-retrospective slowness but equally to the comfortable assumptions of immediacy. And so the issue becomes one of how to integrate this searching existential effort into an attractive cultural narrative. Let's put it bluntly. Why should people choose to make this effort? As Cornelius Castoriadis once asked, 'Are [people] really willing to act…in order to take on their own fate. Do they have this desire, or do they prefer to go on opening their fridge and looking at their TV' (Castoriadis, 1987b: 50). It's a tough question because we can no longer invoke the old modern-moral stories of concerted effort towards progress.

For my money, hope lies not in moral exhortation, but in disclosing the *reward* for this effort. This means tapping the sense, half-buried in the condition of immediacy, that existence is a state of becoming, at once pregnant with possibilities and fragile and precarious. If this raw sensibility is kept to the fore of the cultural narrative, the rewards of applying effort to maintaining feedback loops and continually re-balancing our lives becomes clearer. It is to experience ourselves as capably and sensitively attuned to our fast-moving environment and so as existentially flexible, responsive and resilient.

The promise of the narrative of mechanical speed was order and progress. The attractions of immediacy are lightly achieved comforts and satisfactions. But neither of these can deliver existential fulfilment or security in the face of the temporally compressed contingencies of contemporary acceleration. Virtue to be found in speed is quite different: it is to apply effort to become nimble and graceful life-performers. The goal is balance. The reward is poise.

Notes

1 The best overall guide to the slow movement is the journalist Carl Honore's well-researched and engaging *In Praise of Slow* (2004). But as the title suggests, this is not critically searching. Within this same genre we could place lifestyle-philosophy/self-help books like Bodil Jönsson's sensible *Ten Thoughts about Time* (2003). Within the academic literature there is much less coverage. The slow cities movement occurs from time to time in the literature of urbanism (for example, Knox, 2005) and there are isolated treatments within the broad field of cultural studies – for instance Thierry Paquot's urbane and entertainingly provocative *The Art of the Siesta* (2003). But if there is a comprehensive critical academic exploration of the slow movement, to my shame I have missed it.

2 From Mathew Arnold's poem 'The Scholar Gypsy' – which can itself be read as an elegy for a lost world of spiritual slowness in nature, as contrasted with, 'this strange disease of modern life,/With its sick hurry, its divided aims,/ Its heads o'ertaxed, its palsied hearts…'.

Bibliography

Abrams, Rachel 2006: 'Are You Being Served?' *The Economist: Intelligent Life*, Summer 2006: 13–15.

Ackroyd, Peter 1990: *Dickens*. London: QPD/Sinclair Stevenson.

Adam, Barbara 1990: *Time and Social Theory*. Cambridge: Polity.

Adam, Barbara 1998: *Timescapes of Modernity*. London: Routledge.

Adorno, Theodor 1978: *Minima Moralia: Reflections from Damaged Life*. London: Verso.

Agar, Jon 2003: *Constant Touch: A Global History of the Mobile Phone*. Cambridge: Icon Books.

Agger, Ben 1989: *Fast Capitalism*. Urbana, IL: University of Illinois Press.

Agger, Ben 2005: 'Editorial Introduction', *Fast Capitalism* (www.uta.edu/huma/agger/fastcapitalism/edintro.html).

Albrow, M. 1997: *The Global Age: State and Society Beyond Modernity*. Cambridge: Polity.

Alexander, Jeffrey 1990: 'Between Progress and Apocalypse: Social Theory and the Dream of Reason in the Twentieth Century', in Jeffrey Alexander and Piotr Sztompka (eds), *Rethinking Progress*. London: Unwin Hymand, pp. 15–38.

Althusser, Louis 1971: *Lenin and Philosophy and Other Essays*. New York: Monthly Review Press.

Ang, Tom 2005: 'Seeing the Big Picture', *Technology Guardian*, 24 November: 1.

Apollonio, Umbro (ed.) 1973: *Futurist Manifestos*. London: Thames and Hudson.

Appadurai, Arjun 1990: 'Disjuncture and Difference in the Global Cultural Economy', in Mike Featherstone (ed.), *Global Culture: Nationalism, Globalization and Modernity*. London: Sage, pp. 295–310.

Appadurai, Arjun 1996: *Modernity at Large: Cultural Dimensions of Globalization*. Minneapolis: University of Minnesota Press.

Armitage, John (ed.) 2000: *Paul Virilio: From Modernism to Hypermodernism and Beyond*. London: Sage.

Armitage, John (ed.) 2001: *Virilio Live*. London: Sage.

Auden, W.H. 1966: *Collected Shorter Poems 1927–1957*. London: Faber and Faber.

Augé, Marc 1995: *Non-Places: Introduction to the Anthropology of Supermodernity*. London: Verso.

Balint, Michael 1959: *Thrills and Regression*. New York: International Universities Press.

Ballard, J.G. 1975: *Crash*. London: Panther.

Bate, Jonathan 1991: *Romantic Ecology: Wordsworth and the Environmental Tradition*. London: Routledge.

Baudelaire, Charles 1964: *The Painter of Modern Life and Other Essays*. London: Phaidon. (First published in 1863.)

Bauman, Zygmunt 2000: *Liquid Modernity*. Cambridge: Polity.

Bauman, Zygmunt 2002: 'A Postmodern Grid of the Worldmap? – Interview with Milena Yakimova', *Eurozine Review*, 8 November (www.eurozine.com/articles/2002–11–08–bauman).

Bauman, Zygmunt 2003: *Liquid Love*. Cambridge: Polity.

Bauman, Zygmunt 2005: *Liquid Life*. Cambridge: Polity.

Bayley, Stephen 1986: *Sex, Drink and Fast Cars*. London: Faber and Faber.

BBC Annual Report and Accounts, 2005–2006. London: BBC Publishing.

Beck, Ulrich 1992: *Risk Society: Towards a New Modernity*. London: Sage.

Beck, Ulrich 1994: 'The Reinvention of Politics: Towards a Theory of Reflexive Modernization', in U. Beck, A. Giddens and S. Lash (eds), *Reflexive Modernization*. Cambridge: Polity, pp. 56–109.

Beck, Ulrich 1999: *World Risk Society*. Cambridge: Polity.

Beck, Ulrich and Beck-Gernsheim, Elisabeth 2002: *Individualization: Institutionalized Individualism and its Social and Political Consequences*. London: Sage.

Beckman, Jörg 2004: 'Mobility and Safety', *Theory, Culture and Society*, 21(4–5), 81–100.

Benedikt, M. 1991: *Cyberspace*. Cambridge, MA: MIT Press.

Benjamin, Walter 1979a: 'On Some Motifs in Baudelaire', in *Illuminations*. London: Fontana, pp. 156–202.

Benjamin, Walter 1979b: 'The Work of Art in the Age of Mechanical Reproduction', in *Illuminations*. London: Fontana, pp. 219–53.

Berker, Thomas, Hartmann, Maren, Punie, Yves and Ward, Katie, J. (eds) 2006: *Domestication of Media and Technology*. Maidenhead: Open University Press.

Berman, Marshall 1983: *All that is Solid Melts into Air: The Experience of Modernity*. London: Verso.

Bicknell, Peter (ed.) 1984: *The Illustrated Wordsworth's Guide to the Lakes*. London: Webb and Bower.

Bijker, Wieber, E. and Law, John (eds) 1992: *Shaping Technology/Building Society: Studies in Socio-technical Change*. Cambridge, MA: MIT Press.

Black, Richard 2004: 'E–waste rules still being flouted' *BBC News On-line* (news.bbc.co.uk/1/hi/sci/tech/3549763.stm).

Blakemore, Michael (ed.) 1990: *The Great Railway Show*. York: National Railway Museum.

Braverman, Harry 1974: *Labor and Monopoly Capital: The Degradation of Work in the Twentieth Century*. New York: Monthly Review Press.

Brennan, Teresa 2003: *Globalization and its Terrors: Daily Life in the West*. London: Routledge.

Briggs, Asa and Burke, Peter 2002: *A Social History of the Media*. Cambridge: Polity.

Brook, James and Boal, Iain A. (eds) 1995: *Resisting the Virtual Life*. San Francisco: City Lights.

Brottman, Mikita (ed.) 2001: *Car Crash Culture*. New York: Palgrave.

Callon, Michelle 1987: 'Society in the Making: The Study of Technology as a Tool for Sociological Analysis', in Wiebe E. Bijker, Thomas P. Hughes and Trevor J. Pinch (eds), *The Social Construction of Technological Systems*. Cambridge, MA: MIT Press, pp. 83–103.

Carter, Ian 2001: *Railways and Culture in Britain: The Epitome of Modernity*. Manchester: Manchester University Press.

Castells, M. 1996: *The Rise of The Network Society (The Information Age: Economy, Society and Culture: Volume I)*. Oxford: Blackwell.

Castells, Manuel 1997: *The Power of Identity (The Information Age: Economy, Society and Culture: Volume II)*. Oxford: Blackwell.

Castells, Manuel 2000: 'Information Technology and Global Capitalism', in Will Hutton and Anthony Giddens (eds), *On The Edge: Living with Global Capitalism*. London: Jonathan Cape, pp. 52–75.

Castells, Manuel 2001: *The Internet Galaxy*. Oxford: Oxford University Press.

Castoriadis, Cornelius 1987a: *The Imaginary Constitution of Society*. Cambridge: Polity.

Castoriadis, Cornelius 1987b: in B. Bourne, U. Eichler and D. Herman (eds), *Voices: Modernity and its Discontents*. Nottingham: Spokesman Books.

Chun, Wendy Hui Kyong 2006: 'Introduction: Did Somebody Say New Media?', in Wendy Hui Kyong Chun and Thomas Keenan (eds), *New Media Old Media*. Abingdon: Routledge, pp. 1–10.

Clapham, John H. 1950: *The Early Railway Age 1820–1850*. Cambridge: Cambridge University Press.

Clark, Kenneth 1962: *The Gothic Revival*. Harmondsworth: Penguin.

Clarkson, Jeremy 2004: *The World According to Clarkson*. London: Penguin.

Connolly, William 2002: *Neuropolitics: Thinking, Culture, Speed*. Minneapolis: University of Minnesota Press.

Couldry, Nick 2003: 'Liveness, "Reality" and the Mediated Habitus from Television to the Mobile Phone'. Research paper: Department of Media and Communications, LSE.

Crabtree, James, Nathan, Max and Roberts, Simon: 2003 *MobileUK: Mobile Phones and Everyday Life*. London: The Work Foundation.

Dant, Tim 2004: 'The Driver-car', *Theory, Culture and Society*, 21 (4–5): 61–80.

Davies, William 2006: 'Digital Exuberance', *Institute for Public Policy Research* (www.ippr.org.uk/articles/?id=1918).

Davis, Jim, Hirschl, Thomas and Stack, Michael (eds) 1997: *Cutting Edge: Technology, Information, Capitalism and Social Revolution*. London: Verso.

Davis, John R. 1999: *The Great Exhibition*. Stroud: Sutton Publishing.

Dayan, Daniel and Katz, Elihu 1992: *Media Events: The Live Broadcasting of History*. Cambridge, MA: Harvard University Press.

Delanty, Gerard 1999: *Social Theory in a Changing World*. Cambridge: Polity.

Der Derian, James (ed.) 1998: *The Virilio Reader*. Oxford: Blackwell.

Der Derian, James 2000: 'The Conceptual Cosmology of Paul Virilio', in John Armitage (ed.), *Paul Virilio: From Modernism to Hypermodernism and Beyond*. London: Sage, 215–27.

Derrida, Jacques and Stiegler, Bernard 2002: *Echographies of Television*. Cambridge: Polity.

Dershowitz, Alan M. 2006: *Preemption: A Knife That Cuts Both Ways*. New York: Norton.

Dickens, Charles 2002: *Dombey and Son*. London: Penguin. (First published 1848.)

Disraeli, Benjamin 1900: *Tancred*. London: Longmans Green. (First published in 1847.)

Dodson, Sean 2006: 'Show and Tell Online' *Technology Guardian*, 2 March 1–2.

Donald, James 1997: 'This, Here, Now: Imagining the Modern City', in Sally Westwood and John Williams (eds), *Imagining Cities*. London: Routledge, 181–201.

Dowling, Tim 2006: 'The Rise and Rise of Convenience Food', *The Guardian G2*, 19 May 6–9.

Draut, Tamara et al. 2005: *The Plastic Safety Net: The Reality Behind Debt in America*. Demos US/Centre for Responsible Lending.

Dreyfus, Hubert, L. 2001: *On the Internet*. London: Routledge.

Duff, Oliver 2006: 'Why Your MP3 Player is Already Out of Date', *The Independent*, 14 February: 16–17.

Duffy, Jonathan 2006: 'The MySpace Age', *BBC News Magazine*, 7 March (news.bbc.co.uk/1/hi/magazine/4782118.stm).

Durkheim, Émile 1951: *Suicide*. New York: The Free Press.

Eder, Klaus 1993: *The New Politics of Class: Social Movements and Cultural Dynamics in Advanced Societies*. London: Sage.

Elliott, Larry 2006: 'Even China Cannot Feed a Permanent Bull', *The Guardian*, 15 May: 29.

Ellul, Jacques 1964: *The Technological Society*. New York: Vintage Books.

Eriksen, Thomas Hylland 2001: *Tyranny of the Moment*. London: Pluto Press.

Featherstone, Mike 1991: *Consumer Culture and Postmodernism*. London: Sage.

Featherstone, Mike 2004: 'Automobilities: An Introduction', *Theory, Culture and Society*, 21(4–5): 1–24.

Featherstone, Mike and Burrows, Roger (eds) 1995: 'Cyberspace/Cyberbodies/Cyberpunk', *Body and Society*, 1(3–4).

Featherstone, Mike, Thrift, Nigel and Urry, John (eds) 2004: 'Special Issue on Automobilites', *Theory, Culture and Society* 21(4–5).

Feuer, Jane 1983: 'The Concept of Live Television: Ontology as Ideology', in E. Ann Kaplan (ed.) *Regarding Television*. Los Angeles: American Film Institute, pp. 12–22.

Feuilherade, Peter 2005: 'China "Ripe" for Media Explosion', *BBC Monitoring*, 13 March.

Forster, Edward Morgan 1954: 'The Machine Stops', in *Collected Short Stories*. Harmondsworth: Penguin, pp. 109–46.

Forster, Edward Morgan 1983: *Howards End*. Harmondsworth: Penguin. (First published in 1910.)

Freeman, Michael 1999: *Railways and the Victorian Imagination*. New Haven and London: Yale University Press.

Freud, Sigmund 1953: *Three Essays on the Theory of Sexuality*. London: The Hogarth Press.

Frisby, David 1985: *Fragments of Modernity*. Cambridge: Polity.

Frisby, David 1991: *Sociological Impressionism*. London: Routledge.

Frisby, David 2001: *Cityscapes of Modernity*. Cambridge: Polity.

Frisby, David and Featherstone, Mike (eds) 1997: *Simmel on Culture*. London: Sage.

Garfield, Simon 2002: *The Last Journey of William Huskisson*. London: Faber and Faber.

Gibson, James J. 1979: *The Ecological Approach to Perception*. London: Houghton Mifflin.

Giddens, Anthony 1972: *Politics and Sociology in the Thought of Max Weber*. London: Macmillan.

Giddens, Anthony 1984: *The Constitution of Society*. Cambridge: Polity.

Giddens, Anthony 1990: *The Consequences of Modernity*. Cambridge: Polity.

Giddens, Anthony 1994: 'Living in a Post-traditional Society', in Ulrich Beck, Anthony Giddens and Scott Lash (eds), *Reflexive Modernization*. Cambridge: Polity, pp. 56–109.

Gilloch, Graeme 1996: *Myth and Metropolis: Walter Benjamin and the City*. Cambridge: Polity.

Gilmore, John 1997: *Live Fast, Die Young*. New York: Thunders Mouth Press.

Gissing, George 1953: *The Private Papers of Henry Ryecroft*. London: Phoenix House. (First published in 1903.)

Gleick, James 1999: *Faster: The Acceleration of Just About Everything*. London: Little, Brown.

Gold, John R. 1997: *The Experience of Modernism: Modern Architects and the Future City*. London: E and FN Spon.

Goldman, Robert, Papson, Stephen and Kersey, Noah 2005: 'Speed: Through, Across, and In – The Landscapes of Modernity', *Fast Capitalism*, 1.1 (www.uta.edu/huma/agger/fastcapitalism/1_1/gpk2.html).

Goody, Jack 1997: 'Industrial Food: Towards the Development of a World Cuisine', in C. Counihan and P. van Esterik (eds), *Food and Culture*, London: Routledge, 338–56.

Gorz, Andre 1989: *Critique of Economic Reason*. London: Verso.

Gray, John 1999: *False Dawn: The Delusions of Global Capitalism*. London Granta.

Green, Christopher 2006: 'The Machine', in Christopher Wilk (ed.), *Modernism 1914–1939: Designing a New World*. London: V&A Publications, pp. 71–111.

Greene, Rachel 2004: *Internet Art*. London: Thames and Hudson.

Grint, Keith and Woolgar, Steve 1997: *The Machine at Work: Technology, Work and Organization*. Cambridge: Polity.

Gurney, Peter 2001: 'An Appropriated Space: the Great Exhibition, the Crystal Palace and the Working Class', in Louise Purbeck (ed.), *The Great Exhibition of 1851: New Interdisciplinary Essays*. Manchester: Manchester University Press. 114–45.

Hall, Peter 1996: *Cities of Tomorrow*. Oxford: Blackwell.

Haraway, Donna 1991: *Simians, Cyborgs and Women: The Reinvention of Nature*. London: Free Association Books.

Hardt, Michael and Negri, Antonio 2000: *Empire*. Cambridge, MA: Harvard University Press.

Harvey, David 1989: *The Condition of Postmodernity*. Oxford: Blackwell.

Harvey, David 1999: *The Limits to Capital*. London: Verso.

Hassard, John (ed.) 1990: *The Sociology of Time*. London: Macmillan.

Hayes, R. Dennis 1995: 'Digital Palsy: RSI and Restructuring Capital', in James Brook and Iain A. Boal (eds), *Resisting the Virtual Life*. San Francisco: City Lights, pp. 173–80.

Held, David, McGrew, Tony, Goldblatt, David and Perraton, Jonathan (eds) 1999: *Global Transformations*. Cambridge: Polity.

Hiro, Dilip 2004: *Secrets and Lies: Operation 'Iraq Freedom' and After*. New York: Nation Books.

Hobsbawm, Eric 1999: *Industry and Empire: From 1870 to the Present Day*. London: Penguin.

Hochschild, A.R. 1997: *The Time Bind: When Work Becomes Home and Home Becomes Work*. New York: Metropolitan Books.

Holston, James 1989: *The Modernist City: An Anthropological Critique of Brasilia*. Chicago: University of Chicago Press.

Honoré, Carl 2004: *In Praise of Slow*. London: Orion Books.

Howells, Richard 2003: *Visual Culture*. Cambridge: Polity.

Hughes, Robert 1991: *The Shock of the New*. London: Thames and Hudson.

Hutchby, Ian 2001: *Conversation and Technology: From the Telephone to the Internet*. Cambridge: Polity.

Hutton, Will 2000: 'In Conversation with Anthony Giddens', in Will Hutton and Anthony Giddens (eds), *On The Edge: Living with Global Capitalism*. London: Jonathan Cape, pp. 1–51.

Hutton, Will and Giddens, Anthony (eds) 2000: *On The Edge: Living with Global Capitalism*. London: Jonathan Cape.

Inglis, David 2004: 'Auto Couture: Thinking the Car in Post-war France', *Theory, Culture and Society*, 21(4–5): 197–220.

Jacobs, Jane 1961: *Death and Life of Great Amercian Cities*. New York: Vintage.

Jay, Martin 1993: *Downcast Eyes*. Berkeley: University of California Press.

Jennings, Humphrey 1995: *Pandaemonium 1660–1886: The Coming of the Machine as seen by Contemporary Observers*. London: Macmillan.

Jervis, John 1998: *Exploring the Modern*. Oxford: Blackwell.

Jönsson, Bodil 2003: *Ten Thoughts about Time*. London: Constable and Robinson.

Kaldor, Mary 1999: *New and Old Wars*. Cambridge: Polity.

Katz, Jack 1999: 'Pissed Off in L.A.', in *How Emotions Work*. Chicago: University of Chicago Press, pp. 18–86.

Katz, James E. and Aakhus, Mark (eds) 2002: *Perpetual Contact*. Cambridge: Cambridge University Press.

Kellner, Douglas 1992: *The Persion Gulf TV War*. Boulder, CO: Westview.

Kellner, Douglas 2000: 'Virilio, War and Technology: Some Critical Reflections', in John Armitage (ed.), *Paul Virilio: From Modernism to Hypermodernism and Beyond*. London: Sage, pp. 103–25.

Kern, Stephen 2003: *The Culture of Time and Space 1880–1918*. Cambridge, MA: Harvard University Press. (First published in 1983.)

Kittler, Freidrich, A. 1999: *Gramophone, Film, Typewriter*. Stanford, CA: Stanford University Press.

Knowles, L.C.A. (1921) *The Industrial and Commercial Revolutions in Great Britain during the Nineteenth Century*. London: Routledge and Kegan Paul.

Knox, Paul L. 2005: 'Creating Ordinary Places: Slow Cities in a Fast World', *Journal of Urban Design*, 10(1): 1–11.

Kreitzman, Leon 1999: *The 24 Hour Society*. London: Profile Books.

Kurzweil, Ray 2000: *The Age of Spiritual Machines*. New York: Penguin.

Lasch, Christopher 1991: *The True and Only Heaven*. New York: Norton.

Lash, Scott 2002: *Critique of Information*. London: Sage.

Lash, Scott and Urry, John 1994: *Economies of Signs and Space*. London: Sage.

Latour, Bruno 1992: 'Where are the Missing Masses? The Sociology of a Few Mundane Artefacts', in Wieber E. Bijker and John Law (eds), *Shaping Technology/Building Society: Studies in Socio-technical Change*. Cambridge, MA: MIT Press, pp. 225–58.

Le Corbusier 1959: *Towards a New Architecture*. New York: Praeger. (First published in 1923.)

Le Corbusier 1971: *The City of Tomorrow and its Planning*. London: The Architectural Press. Trans Frederick Etchells. (First published as *l'Urbanism* in 1924.)

Lee, Chin-Chuan, Chan, Joseph Man, Pan, Zhongdang and Clement, Y.K. So 2002: *Global Media Spectacle*. Albany: State University of New York.

Linder, Staffan 1970: *The Harried Leisure Class*. New York: Columbia University Press.

Lipovetsky, Gilles 2005: *Hypermodern Times*. Cambridge: Polity.

Livingstone, Sonia M. 2002: *Young People and New Media: Childhood and the Changing Media Environment*. London: Sage.

Lodder, Christine 2006: 'Searching for Utopia', in Christopher Wilk (ed.), *Modernism 1914–1939: Designing a New World*. London: V&A Publications, pp. 23–69.

Luke, Timothy and Ó Tuathail, Gearóid 1998: 'Global Flowmations, Local Fundamentalisms and Fast Geopolitics: "America" in an Accelerating World Order', in Andrew Herrod, Susan Roberts and Gearóid Ó Tuathail (eds), *An Unruly World: Globalization, Governance and Geography*. London: Routledge, pp. 72–94.

Lupton, Deborah 1999: 'Monsters in Metal Cocoons: "Road Rage" and Cyborg Bodies', *Body and Society*, 5(1): 57–72.

Macnaughton, Phil and Urry, John 1998: *Contested Natures*. London: Sage.

Maënpää, Pasi 2001: 'Mobile Communication as a Way of Urban Life', in Jukka Gronow and Alan Warde (eds), *Ordinary Consumption*. London: Routledge, pp. 107–23.

Maffesoli, Michel 1996: *The Time of the Tribes*. London: Sage.

Manning, Robert, D. 2000: *Credit Card Nation*. New York: Basic Books.

Marcuse, Herbert 1964: *One Dimensional Man*. London: Abacus.

Marinetti, Filippo Tommasso 1973a: 'The Founding and Manifesto of Futurism', in Umbro Apollonio (ed.), *Futurist Manifestos*. London: Thames and Hudson, pp. 19–24. (First published in 1909.)

Marinetti, Filippo Tommasso 1973b: 'Geometric and Mechanical Splendour and the Numerical Sensibility', in Umbro Apollonio (ed.), *Futurist Manifestos*. London: Thames and Hudson, pp. 154–9. (First published in 1914.)

Marx, Karl 1963: *Selected Writings in Sociology and Social Philosophy*. Harmondsworth: Penguin.

Marx, Karl 1973: *Grundrisse*. London: Penguin.

Marx, Karl 1976: *Capital, Volume One*. Harmondsworth: Penguin.

Marx, Karl 1978: *Capital, Volume Two*. Harmondsworth: Penguin.

Marx Karl and Engels, Friedrich 1969: 'Manifesto of the Communist Party', in Lewis S. Feuer (ed.), *Marx and Engels: Basic Writings on Politics and Philosophy*. London: Fontana, pp. 43–82.

McChesney, Robert W., Wood, Ellen Meiksins, Foster, John Bellamy (eds) 1998: *Capitalism and the Information Age: The Political Economy of the Global Communication Revolution*. New York: Monthly Review Press.

McCreery, Sandy 2002: 'Come Together', in Peter Wollen and Joe Kerr (eds), *Autopia: Cars and Culture*. London: Reaktion Books, pp. 307–11.

McCurry, Justin 2006: 'Handset Brings the Mall to You in Japan's M-Shopping Craze', *The Guardian*, 13 February: p. 28.

McKay, George 1996: *Senseless Acts of Beauty: Cultures of Resistance since the 1960s*. London: Verso.

Mcleod, M. 1983: '"Architecture of Revolution": Taylorism, Technocracy and Social Change' *Art Journal*, 43(2): 132–47.

McLuhan, Marshall 1964: *Understanding Media: The Extensions of Man*. London: Routledge and Kegan Paul.

McPherson, Tara 2006: 'Reload: Liveness, Mobility and the Web', in Wendy Hui Kyong Chun and Thomas Keenan (eds), *New Media Old Media*. Abingdon: Routledge, pp. 199–208.

McQuire, Scott: 1998: *Visions of Modernity*. London: Sage.

Melucci, Alberto 1989: *Nomads of the Present: Social Movements and Individual Needs in Contemporary Society*. London: Hutchinson Radius.

Merleau-Ponty, Maurice 1979: *Phenomenology of Perception*. London: Routledge and Kegan Paul.

Meyrowitz, Joshua 1985: *No Sense of Place: The Impact of Electronic Media on Social Behavior*, New York: Oxford University Press.

Millar, Jeremy and Schwarz, Michiel 1998: 'Introduction: Speed is a Vehicle', in Jeremy Millar and Michiel Schwarz (eds), *Speed – Visions of an Accelerated Age*. London: The Photographers Gallery/The Whitechapel Art Gallery, pp. 16–23.

Millar, S. 2001: 'Internet "Could Damage Children's Ability to Learn"', *The Guardian*, October 12: 6.

Miller, Daniel (ed.) 2001 *Car Cultures*. Oxford: Berg.

Miller, Daniel, Jackson, Peter, Thrift, Nigel, Holbrook, Beverley and Rowlands, Michael 1998: *Shopping, Place and Identity*. London: Routledge.

Mirzoeff, Nicholas 2002: *The Visual Culture Reader*. London: Routledge.

Moores, Shaun 1996: *Satellite Television and Everyday Life*. Luton: University of Luton Press.

Morgan, Bryan (ed.) 1963: *The Railway Lover's Companion*. London: Eyre and Spottiswoode.

Morley, David 2000: *Home Territories: Media, Mobility and Identity*. London: Routledge.

Morley, David and Robins, Kevin 1995: *Spaces of Identity: Global Media, Electronic Landscapes and Cultural Boundaries*. London: Routledge.

Morrison, Ken 1995: *Marx, Durkheim, Weber: Formations of Modern Social Thought*. London: Sage.

Mumford, Lewis 1946: *Technics and Civilization*. London: George Routledge and Sons.

Musil, Robert 1995: *The Man Without Qualities*. Trans. Sophie Wilkins and Burton Pike. London: Picador.

Neill, Monty 1995: 'Computers, Thinking, and Schools in the "New World Economic Order"', in James Brook and Iain A. Boal (eds), *Resisting the Virtual Life*. San Francisco: City Lights, pp. 181–94.

Nisbet, Robert 1980: *History of the Idea of Progress*. London: Heinemann.

Nussbaum, Martha 1996: *For Love of Country: Debating the Limits Of Patriotism*. Boston: Beacon.

Paquot, Thierry 2003: *The Art of the Siesta*. London: Marion Boyars.

Parkin, Frank 1982: *Max Weber*. London: Tavistock.

Perkin, Harold 1970: *The Age of the Railway*. London: Panther.

Perloff, Marjorie 2003: *The Futurist Moment*. Chicago, IL: University of Chicago Press.

Peters, John Durham 1999: *Speaking into the Air: A History of the Idea of Communication*. Chicago: University of Chicago Press.

Poster, Mark 1995: *The Second Media Age*. Cambridge: Polity.

Proust, Marcel 1981: *Remembrance of Things Past, Vol 2. The Guermantes Way*. Trans. C.K. Scott Moncrieff and T. Martin. London: Chatto and Windus.

Pryke, Michael and Allen, John 2000: 'Monetized time-space: derivatives – money's "new imaginary"', *Economy and Society*, 29(2): 264–84.

Radford, T. 2000: 'Robotic Future Rushes Towards Us', *The Guardian*, 1 May: 5.

Rai, Milan 2002: *War Plan Iraq*. London: Verso.

Rheingold, Howard 1994: *The Virtual Community*. London: Minerva.

Rifkin, Jeremy 1987: *Time Wars: The Primary Conflict in Human History*. New York: Henry Holt and Company.

Rippin, Hannah 2005: 'The Mobile Phone in Everyday Life', *Fast Capitalism*, 1.1 (www.uta.edu/huma/agger/fastcapitalsim/1_1/rippin.htm).

Ritzer, George 1995: *Expressing America: A Critique of the Global Credit Card Society*. Thousand Oaks, CA: Pine Forge Press.

Ritzer, George 2000: *The McDonaldization of Society*. Thousand Oaks, CA: Pine Forge.

Ritzer, George 2001: *Explorations in the Sociology of Consumption: Fast Food, Credit Cards and Casinos*. London: Sage.

Ritzer, George 2002: 'Revolutionizing the World of Consumption', *Journal of Consumer Culture*, 2(1): 103–18.

Robbins, Michael 1962: *The Railway Age in Britain and its Impact on the World*. London: Routledge and Kegan Paul.

Robertson, Roland 1992: *Globalization: Social Theory and Global Culture*. London: Sage.

Rojek, Chris 1987: *Capitalism and Leisure Theory*. London: Tavistock.

Rojek, Chris 2000: *Leisure and Culture*. London: Macmillan.

Rojek, Chris 2001: *Celebrity*. London: Reaktion Books.

Rojek, Chris 2004: 'The Consumerist Syndrome in Contemporary Society: An Interview with Zygmunt Bauman', *Journal of Consumer Culture*, 4(3): 291–312.

Ronson, Jon 2006: 'Cold Sweat', *The Guardian Weekend* , 28 January: 20–6.

Ross, Kristin 1995: *Fast Cars, Clean Bodies*. Cambridge, MA: The MIT Press.

Royle, Tony 2000: *Working for McDonald's in Europe*. London: Routledge.

Russell, Bertrand 1967: *In Praise of Idleness and other Essays*. London: Unwin Books. (First published in 1935.)

Saatchi, Maurice 2006: 'The Strange Death of Modern Advertising', *Financial Times*, 22 June.

Schiller, Dan 1999: *Digital Capitalism*. Cambridge, MA: The MIT Press.

Schivelbusch, Wolfgang 1980: *The Railway Journey: Trains and Travel in the Nineteenth Century*. Oxford: Basil Blackwell.

Schlosser, Eric 2002: *Fast Food Nation*. New York: Penguin.

Schor, Juliet 1992: *The Overworked American: The Unexpected Decline of Leisure*. New York: Basic Books.

Seager, Ashley 2006: 'Debt Problem Soars as 1m Face Threat of Bankruptcy', *The Guardian*, 22 May: 30.

Sennett, Richard 1998: *The Corrosion of Character*. New York: W.W. Norton.

Sennett, Richard 2000: 'Street and Office: Two Sources of Identity', in Will Hutton and Anthony Giddens (eds), *On The Edge: Living with Global Capitalism*. London: Jonathan Cape, pp. 175–90.

Sennett, Richard 2006: *The Culture of the New Capitalism*. New Haven:Yale University Press.

Setright, L.J.K. 2002: *Drive On!: A Social History of the Motor Car*. London: Granta.

Sheller, Mimi 2004: 'Automotive Reactions: Feeling the Car', *Theory, Culture and Society*, 21(4–5): 221–42.

Shepard, Benjamin and Hayduk, Ronald (eds) 2002: *From ACT UP to the WTO: Urban Protest and Community Building in the Era of Globalization*. London: Verso.

Shields, Rob 1997: 'Flow as a New Paradigm', *Space and Culture*, 1: 1–4.

Shove, Elizabeth 2003: *Comfort, Cleanliness and Convenience: The Social Organization of Normality*. Oxford: Berg.

Sillitoe, Alan 1973: *Saturday Night and Sunday Morning*. London: W.H. Allen.

Silverstone, Roger and Hirsch, Eric 1992 (eds): *Consuming Technologies: Media and Information in Domestic Spaces*. London: Routledge.

Simmel, Georg 1978: *The Philosophy of Money*. Trans. Tom Bottomore and David Frisby. London: Routledge and Kegan Paul. (First published in 1900.)

Simmel, Georg 1997a: 'The Philosophy of Fashion'. Trans. Mark Ritter and David Frisby, in David Frisby and Mike Featherstone (eds), *Simmel on Culture*. London: Sage, pp. 187–205. (First published in 1905.)

Simmel, Georg 1997b: 'The Metropolis and Mental Life'. Trans. Hans Gerth, in David Frisby and Mike Featherstone (eds), *Simmel on Culture*. London: Sage, pp. 174–85. (First published in 1903.)

Simmons, Jack 1968: *The Railways of Britain: An Historical Introduction*. London: Macmillan.

Simmons, Jack and Biddle, Gordon (eds) 1997: *The Oxford Companion to British Railway History*. Oxford: Oxford University Press.

Slater, Don 1997: *Consumer Culture and Modernity*. Cambridge: Polity.

Smart, Barry 2003: *Economy, Culture and Society: A Sociological Critique of Neo-Liberalism*. Buckingham: Open University Press.

Soros, George 1998: *The Crisis of Global Capitalism*. London: Little, Brown.

Spigel, Lynn 1992: *Make Room for TV: Television and the Family Ideal in Postwar America*. Chicago: University of Chicago Press.

Spufford, Francis and Uglow, Jenny (eds) 1996: *Cultural Babbage: Technology, Time and Invention*. London: Faber and Faber.

Stallybrass, Oliver 1983: 'Editor's Introduction' to *Howards End*. Harmondsworth: Penguin, pp. 7–17.

Standage, Tom 1999: *The Victorian Internet*. London: Phoenix.

Strange, Susan 1996: *The Retreat of the State: The Diffusion of Power in the World Economy*. Cambridge: Cambridge University Press.

Sun, Tzu 1998: *The Art of War*. Trans. Yuan Shibing. Ware: Wordsworth Editions.

Sztompka, Piotr 1993: 'Vicissitudes of the Idea of Progress' in *The Sociology of Social Change*. Oxford: Blackwell, pp. 24–40.

Taylor, Frederick Winslow 1967: *The Principles of Scientific Management*. New York: W.W. Norton. (First published in 1911.)

Therborn, Gören 1995: *European Modernity and Beyond*. London: Sage.

Thompson, Edward, P. 1991: ' Time, Work Discipline and Industrial Capitalism', in *Customs in Common*. London: The Merlin Press, pp. 352–403.

Thompson, John B. 1995: *The Media and Modernity*. Cambridge: Polity.

Thrift, Nigel 1997: 'The Rise of Soft Capitalism', *Cultural Values*, 1: 29–57.

Thrift, Nigel 2005: *Knowing Capitalism*. London: Sage.

Tilly, Charles 2002: *Stories, Identities, and Political Change*. Oxford: Rowman and Littlefield.

Tisdall, Caroline and Bozzolla, Angelo 1977: *Futurism*. London: Thames and Hudson.

Toffler, Alvin 1971: *Future Shock*. London: Pan.

Tomlinson, John 1991: *Cultural Imperialism*. London: Cassell.

Tomlinson, John 1999: *Globalization and Culture*. Cambridge: Polity.

Tomlinson, John 2001: 'Proximity Politics', in Frank Webster (ed.), *Culture and Politics in the Information Age*. London: Routledge, pp. 52–62.

Tomlinson, John 2002: 'Interests and Identities in Cosmopolitan Politics', in Steve Vertovek and Robin Cohen (eds), *Conceiving Cosmopolitanism*. Oxford: Oxford University Press, pp. 240–53.

Touraine, Alain 1965: *Sociologie de l'action*. Paris: Seuil.

Touraine, Alain 1978: *The Voice and the Eye: The Analysis of Social Movements*. Cambridge: Cambridge University Press.

Tuan, Yi-.Fu 1996: *Cosmos and Hearth: A Cosmopolite's Viewpoint*. Minneapolis: University of Minnesota Press.

Twist, Jo 2005: 'Gadget Growth Fuels Eco Concerns', *BBC News On-line* (news.bbc.co.uk/go/pr/fr/-/1/hi/technology/4183969.stm).

Uhlig, Robert 2003: 'Almost All Teenagers Now Own a Mobile Phone', *The Daily Telegraph*, 27 November: 11.

Urry, John 2000: *Sociology Beyond Societies: Mobilities for the Twenty-first Century*. London: Routledge.

Urry, John 2003: *Global Complexity*. Cambridge: Polity.

van Dijk, Jan 2005: *The Deepening Divide: Inequality in the Information Society*. London: Sage.

Virilio, Paul 1986: *Speed and Politics*. New York: Semiotext(e).

Virilio, Paul 1997: *Open Sky*. London: Verso.

Virilio, Paul 2000a: *Strategy of Deception*. London:Verso.

Virilio, Paul 2000b: *Polar Inertia*. London: Sage.

Virilio, Paul 2000c: 'From Modernism to Hypermodernism and Beyond' (interview with John Armitage) in John Armitage (ed.), *Paul Virilio: From Modernism to Hypermodernism and Beyond*. London: Sage, pp. 25–56.

Virilio, Paul 2001a: *Desert Screen: War at the Speed of Light*. London: The Athlone Press.

Virilio, Paul 2001b: 'Perception, Politics and the Individual' (interview with Neils Brugger) in John Armitage (ed.), *Virilio Live: Selected Interviews*. London: Sage, pp. 82–96.

Walzer, Michael 1994: *Thick and Thin: Moral Argument at Home and Abroad*. Notre Dame, IN: University of Notre Dame Press.

Ward, Mark 2006: 'Searching for the Net's Big Thing', *BBC News On-line* (news.bbc.co.uk/1/hi/technology/4780648.stm).

Ward, Mark 2006: 'Teen Craze over Networking Sites', *BBC New On-line*, 23 March (news.bbc.co.uk/1/hi/technology/4826218.stm).

Warde, Alan 1997: *Consumption, Food and Taste*. London: Sage.

Warde, Alan 2002: 'Setting the Scene: Changing Conceptions of Consumption', in Steven Miles, Alison Anderson and Kevin Meethan (eds), *The Changing Consumer: Markets and Meanings*. London: Routledge, pp. 10–24.

Weber, Max 1970: 'The Social Psychology of the World Religions', in H.H. Gerth and C. Wright Mills (eds), *From Max Weber*. London: Routledge and Kegan Paul, pp. 267–301.

Weber, Max 1978: *Economy and Society* (Vols 1 and 2). Guenther Roth and Claus Wittich (eds). Berkeley: University of California Press.

Webster, Ben 2005: 'March of Speed Cameras Halted', *The Times*, 5 November. (www.timesonline.co.uk/article/0,,1858368,00).

Wells, H.G. 1924: *Ann Veronica*. London: T. Fisher Unwin Ltd.

Wells, H.G. 1980a: 'Preface' in *The Time Machine and Other Stories*, London: Book Club Associates, pp. 15–17. (First published in 1933.)

Wells, H.G. 1980b: 'In the Days of the Comet' in *The Time Machine and Other Stories*, London: Book Club Associates, pp. 551–709. (First published in 1906.)

Williams, Raymond 1963: *Culture and Society 1780–1950*. Harmondsworth: Penguin.

Williams, Raymond 1977: *Marxism and Literature*. Oxford: Oxford University Press.

Williams, Raymond 1981: *Culture*. London: Fontana.

Williams, Raymond 1983: 'Culture and Technology', in *Towards 2000*. London: Chatto and Windus, pp. 128–52.

Williams, Raymond 1989: *Resources of Hope: Culture, Democracy, Socialism*. London: Verso.

Williams, Raymond 1989: 'Problems of the Coming Period' in *Resources of Hope: Culture, Democracy, Socialism*. London: Verso, pp. 161–74. (First published in 1983.)

Wilson, A.N. 2002: *The Victorians*. London: Hutchinson.

Winston, Brian 1998: *Media Technology and Society: A History from the Telegraph to the Internet*. London: Routledge.

Wolin, Richard 1982: *Walter Benjamin: An Aesthetic of Redemption*. New York: Columbia University Press.

Wolin, Sheldon 1997: 'What Time Is it?', *Theory and Event*, 1(1).

Wollen, Peter 1998: 'The Crowd Roars – Suspense and the Cinema', in Jeremy Miller and Michiel Schwarz (eds), *Speed–Visions of an Accelerated Age*. London: The Photographers Gallery/The Whitechapel Art Gallery, pp. 77–86.

Wollen, Peter 2002: 'Cars and Culture', in Peter Wollen and Joe Kerr (eds), *Autopia: Cars and Culture*. London: Reaktion Books, pp. 10–20.

Wollen, Peter and Kerr, Joe (eds) 2002: *Autopia: Cars and Culture*. London: Reaktion Books.

Wordsworth, William (1844) 'Kendal and Windermere Railway: Two Letters to the Morning Post', in Peter Bicknell (ed.), *The Illustrated Wordsworth's Guide to the Lakes*. London: Webb and Bower.

Index

Aakhus, Mark   103
Abrams, Rachel   145n.13
abstention   150–1
acceleration   1, 6, 7, 11, 23, 25, 26,
    32, 39, 63, 67, 73, 74, 78, 86, 88,
    124, 140, 154–5, 156
Ackroyd, Peter   15
Actor Network Theory   11
Adam, Barbara   13n.2
Adams, John   94
Adorno, Theodor   152–3
advertising   31, 103, 120,
    121n.6, 129
affordances   132, 143n.7
Agar, Jon   103
Agger, Ben   81
Albrow, Martin   92n.5
Alexander, Jeffrey   41n.18
Allen, John   82
Althusser, Louis   137
*American Nervousness: Its Causes and
    Consequences*   36
Ang, Tom   132
annihilation of space by time   17
anticipation   83, 133
Apocalypse Now   56
Apollonio, Umbro   45, 68n.1
Appadurai, Arjun   75, 145n.21
appropriation   80, 125, 128, 137
Armitage, John   69n.20
The Art of War   57
Auden, W.H.   19
Augé, Marc   135
automaton   83

Babbage, Charles   16, 40n.5
balance   153, 154, 158
balance-as-control   152–4
Balint, Michael   49
Balla, Giacomo   45
Ballard, J.G.   69n.15
bargain with capitalism   86–7
bargain with modernity   22

'Basel Convention on the
    Transboundary Movements of
    Hazardous Wastes and their
    Disposal'   141
Bate, Jonathan   23
Baudelaire, Charles   36, 92n.3
Bauman, Zygmunt   75, 76, 77, 78, 79,
    80, 91, 92, 104, 126, 127, 128,
    129, 138, 141
Baumeister, Willi   51
Bayley, Stephen   50
BBC Annual Report and Accounts
    122n.12
Beard, George M.   36
Beck, Ulrich   66, 68n.6, 142, 143n.6
Beck-Gernsheim, Elisabeth   143n.6
Beckman, Jörg   70n.29
Benedikt, M.   103
Benjamin, Walter   40n.10, 43n.33, 56,
    63–4, 68n.8, 122n.13, 123n.20
Berker, Thomas   95
Berman, Marshall   32–3, 76, 79
Bicknell, Peter   24, 42nn.21, 22
Biddle, Gordon   40n.4
Bijker, Wieber E.   11
Black, Richard   141
Blair, Tony   23
Blakemore, Michael   41n.12
blasé attitude   37, 133, 139
Bleak House   19
Boccioni, Umberto   45, 57
Bogart, Humphrey   53
Bozzolla, Angelo   45, 46, 57, 68n.2,
    69n.12
brain chemistry
    and modern speed   48
Braverman, Harry   28, 29, 30
Brennan, Teresa   42n.23, 83, 84, 85,
    88, 89, 142
Briggs, Asa   121n.3
British Trades Union Congress   27
Britten, Benjamin   19
Brottman, Mikita   53

bureaucracy 6
Burke, Peter 121n.3
Burrows, Roger 51

Caché (Michael Haneke) 101
Callon, Michelle 11
Campbell, Donald 54–5
Campbell, Malcolm 54–5
Capital 5, 25, 136
capitalism 5–6, 25–6, 28, 31–2,
    79, 148
capitalist market economy 82
Carter, Ian 15, 40n.4, 122n.17
cashback facilities 136
Castells, Manuel 8, 75, 82, 83,
    121n.1, 122n.8, 147–8
Castoriadis, Cornelius 89, 159
Chan, Joseph Man 100
change, ideology of 22, 85
Chaplin, Charlie 28, 42n.24
Charles (Prince of Wales) 1
cheques 134, 135
China 17, 22, 121n.1, 141
Chun, Wendy Hui Kyong 121n.4
CittàSlow movement 146, 147
    see also slow cities movement
city *see* metropolis
Clapham, John H. 40n.4
Clark, Kenneth 104
Clarkson, Jeremy 48, 66, 68n.5, 70n.32
Clement, Y.K. So 100
'closure of the gap' 74, 90, 91, 120
Cold War 58, 59
communications technologies 58, 75,
    80, 94, 103, 105, 106
    see also keyboards; keypad; mobile
        phone technology; screens
The Communist Manifesto 6, 14, 75–6
Connolly, William 154, 155, 156,
    157, 158
conquest of space 78
consumer expectation
    low horizons in 137–40
consumer immediacy, concerted
        incitements to 128–37
    market for convenience 130–1
    media technologies, as impatient and
        immoderate 131–3
    spending, new technologies 133–7
consumerism 89, 126, 128, 138,
    140, 141
consumerist syndrome 126, 127
consumption 88–9, 111, 129, 131,
    132, 138–9, 142, 144n.10
    importance 138

sphere, immediacy in 125–8
in teletechnologies 117–20
contemporary consumerism
    127, 136
    criticism 142
    see also consumerism
contrivance of redundancy 139–40
convenience goods 130–1
Corn Laws (1815) 25–6
cosmopolitanism 157
Couldry, Nick 99
Crabtree, James 103
credit card 134, 135–6, 141, 145n.14
cultural imagination 19, 91
cultural modernity 8, 149
cultural-political pluralism 156
cultural politics 154
cultural significance 1
cultural values 3, 5, 149
cyborg culture 50–2
cynicism 20, 54, 129, 139

The Daily News 15
Dant, Tim 51, 52, 69n.11
Davies, William 129
Davis, Jim 82
Davis, John R. 40n.9
Dayan, Daniel 100
Dean, James 53
debit card 134, 135–6, 145n.14
deceleration 146
    and democratic cultural life,
        connection 155–9
    slow movement, significance
        of 146–9
    slow values 149–54
Delanty, Gerard 41n.15
deliberate slow working 29
delivery 111, 124
    concerted incitements, to consumer
        immediacy 128–37
        market for convenience 130–1
        media technologies, impatient and
            immoderate 131–3
        spending, new technologies
            of 133–7
    critique 140–2
    immediacy, in consumption sphere
        125–8
    low horizons, in consumer
        expectation 137–40
Der Derian, James 69nn.20, 21
deregulation 86, 141
Derrida, Jacques 92n.4, 100, 154
Dershowitz, Alan M. 63, 70n.24

Desert Screen: War at the Speed of Light 59
'Destruction of Syntax – Imagination without Strings – Words-in-Freedom' (Marinetti) 46
Dickens, Charles 14, 15, 19
Disraeli, Benjamin 151
Dodson, Sean 120
Dombey and Son 14
Donald, James 33
Dowling, Tim 143n.5
'downshifting' 150
Draut, Tamara 141
Dreyfus, Hubert L. 114–15, 116, 123n.25
'driver-car' concept 51, 52
Duchamp, Marcel 51
Duff, Oliver 144n.8
Duffy, Jonathan 120, 121
Durkheim, Émile 5, 128–9
dynamic money economy 7
dynamism 23, 158

Economic and Philosophical Manuscripts 136
Economy and Society 6
Eder, Klaus 147
electronic media 98, 99, 105, 122n.11
electronic purchase
  see credit card; debit card
Elliott, Larry 140
Ellul, Jacques 41n.17
Emerson, Ralph Waldo 21
Engels, Friedrich 6, 14, 75–6
eotechnology 16
Eriksen, Thomas Hylland 13n.2
European Union 27
'E-waste' 141
existential focus 152, 153

Fascism 45, 63
fashion 7
fast capitalism 81–9, 111, 118, 120, 138, 142, 155
Fast Capitalism 81
fast-short life 53–5
Featherstone, Mike 51, 65, 66, 70n.29, 143n.2
Ferrari, Enzo 50
Feuer, Jane 99
Feuilherade, Peter 121n.1
First World War 44
fluidity 75–6, 92n.2
fluid modernity 80, 91, 103

Forster, Edward Morgan 112, 113, 114, 115, 116, 123n.24
Foster, John Bellamy 122n.8
Freeman, Michael 17, 24, 25, 39–40n.3, 40nn.4, 6, 41n.20, 104, 122n.17
Freud, Sigmund 49, 68n.7
Frisby, David 7, 34, 37, 40n.10, 42n.29, 92n.3
frugal simplicity 150
fundamentalism 156
The Future of Success 129
Future Shock 8
Futurism 45, 46–7, 68n.1
Futurist 8
  modern speed, celebration of 47
  movement 44
Futurist Manifesto 44, 56, 112

Garfield, Simon 40n.4
Gibson, James J. 143n.7
Giddens, Anthony 8, 13n.2, 38, 52, 58, 68n.6, 69n.18, 82, 93nn.7,8, 134
Gilloch, Graeme 36
Gilmore, John 53
Gissing, George 42n.23
glacial time 2
Gladstone, William 23
Gleick, James 13n.2
global fluids 76
globalization 8, 46, 83, 148
globalized capitalism, Brennan's critique 84
global modernity 11, 81
Gold, John R. 33, 42n.32, 43n.34
Goldblatt, David 8, 82
Goldman, Robert 82, 84
Goody, Jack 143n.5
Gorz, Andre 126
Graham, Thomas 26
Gramsci, Antonio 9
Gray, John 82
The Great Exhibition (1851) 18
Green, Christopher 51
Greene, Rachel 101–2
Grierson, John 19
Grint, Keith 11
Grundrisse 5, 17
Gulf War (1991) 59, 64
Gurney, Peter 40n.9

Hall, Peter 42n.32
handsets
  see mobile phone technology

Haneke, Michael   101
Haraway, Donna   51
Hardt, Michael   28
Hard Times   19
The Harried Leisure Class   130
Hartmann, Maren   95
Harvey, David   6, 13n.2, 93n.7
Hassard, John   13n.2
Hayduk, Ronald   142
Hayes, R. Dennis   112
heavy modernity   77–8
hedge funds   82–3
Held, David   8, 82
Hiro, Dilip   62, 70n.25
Hirsch, Eric   95, 131
Hirschl, Thomas   82
Hobsbawm, Eric   15
Hochschild, A.R.   130
Holbrook, Beverley   143n.2
Holston, James   42n.32
Honoré, Carl   148, 159n.1
Howard's End   115, 116
Howells, Richard   123n.19
Hughes, Robert   45, 51
human–machine interaction   50–2
Hutchby, Ian   143n.7
Hutton, Will   82
hyperconsumption   125
hypermodernity   125

imaginary significations   89
immediacy   106, 107, 119, 158
    condition of   10, 12, 72, 149–50
        fast capitalism   81–9, 111, 118,
            120, 138, 142, 155
        fluidity   75–6, 92n.2
        lightness   79–81, 91, 111, 135
        speed without progress, arrival
            without departure   89–92
    consumer immediacy, concerted
        incitements to   128–37
        market for convenience   130–1
        media technologies, as
            impatient and immoderate
            131–3
        spending, new technologies   133–7
    and media   97–102
        professional/stylistic developments
            99–100
        technical improvements and
            innovations   99
        technological and professional/
            stylistic developments,
            mediation of   100–1
    in sphere of consumption   125–8

India   141
individualism   65, 66, 85
industrialization   16, 17–18, 104,
    105, 109
industrialization of war   58
industrial production   18, 25
Inglis, David   33
instantaneity culture   74, 91
instrumental rationality   34, 78
Iraq War (2003)   57
irrationality   58, 65, 129
Italy   146

Jackson, Peter   143n.2
Jacobs, Jane   42n.32
James, Henry   109
Jay, Martin   123n.19
Jennings, Humphrey   17, 18, 23,
    40–1n.11, 79
Jeremijenko, Natalie   102
Jervis, John   79, 122n.13
Jones, Sir Digby   27
Jönsson, Bodil   159n.1
Juggernaut of modernity
    (Giddens)   38

Kaldor, Mary   58, 69n.19
Katz, Elihu   100
Katz, Jack   71n.34, 100
Katz, James E.   103
Kellner, Douglas   69, 70
Kern, Stephen   13n.2, 36, 38, 39,
    123nn.28, 29
Kersey, Noah   82, 84
keyboards   107–11
keypad   73, 81, 94, 108
Kierkegaard, Søren   115
Kilgore, Lieutenant-Colonel   56
Kittler, Freidrich A.   108, 109, 110,
    123n.21
Knock on any Door   53
Knowles, L.C.A.   40n.8
Knox, Paul L.   159n.1
Kosovo conflict (1999)   59
Kreitzman, Leon   13n.2
Kurzweil, Ray   123n.25

A la Recherche du Temps Perdu   117
Lasch, Christopher   41n.18
Lash, Scott   93n.7, 122n.10
Latour, Bruno   11
Law, John   11
law of proximity   90
Le Corbusier   32–6, 37, 38, 39,
    42nn.28, 30, 31, 32

Lee, Chin-Chuan 100
Le Figaro 44
legerdemain 80–1
Lenin, Vladimir 9
'life getting faster' 2
lightness 79–81, 91, 109, 111, 135
Linder, Staffan 130
Lipovetsky, Gilles 124, 125, 126, 127, 143n.3
liquefaction 76
liquidity 75–9
liquid modernity 76, 77, 78
Little Dorrit 19
'live fast, die young' 53, 54, 55, 124
Lives of the Engineers (1861) 19
Live Wire 102
Livingstone, Sonia M. 121–2n.6
Lodder, Christine 42n.32, 68n.1
Luke, Timothy 75
Lupton, Deborah 51, 67
l'Urbanisme 32, 33

machinery 18
  bureautic organization, comparison with 6
  and progress of culture 20–5
machines 15–20
machine speed 14
  cultural contradictions, in unruly culture 64–8
  machines 15–20
  metropolis 32–9
  money 25–32, 134
  and progress of culture 20–5
  sensuality of 47–52
The Machine Stops 112–13, 116
Mackendrick, Alexander 21
Macnaughton, Phil 16
MAD (Mutually Assured Destruction) 58
Maënpää, Pasi 103
Maffesoli, Michel 142
Manning, Robert D. 137
The Man Without Qualities 37
Marcuse, Herbert 89
Marinetti, Filippo Tommasso 8, 33, 44–5, 46, 51, 52, 56, 57, 63, 64, 68nn.2, 4, 69n.17
marketing 128, 129, 133, 137, 139
Marx, Karl 5–6, 14, 17, 25, 40n.8, 9, 75–6, 80, 136
Maschinenbilder 51
mass society 7
Mayhew, Henry 18

McChesney, Robert W. 122n.8
McCreery, Sandy 70n.32
McCurry, Justin 144n.13
McDonald's restaurants, labour relations in 29–30
McGrew, Tony 8, 82
McKay, George 142
Mcleod, M. 35
McLuhan, Marshall 122n.10
McPherson, Tara 99, 120
McQuire, Scott 41n.18
mechanical modernity 67, 80–1, 90, 109, 153–4
  changing terminals in 102–7
mechanical speed 17, 20, 23, 74, 89, 149–50
  versus natural speed 15–17
mechanical velocity 19, 74, 78, 109
media 74–5, 94
  connections 111–16
  dispensability of 96
  and immediacy 97–102
  integrating with physical mobility in fluid modernity 102–7
  as intervening substance 98
  keeping in touch 117–20
  keyboards, assessing and communicating with 107–11
  proportion, sense of 95–7
  reification of 98–9
  spatial separation 97–8
media technologies 88, 94, 95, 96, 97, 99, 107, 108, 118
  as impatient and immoderate 131–3
  speed in 11–12
Melucci, Alberto 147
Menezes, Jean Charles de
  mis-identified killing of 62
Merleau-Ponty, Maurice 8, 115, 123n.26
metropolis 32–9, 65, 105
Meyrowitz, Joshua 122n.9
Millar, Jeremy 68n.1
Millar, S. 112
Miller, Daniel 65, 112, 143n.2
Milton, John 17
Mirzoeff, Nicholas 123
mobile phone technology 91, 103, 106, 112, 116, 119, 120
modern cultural imagination, themes 15, 47, 126, 158
  sensuality of machine speed 47–52
  speed-heroism 52–6
  violence and war 56–64
  see also cultural imagination

modernity   65, 74, 78, 153, 154, 158
   speed in   5–9
   see also individual entries
Modern Times   28
money   7, 25–32, 37, 134, 135
   Marx's view   136
Moores, Shaun   103
Morgan, Bryan   40n.4
Morley, David   95, 122n.9
Morrison, Ken   6, 93n.8, 129
'M-shopping'   144–5n.13
Mumford, Lewis   17, 44
Musil, Robert   37–8, 39
Mussolini, Benito   45, 69n.17

Nathan, Max   103
natural soldiering   29
natural speed versus mechanical
   speed   15–17
Naysmith, James   17–18, 40n.7
'near field communication technology'
   145n.17
Negri, Antonio   28
Neill, Monty   112
neurasthenia   36
*Neuropolitics: Thinking, Culture,
   Speed*   154
'New Labour'   23, 25, 27
'New Man'   43n.34, 46, 51
Nietzsche, Friedrich   109, 115
Night Mail   19, 20, 41n.13
Nisbet, Robert   20, 21
Nixon in China   94
normalizing of technologies
   of immediacy   130
Nussbaum, Martha   157

ocnophiles   49
On the Internet   114
organic time, myth of   84
Ó Tuathail, Gearóid   75
The Overworked American   130

pace of life   1–3, 5, 7–8, 22, 25, 32,
   36, 44, 111, 146, 148, 156
'Paleotechnic Age'   17
Pan, Zhongdang   100
Pandaemonium   17
Papson, Stephen   82, 84
Paquot, Thierry   159n.1
Parkin, Frank   6
patience   151–2
Paxton, Joseph   15, 18
Penrith Tea Shop   124
Perkin, Harold   40n.4

Perloff, Marjorie   45
Perraton, Jonathan   8, 82
personal indebtedness   140–1
Peters, John Durham   99, 122n.7
Petrini, Carlo   146
philobats   49
Philosophy of Money   7
Picabia, Francis   51
plastic cards
   see credit card; debit card
Poster, Mark   121n.4
In Praise of Slow website   148
pre-eminence of the present   125, 127
*Preemption: A Knife That Cuts Both
   Ways*   63
preemption culture   61–2
Preemptive doctrine, Kofi Annan,
   criticism of   70n
prepaid (offline) contactless card
   payment systems   145n.17
primum mobile   25, 60
The Principles of Scientific Management
   28, 29, 44
production   31–2, 46, 82, 88, 126
productivism   153
professional/stylistic developments, in
   media   99–100
   and technological developments,
      mediation of   100–1
progress of culture and machinery
   20–5
proportionality   95–7, 106, 115
proto-cyborg fantasy   51
   see also cyborg culture
Proust, Marcel   117–18, 120
Pryke, Michael   82
psychoanalysis
   and modern speed   49–50
Punie, Yves   95
'pure war'   58

Radford, T.   123n.18
Rai, Milan   70
Railroad Mania   14
The Railway Companion (1833)   16
Railway Movement   26
rationality   34, 39, 44, 57, 65,
   113, 131
rational-progressive speed   17, 39, 47,
   57, 153–4
   and unruly speed, distinction
      between   51–2
Ray, Nicholas   53
Rebel without a Cause   53
redundancy   90, 91, 140, 141

Reich, Robert   129
retail therapy   89
Rheingold, Howard   103
Rifkin, Jeremy   13n.2
Rippin, Hannah   103, 119
Ritzer, George   29, 137, 140, 143n.2,
      144–5n.13, 145n.18
road-rage   3
road safety   65–6
Robbins, Michael   40n.4, 122n.9
Roberts, Simon   103
Robertson, Roland   8
Robins, Kevin   122n.9
Rojek, Chris   54, 126, 143n.2
Ronson, Jon   145n.19
Ross, Kristin   42n.32, 70n.33
Rowlands, Michael   143n.2
Royle, Tony   29
Ruskin, John   23, 24, 93n.14
Russell, Bertrand   20, 41n.13
Russolo, Luigi   45, 57

Saatchi, Maurice   121–2n.6
Saddam Hussein   61–2
Sant'Elia, Antonio   57
Saturday Night and Sunday
      Morning   30
Schiller, Dan   82, 122n.8
Schivelbusch, Wolfgang   15, 16, 25–6,
      40n.4, 93n.14, 104–5
Schlosser, Eric   29
Schor, Juliet   130
Schwarz, Michiel   68n.1
Scientific Management   28
screens   73, 99, 101, 144nn.11, 12
Seager, Ashley   141
secularization   54, 122n.16
sedentary life   3, 103, 112, 114
sedentary speed
      see sedentary life
Sennett, Richard   1, 82, 85, 86,
      93n.13, 144n.10
sensuality of machine speed   47–52
      reasons described
            using brain chemistry   48
            using 'ergonomic' pleasure
                  concept   50
            using psychoanalysis   49–50
Setright, L.J.K.   16, 129
Sheller, Mimi   50, 69n.10
Shepard, Benjamin   142
Shields, Rob   75
Shove, Elizabeth   130, 131, 132
Sillitoe, Alan   30, 42n.26
Silverstone, Roger   95, 131

Simmel, Georg   7, 37, 39, 43n.33, 139
Simmons, Jack   40n.4
Simple Living Network   147, 150
simplicity   150, 151
Sitte, Camillo   34, 42n.29
Slater, Don   143
sleep function   96
slow cities movement   2, 147, 159n.1
      see also CittàSlow movement
Slow Food movement   2, 146, 147
SlowLab   147
slowlondon website   147, 148–9,
      152, 153
slow movement   1, 10, 22, 146–9
      aims   148–9
      categorization   148
      characteristics   148
      cultural value   149–54
      significance of   146–9
      societal goal   148
      see also slow cities movement;
            Slow Food movement
slow values   149–54
      abstention   150–1
      balance-as-control   152–4
      focus   152–3
      patience   151–2
Smart, Barry   126, 140
Smiles, Samuel   19
social constructivism   12, 85, 143n.7
Society for the Deceleration of
      Time   147
soft capitalism   79
softness   80, 88, 109, 110
soldiering   29
Soros, George   83
space   59, 74, 77, 78, 104–5, 118
speed   2–5
      as cultural value   3–4
      and modernity   5–9
      as physical movement   2–3
      see also individual entries
Speed and Politics   58, 59
speed cameras   65–6
speed-heroism   52–6
speed-inflected disposition   53
Spigel, Lynn   95
Spufford, Francis   40n.5
Stack, Michael   82
Stallybrass, Oliver   123n.27
Standage, Tom   121n.5, 123n.30
Stephenson, George   15, 39nn.2, 3
Stiegler, Bernard   92n.4, 100, 154
Strange, Susan   82
Strategy of Deception   59

Suicide   128
Sun Tzu   57
systematic soldiering   29
Sztompka, Piotr   41n.18

task orientation   87–8
Taylor, Frederick Winslow   28, 29,
      30, 44
Taylorism   9, 28–30, 35, 38, 42n.25,
      87, 145n.19
   critique   29
technical improvements and
      innovations, in media   99
technological determinism   11,
      12, 143n.7
   criticism   122n.10
telemediated society   10
telemediatization   74, 94, 102, 103,
      106, 107, 108, 111–20
   and immediacy   97–102
   naturalization of   101
   proportion, sense of   95–7
   see also media
telepresence   111–16, 121
   Hubert Dreyfus, critiques
         of   114–15
   presencing, existential mode
         of   117–20
television   94–5, 100, 121–2n.6,
      144n.12
Tempo Giusto   147
terminal   103–6
Therborn, Gören   92n.5
Thompson, Edward, P.   42n.23,
      87, 88
Thompson, John B.   122n.9
Thrift, Nigel   65, 79, 82, 122n.7,
      143n.2
Thrills and Regression   49
Tilly, Charles   30, 42n.27
time   5, 31, 33, 45, 59, 74, 77, 87–8,
      118, 130, 156
   see also individual entries
'Time is Money'   26–7
time poverty   22, 130
The Times   15
time saving   130
Tisdall, Caroline   45, 46, 57, 68n.2,
      69n.12
Toffler, Alvin   7–8
Top Gear   66, 68n.5
Touraine, Alain   147
Towards a New Architecture   33
traditional values, preservation of   22
transgressive speed   67

transportation systems   6
*A Treatise on Internal Intercourse
      and Communication in Civilised
      States*   26
Tuan, Yi-Fu   119
Twist, Jo   141
typewriter   109, 110, 123n.21

Uglow, Jenny   40n.5
Uhlig, Robert   119
uncluttered simplicity   150
United Kingdom   16, 27, 29, 62,
      140, 141, 146
United States   29, 140
unruly speed   9, 44
   cultural contradictions, of machine
         speed   64–8
   Futurism   44–7
   and rational-progressive speed,
         distinction between   51–2
   sensuality of machine speed   47–52
   speed-heroism   52–6
   violence and war   56–64
urbanism   11, 22, 32, 33, 35–8,
      42nn.31, 32, 43n.33, 146, 159n.1
Urry, John   16, 51, 65, 75, 76, 93n.7,
      103, 123n.19
utilitarianism   19

value of speed, in relation to other
      social goods   24–5
van Dijk, Jan   121n.1
velocity   5, 14, 15, 19, 20, 54, 74,
      78, 89, 109
violence   56–64
Virilio, Paul   8, 58, 59–60, 69n.20,
      21, 90, 91, 93nn.14, 15, 102–3,
      104, 123n.18, 155
virtual mobility   103
virtual travel   103
virtuous patience   151, 152
Voisin Plan   34, 42n.31

wallet phones   145n.17
Walzer, Michael   157
war   56–64
Ward, Katie J.   95
Ward, Mark   120, 132
Warde, Alan   143nn.2, 5
war on terror   61
Watt, Harry   19
weapons of mass destruction (WMDs)
      58, 61–2
Weber, Max   6, 93n.8
Webster, Ben   66

Wells, H.G.   112, 123nn.22, 23
Williams, Raymond   11, 40n.7, 67,
    98–9, 102, 122nn.10, 11, 16
Wilson, A.N.   18–19, 39n.1, 104,
    122n.16
Winston, Brian   95, 96, 121n.3,
    123n.30
Withnail and I   124, 143n.1
Wolin, Richard   43n.33
Wolin, Sheldon   155
Wollen, Peter   49
Wood, Ellen Meiksins   122n.8
Wood, Nicholas   16

Woolgar, Steve   11
Wordsworth, William   23–4,
    42nn.21, 22
work–home life integration   87–8
working class, attitude of   18
working long hours   27, 28
work narrative   85–6
World Health Organization
    report, for road safety   65, 66
Wright, Basil   19

youth   18, 52–3, 54, 73, 93n.12,
    103, 124